CW01521870

ARE WE TOGETHER?

COMMUNITY LIFE IN ACTION
(REVISED EDITION)

David Gibson

CLUAIN MHUIRE PRESS
2014

Published by Cluain Mhuire Press and Createspace

Set in 11 point Cambria

ISBN-13:978-1497500655
ISBN-10:1497500656

To Johnny Moore and Stanis McGuire
who taught me how to be a Brother

ACKNOWLEDGEMENTS

I want to acknowledge the generous assistance of Dr Cathy McQuaid and Dr Ian Stewart who offered very welcome comments on the drafts of the book, and whose suggestions have made all the difference. I take full responsibility, however, for the ideas I have expressed in *Are We Together?* My ideas and understanding of Transactional Analysis may not always concur with the views of my dear colleagues, but that makes for a healthy debate!

I also thank Br Greg Wall for the careful editing he so unselfishly undertook. Many a mistake was avoided thanks to his careful scrutiny of the text.

And to my community in Rome, I want to express my deep appreciation for the support they gave me, and the interest they have shown in the birth of the book. They had to put up with my daily references to the various drafts that I undertook, and to the overall progress of the project. Their encouragement and forbearance was a real gift.

CONTENTS

List of Figures and Tables

Figures

Tables

Introduction

Are We Together? is written principally for use by religious communities, although I can see how it could also be very valuable for any group of people who either work or live together, or who assemble on a regular basis as a group, and want to deepen the quality of their group interaction.

When I remember my own religious formation in the novitiate, I think back on the content of the programme that was available at the time. Much of the course involved a concentration on the spirituality of Brotherhood. We studied the vows, meditation, the teachings of the Church, and many other aspects of the spiritual life.

What was missing in the formation process was any focus on the psychological structure of the individual, and the dynamics of community or group living. Human development was not seen as an explicit topic for discussion. We lived together in the formation house, and the life together was meant to teach us how to live in community. This was an unfortunate omission.

Even today, I am not sure how much input is devoted to the dynamics of community living. There is some attention given to the psychological development of the person, but how much focuses on the psychological basis for group life? I suspect very little.

The Constitutions of many religious orders will have at least one chapter that outlines the importance of community and the value of the shared dimension of Religious Life. In the Constitutions of the Christian Brothers, for example, the emphasis on community living is unambiguous. Constitution 34 states:

> *Brotherhood in community is a principal source of our companionship and a privileged context for our personal growth. Our personalities develop as each of us accepts responsibility to make a unique contribution to the life and mission of the community. It is from community that we carry our gifts to others. We in turn are enriched as the lives of others touch our own.*
> (Christian Brothers, 1984: Const. 34).

Such a statement from the Christian Brothers' Constitution makes community living constitutive of Religious Life. It portrays community life as the very locus for a consecrated way of life. Without the communal dimension, it would appear that Religious Life has an essential element missing.

Quite a few men and women, however, find it very difficult, if not impossible, to continue living in a religious community. While some religious live alone because of ministry requirements, there are many religious who have opted to live on their own because of negative experiences in community. There are religious who dread the idea of community meetings, and prefer to retire to their bedrooms instead of spending time with the community. *Are We Together?* explains why community living can be difficult unless there is a high level of individual and interpersonal awareness.

Are We Together? offers some insights into the individual and group psychological dynamics that can contribute to improving the quality of community living. By so doing, I hope that I can help obviate some of the difficulties that inevitably arise when people are grouped together to form community.

The principal aim in writing *Are We Together?* is to share the insights that Transactional Analysis (TA) has to offer in understanding the individual and group dynamics of community or group life. Having run many workshops on the basics of TA for religious in different continents, I can see how valuable even a cursory knowledge of this approach can be in assisting people to understand some of the unconscious dynamics that create difficulties in community living.

Formation programmes that prepare young people for religious life will benefit from studying *Are We Together?*, by providing them with key concepts that will assist them in dealing with personality differences, conflicts, misunderstandings and many other unconscious psychological processes that inevitably arise when people come together. Because such information is often lacking, many religious have to struggle to understand what actually goes on when conflicts and misunderstandings arise, and many people blame themselves or others for causing such upsets. Often the reasons for the discomfort are far more complex than they seem at the outset.

And as well as religious communities, I believe that other groups can benefit greatly from an understanding of the theory and practice of TA. Any group will have many similar challenges that religious communities have. By studying TA, they will have a theory that will help them resolve some of their difficulties.

Dr Eric Berne (1910-1970) created the theory of TA, and became famous for his book *Games People Play,* first published in 1964. He was initially trained as a psychoanalyst and had Eric Erikson as his therapist for some years. Gradually, however, he became disenchanted with psychoanalysis, and felt that its arcane language and its demand for many years of treatment made it inaccessible for many people. In 1961, he wrote *Transactional Analysis and Psychotherapy* wherein he outlined an alternative approach to individual and group treatment. This was followed by a steady flow of publications up to his untimely death in 1970.

Are We Together? explores the main concepts of Eric Berne as they apply to the individual living a community life, and offers religious and other people who live in various group configurations some insights and methods for improving the quality of their communal life.

Students of TA may also find *Are We Together?* very useful as it offers a succinct outline of the main ideas of TA relevant to the needs of people who live and work in group settings. In addition, students may find the many TA references included in the text and found at the end of the book, a rich source for further study.

The approach of *Are We Together?* focuses first on the structure of the individual within the community. Berne said that 'The character of a group arises from the psychological mechanisms which it favours for handling individual anxieties.'(Berne, 1963:22). When individuals have not dealt with their own issues, this impacts greatly on how a community will function. A healthy community needs to be composed of people who have a psychological awareness of their own proclivities or dysfunctional ways of fulfilling their needs (*Ibid:* 57). Without an understanding of the person, much of the group dynamics becomes unintelligible. It is also my belief that the community in itself has not the capacity to compensate for the immaturity of the individual. No matter how good a community is, it cannot replace the need for individual religious attending to their own psychological health.

No community can satisfactorily cope with individual pathology. In the words of Eric Berne, 'All the dystonic proclivities added together comprise the internal disorganizing forces of any group or organisation' (*Ibid:* 57). By 'dystonic proclivities' he means those aspects of the person that are clearly and consciously acknowledged as a problem. Individual psychological difficulties will affect the group process, and therefore need to be addressed as the person prepares to join a community.

Consequently, the first three parts of the book deals with the structure and function of the individual member, and how he or she interacts with other people in community.

Part 1 focuses on Script, a key concept of Eric Berne, and explains how and why the Script is formed, and how it is maintained. In this section we also focus on the structure and function of ego states, which explain how the individual incorporates the memories of childhood, and the influence of parents into the psychological make-up of the person. A good understanding of the intrapsychic (within the mind) structure of the person provides a solid basis for exploring the interpersonal dynamics of community.

Part 2 examines how the interpersonal dynamics function as we communicate within a community setting. Communication lies at the heart of community, and many communities struggle with how to maintain a healthy level of communication in the face of conflict. This section offers some ideas and suggestions about conflict management, and about how to create a climate in community that lessens the impact of the inevitable presence of conflict in any community.

Part 3 highlights the phenomenon of how we distort reality to fit in with our view of the world, or more exactly with our Script. The way we discount many aspects of reality, and passively behave in the face of our Script often leads us to a type of symbiotic relationship that limits our capacity to be autonomous. Discounting and passivity impact greatly on our willingness to enter into healthy interpersonal community relationships.

Part 4 offers some insight into the group process where we come to understand how a group needs to balance the group task – the reason for which it exists - and the group process, or how the individual members work to create a cohesive unit in the face of individual differences, and a multitude of Scripts. In this section we also discuss the role and qualities of leadership in maintaining a group spirit.

Part 5 offers a glimpse of the potential of religious to live a life in community in a wholesome, integrated and mature way. In this section, we come to appreciate how vital is it for religious be committed to their own growth, and to the development of the community. Only when religious live healthy personal and interpersonal lives will their ministry be a ministry of integrity.

At the conclusion to the book, I offer a case study that underlines the value of using TA for developing vibrant communities. Some may want to read this first!

How to Use this Book

My hope is that you will find *Are We Together?* a valuable resource in improving the quality of life *within* the community. You will find many concepts from Transactional Analysis useful both personally and professionally. The best way to use this book is to read it in the context of community meetings, or over the course of a series of community workshops.

It may also be important to say that the concepts of TA require careful study if we are going to apply them to improve the dynamics of community life. Studying *Are We Together?* as a group is, therefore, a great way to undertake this work.

In each chapter I introduce a key concept of TA, and my hope is that readers will gradually assimilate TA theory into their analysis of their own community experience, and further use the theory to develop a richer quality of community living.

At the conclusion to each chapter, there are a number of exercises designed to help you assimilate the content of the chapter in question. Doing the exercises, while not essential, is highly recommended. Even more valuable is when you work on the exercises with the members of your group or community. The sharing of experiences and understandings, not only deepens your own appreciation of the dynamics of community life, but also can provide a fascinating insight into the people with whom you live, and an opportunity for them to come to know you more fully.

My hope also is that *Are We Together?* could form the basis for that aspect of formation programmes that focuses on how to understand the inner workings of community, and how to live community in rich and healthy ways.

At the end of *Are We Together?* I have listed various texts that are very useful for people who wish to pursue more deeply their study of TA.

The Title: Are We Together?

I conclude the introduction with word of explanation on the title of the book. Recently, I was in Africa with a selected group of Brothers who were preparing to be part of a task force in restructuring their Congregation. As part of the programme, we had the privilege of meeting some very inspiring African people who gave input into the process. When some of the presenters wanted to know if the Brothers were following the material they were giving, they would ask, 'Are we together?' meaning 'Do you understand what I am saying?'

So, when thinking about a title for this book on the development of community, I thought the phrase most apt in seeking to communicate the theory of TA to a wider audience of people who want to form vibrant and cohesive communities. The question, 'Are We Together?' not only seeks to find out whether the readership understands the concepts of TA, but also poses the question as to how united a community is in living religious community life.

I do hope that somehow this book will contribute to bringing people together in a spirit of unity and love.

The Revised Edition

The revised edition has corrected some typographical errors and has included the concept of Antiscript, which had been omitted in the previous edition (*pp.* 76-77). Other minor changes have also been included as a result of feedback from readers.

August 2014

ARE WE TOGETHER?

COMMUNITY LIFE IN ACTION
(REVISED EDITION)

Our Script

"You write your life story by the choices you make.
You never know if they have been a mistake.
Those moments of decision are so difficult."
Helen Mirren

At a recent workshop that I attended introducing people to Transactional Analysis (TA), I was surprised that Mark Head, the facilitator, opened the sessions with the topic of Script (Head, 2014). The facilitator's reason for starting with Script, he said, was that Script affects our whole life, and that understanding Script at the outset, puts ego states, transactions and games in context. I liked his reasoning.

This book, therefore, will begin by presenting the idea of Script and how Script situates us in a particular life position (Chapters 1 and 2). Once we understand how our Script shapes our lives, we introduce Structural and Functional Analysis of ego states (Chapters 3 and 4), the former analysis referring to the content of our ego states and the latter dealing with how our ego states function in real life. With a clear idea of the 'what' and the 'how' of the ego states, we can then examine how ego states can be contaminated (Chapter 5). When we talk about contamination, we are highlighting the fact that many people may have the impression that they are acting in a mature fashion, when in reality, they may be working from prejudice or indeed from delusion. Therefore, it is very valuable to be able to diagnose which ego state a person is acting from, and Chapter 6 offers four different levels of diagnosis. Chapters 7 and 8 focus on how the family influence plays a significant role in the creation of our Script. These chapters also discuss how the various levels of contamination in our Adult ego state can be the result of inter-generational contamination. Chapter 9 shows how Script is played out in the context of our day-to-day living and especially in connection with our relationship with time.

Note Well!

A note with regard to the anecdotes scattered throughout the text. All of the incidents are real and most of them happened! However, I have protected the identity of the people either by interchanging male and female characters, or by so disguising the people and the situations, so that no person can be identified. Any likeness to a person you know is purely coincidental.

Chapter One

Our Script

"There is no greater agony
than bearing an untold story inside you."
Maya Angelou

Sister Joan was the leader of her community, and had been appointed for a three-year term. She came across as a domineering, controlling and somewhat paranoid person, who easily took offence when the members of her community did not immediately greet her ideas or suggestions with approval. She was constantly on guard to prevent any member of the community going against her wishes. Often she felt that the community was non-cooperative and even rebellious, and so she felt that the only way to control matters was to be a step ahead of the sisters, and quash any hint of rebellion or disagreement.

For the community, Sister Joan was a nightmare. Any sense of freedom and creativity on their part was considered a threat to her, and so for peace sake, the community simply went along with what Sr Joan wanted even though this was done with an underlying feeling of resentment and rebellion. The community often grumbled about the way leadership was being exercised, but most were too afraid of the power and rigidity with which St Joan exercised her authority to voice their dissatisfaction openly.

How did Sister Joan become so powerful, so dominant and so abusive? She was not born that way, and yet it seemed that she was incapable of being otherwise. As long as people knew her, Sister Joan always came across as strong and definite about her views and attitudes. It seemed that no matter how many courses she undertook, she seemed impervious to change. Her previous communities had found her extremely difficult, and her superiors wondered if giving her some measure of authority would help her understand the need for leading a community instead of driving it, for listening instead of telling people what to do. They discovered too late that Sister Joan was even more dysfunctional in leadership than she had been as a member of a community. Then she was constantly at odds with her higher superiors, and now, little had changed.

The description of Sister Joan highlights the phenomenon of Script where Sister Joan had become the person she was as a result of an early decision she made in childhood which led her to think, feel and behave in such an authoritarian manner. From an early age, Joan realised that she could only survive if she became controlling and dominating, thus ensuring that nobody could hurt or control her. Having grown up in a family where her parents were inconsistent in the way they treated her, sometimes offering love and affection, and at other times punishing and demeaning her, Joan made an early decision that she would make sure that nobody was going to hurt her in the future. She would attack first in order to defend herself from being hurt. She formed a Script that had her as the victor of any battle that loomed on the horizon. This Script had a beginning, middle and end, and the end had her as a victorious but lone warrior triumphant after a bloody battle. In summary, her Script was 'I must always defend myself against attack and the best form of defence is attack first.'

A Definition of Script

Eric Berne said that each of us from an early age writes a Script that will determine the way our life unfolds (Berne, 1961:117). He was particularly interested in those Scripts that are confining rather than liberating. No doubt some people have a Script that is healthy and positive, and we will discuss healthy Scripts anon. However, when Berne talked about Script, he was dealing mainly with limiting Scripts. We focus in this chapter, therefore, on those Scripts that prevent the person from living a full and integrated individual life, and from leading a rich and dynamic community life.

Berne defined a Script as:

> 'A life plan based on a decision made in childhood, reinforced by the parents, justified by subsequent events, and culminating in a chosen alternative.' (Berne, 1972:493)

Like any Script for a novel or play, a life Script has a beginning, a middle and an end, and so when we write our Script, we unconsciously work out how this Script will unfold in the course of our life. The Script is what the person plans to do, and then life shows how this Script will work out. Berne calls this development of Script the 'life course', indicating what happens when a person lives according to their Script (*Ibid:*75).

It may be useful to take the various elements of Berne's definition of Script quoted above to understand what is involved in each aspect of a person's Script.

A Life Plan

It is difficult to imagine that a child from an early age would have a definite plan for his or her life, but Berne believed that by the age of six, and even as early as three, a child will have formed a definite life plan (Berne: 1972: 122).

When we talk about a life plan, we are not simply talking about a general view of life, or of the world, or of the future. The plan refers to how children will relate to the people they meet, and how they will face the moments of success and failure. It details how children will work out the way their life will unfold, how they will manage the various challenges facing them, and how ultimately they will face the final moment of death.

The plan may be somewhat determined by physical, emotional and environmental factors, but no one factor will decide the type of Script that the person writes. Woollams and Brown call this level of determination, the 'vulnerability quotient' (1978:152). The physical make up of the person, whether they are healthy, intelligent, or handicapped in any way will impact on the quality of life they lead. Whether they are born into a poor or wealthy family will also have some implications as to their future. The influence that people with whom they interact early on in their life will, in addition, impact positively or negatively on how they view themselves, others and the future that they envisage for their life.

Berne describes the initial Script as a household drama that is played out very early on in life (Berne, 1961:117). He calls this early Script, the *protocol,* which is the earliest draft of the Script. The *protocol* lays the foundation for the *Script proper,* which is formed later after a number of revisions of the initial *protocol.* The various revisions occur at different moments in early childhood and adolescence.

Like the medieval monks who had to correct misspells or mistakes in their original manuscript (protocol) by scraping the vellum to remove the error, and writing the correct version (palimpsest) instead, so the Script can be changed to create a *palimpsest* – a *Script proper* on which corrections or modifications to the basic *protocol* can be made. As the child grows and develops up to the age of adolescence, and is exposed to a wider environment, parts of the early elements of the Script will be modified in some of the details, although it is unlikely that the major thrust will change radically. Hence, we can appreciate Berne's metaphor of the *palimpsest* as a revision of the initial *protocol* until the Script is finally written. While the child adapts to various circumstances – Berne calls this *the adaptation* – the basic plan or Script is established by the time the person reaches adolescence.

When we talk about Script as an *'unconscious life plan'* (Berne, 1966:228) we are referring to the initial *protocol* which is out of awareness. The child formed this early Script before she had any level of self-consciousness. Hence, it is almost impossible to access that early life plan (protocol) even with the help of some form of therapy. And because the Script is unconscious, the person is inclined to replay the Script throughout his or her life. Freud called the tendency to re-live the Script in daily life, a 'destiny compulsion' where at an unconscious level, the person feels unable to resist the basic compulsion to live according to the early life plan (Freud, 1922: 43ff).

Based on a decision made in childhood

The decisional nature of Script points to the belief that we have the capacity to determine how our life should unfold. It may be that our level of freedom is quite limited, but nevertheless, Berne held that we do have a certain level of freedom to choose despite the powerful forces impacting on us from an early age. Script decisions refer to certain decisions made in childhood in response to far from ideal situations. These decisions determine to a great extent how the child will respond to similar situations in the future. Just as Script is understood as a compulsion to repeat in the present some of the patterns from the past, it should be noted that two children from a similar background might decide to respond in two very different ways. Theoretically then, we could conceive that for one child the response to their environment would lead to tragic Script decisions, whereas the other child's response could avoid such a negative outcome.

Berne (1972:137) cites the example of a mother who responds exasperatedly to her two sons who were annoying her, and behaving outrageously, by saying, "You'll both end up in a psychiatric ward!' Both of them did: one as a patient and the other as a consultant psychiatrist! In the face of similar situations, the decisional quality of our response lies within our capacity to choose. Then, as a result of the actual decisions that we make, we create our own future.

The decisional nature of the Script needs, as well, to be understood within an awareness of the limitations of a child's capacity to decide. Naturally, a child has not developed the intellectual capacity from an early age to weigh up all the pros and cons in a given situation. Consequently, it should be noted that the decisional nature of the response could be more an emotional and reflex reaction to a given situation rather than a fully worked-out rational decision.

Reinforced by Parents

Berne describes how a Script is 'transmitted' through the directives handed down from parents to their children (Berne: 1972:314). We will see later how this mechanism works, but suffice it to say for the moment that, although the impact of parents is not determinant in the creation of the Script, it plays a very important part in the Script formation.

The word 'reinforced' implies that the parent simply colludes with the child's initial Script decisions. This may be a rather simplistic notion that underplays the vital role of parents in the actual formation of the initial *protocol.* Developments in neuroscience emphasise the crucial impact of the caregiver's influence on the very formation of the child's emotional life (Schore, 2003; 2012). The very growth of brain of the child is significantly dependent on the loving gaze of the caregivers.

It is also interesting to see how more recent views on the role of parents in the formation of Script is seen as more bi-directional (Summers &Tudor, 2000: 24ff; Cornell, 1988:277). By this we mean that the child can impact on the parent just as much as the parent impacts on the child. The behaviour of infants – how calm or troubled they are, for example – has its effect on the responses of parents to the infant. So, the child is not simply a passive recipient of the parents' attitudes and behaviours, but is an active player in the drama of early life (Barr, 1987:135ff).

Justified by subsequent events

When a person has formed their Script, they then view the world from the perspective of that decisional stance. So, for instance, when Sister Joan's Script was based on the belief that she had to fight her corner because the world was out to get her, she then viewed every event and most people as threats to her very existence. Every event confirmed or justified her original Script, and further convinced her of the need to be vigilant and aggressive even when objectively there was no obvious danger. Berne (1972:137) calls the outcome of the Script the *payoff,* where the outcome of the Script justifies the Script, and confirms the validity of the Script in the mind of the Script-bound person. Every time Sister Joan met with any form of opposition, she confirmed the validity of her original decisional stance that she took before people and the world at large.

And culminating in a chosen alternative

The chosen alternative further highlights the decisional nature of Script and implies that a variety of choices are possible in the moment when the Script is established. Berne (Berne, 1972: 223; 251) talks about 'winning' and 'non-winning' Scripts and Steiner classifies the tragic Scripts as loveless, joyless or mindless, (Steiner, 1974: 77).

At each moment of a person's life there is the decisional moment to view life from a positive or negative stance, and what is somewhat comforting in this rather deterministic view of life is that the decisions taken early on in life can be changed (Berne, 1966:268). We can make new decisions that counter the early Script or to use Berne's phrase, 'we can close the show and put a better one on the road' (Berne, 1961: 118). This can happen when the person seeks therapy to confront their tragic Script, or when the person experiences relationships that go to heal the hurts of the past.

Script and Community Life

Each member of a community will have their own Script that may be a winning, a losing or a banal Script.

The winning Script is one where the person sets out to achieve a goal and ends up achieving it (Berne, 1972:234). The winning Script, Berne says, turns us into Princes and Princesses, while the losing Script turns us into frogs! (*Ibid:*58). In the winning Script, the person fulfils the contract they have with themselves and with the world. They have a sense of achievement and satisfaction having accomplished what they set out to do. They have fulfilled their 'declared purpose' in life (Berne, 1972:497). In a sense, we could say that a people are winners when they are not 'in Script', that is, when they are not confined by an unconscious life plan that has been shaped by the inadequacies of parents and tragic events. The person is 'Script free'.

The losing Script is where people never achieve what they set out to do. They become frogs instead of princes and princesses (*Ibid:*58;115). They may have glorious plans but they never materialise. Consequently, people could appear to be very successful, achieving many feats, gaining academic honours and awards, and could still be a loser because their declared purpose in life was not fulfilled. We all know people who seem to have everything, who have achieved amazing successes, receiving much acclaim, and yet they are not content. This is due to the fact that they have a losing Script where their aim in life has not come to fruition.

The banal or non-winning Script is described by Steiner as those that '...go unnoticed like water running down the drain' and who at the end of their lives realise '...that their potentialities as human beings have in some mysterious ways been betrayed and defeated' (Steiner, 1974:97). They may be religious who spend most of the day in silent adoration before the television, or who prefer to avoid assuming any form of responsibility for fear of making a mistake. For them it is better not to have tried at all rather than have tried and failed.

And losing and banal Scripts can be further categorised as mindless, joyless or loveless.

A mindless Script is one that ignores various elements of rationality that would benefit a person in making sense of their life. People, who seem to resist any desire to have self-knowledge or awareness, fall into this category (*Ibid:*118ff). People with mindless Scripts seem to be locked into their own small back yard, and have no interest in the wider world, or in the lives of other people and nations. Often, they are so focussed on concrete reality, that they discount intuition, and limit their view to what is observable. Religious men and women with mindless Scripts accept the *status quo* blindly, afraid to challenge the orthodox way of viewing life, and comfortable with the accepted norms.

Joyless Scripts come from situations where the very creativity of children (or religious for that matter) was crushed due to over-control or criticism from their parents (*Ibid:*139ff). Their parents' constant criticism blocks the natural exuberance that is so often evident in young children. Spontaneity is replaced by fear of taking initiative, or of being creatively different. With a joyless Script, the very heart of the child is changed from being a heart of flesh to a heart of stone. Religious who live joyless Scripts appear as God's frozen people instead of God's chosen people! They are not good specimens for vocation literature, nor are they very easy people in community, because any form of exuberance, spontaneity and freedom creates high anxiety in them.

Loveless Scripts are characterised by a lack of human contact or what Steiner described as strokes (*Ibid:*105ff). The experience of being held lovingly by the mother creates in the child, a sense of being loved and cared for. The absence of such human contact means that the child shrivels up and dies either literally or metaphorically. Berne called this need for touch, *stimulus hunger* that is almost more important than food itself (Berne, 1961: 83). Adults too need the support of touch, be it physical touch or simply the recognition by others that they exist. How easy it is for people in community to simply disappear due to the lack of recognition. They simply fade into the woodwork and become invisible to each other. In situations where workaholism dominates the life of the community, religious can find themselves as simple cogs in an impersonal wheel of efficiency and end up loveless and lifeless.

We all come from families where our needs were either met fully (hence a winning Script) or, for the most of us, where we perceived that somehow we did not receive the necessary love, acceptance, support or encouragement that we needed to develop into a fully mature and contented adult. In the light of such deficits, our approach to life will be Script-bound in one way or the other. Our behaviour in a community setting will, therefore, result in various behaviours that often may inhibit a healthy way of interacting within a group.

It is only as we begin to reflect on our own behaviour, and that of the other members of the community, that we can come to a compassionate understanding of why we, or others in the community, behave or interact in ways that may not be helpful in creating a positive community spirit.

The challenge for each of us is to begin to diagnose our own Script before we seek to identify other's Scripts. Or if we begin with the analysis of other's Scripts, we also need to pay attention to our own way of being within the community.

Because the formation of Script is an initially unconscious process, it is often very difficult to get in touch with the early Script decisions that have formed our ways of thinking, feeling and behaving. Some of the exercises offered at the end of the chapter may help in identifying some of the elements of a person's Script, and offer an opportunity to apply the theory to our own situation. Simply reading the theory has not the same effect as working through the exercises in a systematic way.

When the members of the community work together on finding out more about each other, the quality of the community life is enriched. Needless to say, such sharing at a community level is challenging and not without risk. It can, therefore, be useful to have a facilitator to assist the community in its growth and development.

Conclusion

What we have highlighted in this chapter is the reality that people come to community each with a different history and a different story. At the basis of each story is a set of beliefs about the person themselves, about other people, and about how they view the world and their future. These beliefs impact on the person internally, even physiologically, and form the way the person views the world. Recognition of the differences between people offers us an insight into the richness of community living, and presents an invitation to a community to draw on this rich tapestry of personal stories in order for the quality of life together to be enhanced. It is only when people feel free enough to explore the various elements of their Script that the members of the community can begin to grow in mutual understanding and acceptance.

Exercises

1. Pick a favourite fairy story or other type of story that you remember from your childhood. Write it down in as much detail as you can remember, even adding to it if you like! In writing the story, describe the characters, noting their thoughts and feelings. When you have finished writing the story, share the story with the rest of the community. Then ask them to tell you how they think the story reflects some aspects of your life. And finally, share how you think the story applies to your way of thinking, feeling and behaving.

2. If you were to write your own epitaph what would it be? Share this with your community and ask them what epitaph they think would suit you better and why.

3. What are your declared goals in life? Are you achieving them?

4. In a sentence write down the core belief you have about yourself, others and the future that lies before you.

5. Were you to describe your Script as mindless, joyless or loveless which one would you pick to apply to yourself? And why? Give examples that illustrate your point.

6. What one thing would you want to change in order to begin to change or modify your Script?

Chapter Two

Life Positions

"Two looked out through prison bars;
one saw mud, the other stars."
Oscar Wilde

How is it that within the one community there can be such a variety of temperaments, personalities and philosophies of life? The simple answer is that people's personalities, temperaments and philosophies vary for a multiplicity of reasons that often defy explanation. People have very differing views of themselves, others and the world due to the way they position themselves *vis-à-vis* life, and often such positions are made very early in life.

Br John seems to be the epitome of an integrated adult. He is pleasant with everyone and manages to weather misunderstandings and pettiness with aplomb that at times infuriates other members of the community. He appears to have an even temper that seldom changes, and yet he is able to be assertive when he needs to be without being aggressive.

In the same community is Br Michael who feels that he is not good enough in comparison with others who seem more qualified, more intelligent and better teachers. Because he lacks confidence and fears failure, he often avoids any role of responsibility, and suffers from a mild form of depression. He finds life in community difficult, and often retires to his room outside the times of prayer and meals, or he takes comfort in alcohol to the extent that it is becoming a problem.

Br Anthony is inclined to be very dominant and opinionated, and the other members of the community often react by avoiding any form of disagreement with him. He seems to think that it is his way or the highway, and even though he is not the officially appointed leader of the community, it appears that he has self-appointed himself as the local superior. He has an opinion on almost everything and when he expresses his views, he gives the impression that no other view could possibly exist.

Each of the above characters live in the same community and Br Michael and Br Anthony find it quite difficult for different reasons to interact with the other members of the community in a way that is healthy and mature. Nor was it easy for the mature Br John, although he has enough resources to manage the various levels of dysfunction that are only too evident to him.

No community is without people who struggle to live a healthy and positive interpersonal life. By understanding why people can become depressed, aggressive or despondent, we can have a more compassionate view of 'difficult' members, but more importantly, we can understand how we ourselves function on a day-to-day basis, and under differing circumstances. This chapter seeks to explain how such a variety of characters can develop through what Berne called 'life-positions' (Berne, 1962:23; 1966: 270).

Existential life positions are closely related to the idea of Script, where the position a person assumes very early in life becomes the foundation for the development of Script. Berne says that these positions are more or less fixed by as early as three years of age, while some others see that a child could have adopted their life position even earlier than that (Steiner, 1971:74). Subsequent to the choice of life-positions, the Script begins to be formed along the lines suggested by the life-position.

Berne classified the life positions as:

> I'm OK – You're OK
> I'm Not OK – You're OK
> I'm OK – You're Not OK
> I'm Not OK – You're Not OK

These four positions track how a person views both themselves and others, and how these positions impact on the way a person relates to other people. In outlining the elements of the four positions, Franklin Ernst indicated how each position is characterised by the manner in which we relate to other people (Ernst, 1971: 33ff) and this classification of behaviours he termed *an operation,* that is, how people operate socially from a particular standpoint (Fig. 1).

You are OK

Get Away From (*operation*) I'm Not OK- You're OK Flight Humble – (depressive)	Get On With (*operation*) I'm OK – You're OK Free Healthy
Get Nowhere with (*operation*) I'm Not OK – You're Not OK Freeze Hopeless (Schizoid)	Get Rid Of (*operation*) I'm OK – You're Not OK Fight Hurtful (Paranoid)

I am Not OK *(left)*   I am OK *(right)*

You are Not OK

Fig.1 The OK Corral: Grid for What's Happening (Ernst 1971 adapted)

I'm OK – You're OK

The healthy position (I'm OK – You're OK) is where people have a positive self-image and a healthy level of self-acceptance. They recognise their strengths and weaknesses, and are open to growth and personal development. Being OK does not mean being perfect, but rather is an attitude of willingness to change and explore possibilities. The I'm OK – You're OK person views others in a positive light. They are not blind to the faults and weaknesses of others, but they accept the person 'warts and all'. They may not see the other's behaviour as OK, but they do not equate the behaviour with the essential value of each person. So, they can well be critical of the behaviour of a person while, at the same time, demonstrating positive regard for the person not withstanding everything. They are characterised by a level of freedom both personal and interpersonal where they relate to people in an adult fashion. So, in terms of Ernst's *operations* mentioned above, these people *get on with* others, and overall have a positive impact on a community, helping to create harmony and peace.

I'm Not OK- You're OK

The humble position (I'm Not OK – You're OK) is characterised by people with a sense of inferiority where they view others as better than themselves, and where they fail to see many positive qualities that they themselves may have. They are only too well aware of their weaknesses, and find themselves, to a greater or lesser extent, paralysed by the belief that they cannot achieve what they see others achieving. They are inclined to constantly compare themselves with others, and invariably come out second best. They are blind to their own gifts, and blind to the limitations of others. So, the other person is seen as perfect, and they consider themselves as somehow damaged or flawed. They are in the one-down position. As they view other people, they imagine that others have solved life's problems and are simply sailing though life while their life is a continual struggle. In terms of Ernst's *operations* they seek to *get away from* people or using the flight, fight or freeze image, they *flee* human contact because the interaction with others whom they consider better than themselves only makes their lives more miserable. Depression is often present in people who have this view of life. People who find themselves in this position are frequently inclined to spend a lot of their time in their rooms, or find themselves before the television in the hope of avoiding any form of intimacy or even superficial conversation.

I'm OK – You're Not OK

The hurtful position (I'm OK – You're Not OK), also seen as the paranoid position, is where people view themselves as strong, independent and generally superior to others. They are often characterised by a certain lack of empathy and intolerance for those who are weak or not as OK as they consider themselves to be. The paranoid aspect of this position reveals itself in a hypersensitivity to any form of potential threat, where this person decides to attack rather than leave him or herself open to criticism or blame. A community with such a person appears to be walking on eggshells, afraid of incurring the anger or disapproval of the angry person. Often paranoid people are so sensitive to potential slights that they become almost totally insensitive to the impact of their behaviour on others in the community. It is in this community that the dictum 'peace at any price' often predominates. In terms of Ernst's *operations,* the paranoid's position is how to *get rid of* those who are considered a nuisance or simply of no use to the person. These are the people who never resort to *flight* because they are always ready to *fight.*

I'm Not OK – You're Not OK

The hopeless position (I'm Not OK – You're Not OK) describes the person who sees little light at the end of the tunnel. Their view of themselves is marked by self-criticism, depression, anger and other difficult emotions that seem never to lift. Their view of themselves, others and the future is a gloomy one, and they struggle to see the positive side in people and situations. They display a high level of passivity, and perceive challenges as insuperable burdens that they consider impossible to carry. They are stuck or they *freeze,* caught in a web of discontent, sadness and hopelessness, which can lead them to feel that they are going crazy. So, Ernst categorises this hopeless position as one where the person *gets nowhere with* either people or situations. The psychiatric label would identify them as schizoid. They seem to imagine that nothing can be done. They *freeze* instead of using *fight* or *flight.* In the extreme, a member of a community that suffers from such a debilitating outlook may need some form of psychiatric care or medication. They can drain the efforts of the members of the community who seek to raise their spirits, or offer any form of comfort or reassurance.

Needless to say, the above descriptions of the three difficult life positions are rather extreme examples and, therefore, we may not find it easy to situate ourselves fully in any one quadrant. It is important to stress, however, that each life-position can have broad continuum along which we can place ourselves. We all recognise some aspects of any one or more of the positions in both others and ourselves. Most people find that they situate themselves in a number of the quadrants depending on the situation in which they find themselves. There may be times when we are more in one space than in the other. However, since we are talking about our Script position, where the Script is heavily influenced by the position we take, we will probably find that we favour one quadrant over the others. So, our choice is between the humble, the hurtful or the hopeless quadrants when we are talking about Script.

The Corralogram

Franklin Ernst devised a method for charting the moments we spend in any one of the quadrants during the course of the day. He called the device, the *Corralogram*, which invites the person to chart where they are either in any one normal day, or indeed in specific situations (Ernst, 1982:5ff). A typical chart could look like what we see in Fig. 2. (Note the abbreviations of U+, U-. I+. I- for You're OK- You're not OK and I'm Ok, I'm Not OK etc.). In the exercises that follow we will have the opportunity to draw up our own corralogram.

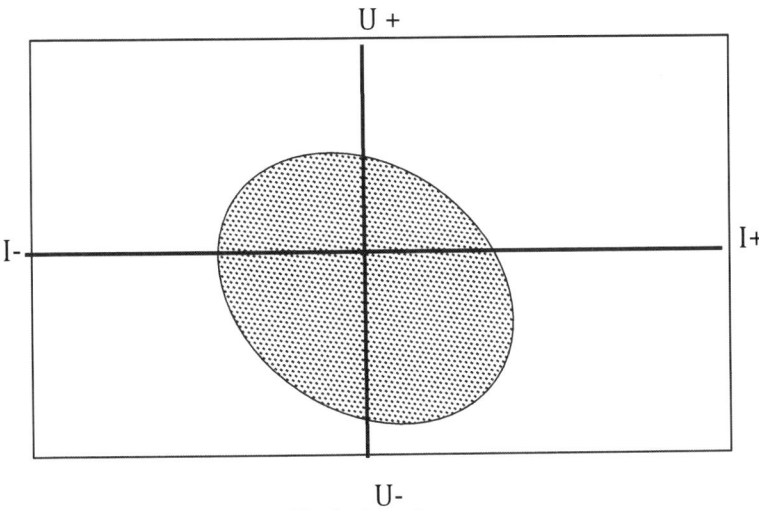

Fig. 2 Corralogram

Can we move Positions?

To the question 'Can a person move from one position to another one?' Stewart and Joines (2012:127) respond in the affirmative. So, for the person in the Humble position (I-U+), they may need to move from the Humble position through the Hurtful position (I+U-) where they feel stronger and even superior to others, before they move to the Healthy position (I+U+), where both people are seen as OK.

Likewise, someone in the Hopeless position (I-U-) may need to move first through the Humble position (I-U+) where they see at least that some people are OK, and then move through the Hurtful position (I+U-) where they gain some confidence in themselves before they move to the Healthy position (I+U+).

And finally, the person in the Hurtful position (I+U-) needs to move through the Humble position (I-U+) because the position of the paranoid seeing themselves as OK is a defence against a basic sense of inferiority. Once they accept their own limitations, they can then move to the Healthy position (I+U+).

Such movements can be assisted by therapy, friendship and/or spiritual direction. The changes from one position to a healthier position requires effort and some assistance, especially when one of the quadrants is very pronounced in the life of the person.

Conclusion

So far we have dealt with our Script and our life-positions where, at an early age, we made decisions for our future according to the way we viewed life. Naturally, these decisions are based on the very limited knowledge available to a child at the time of forming their Script, and situating themselves in one of the life-positions. Even the information available to them at the time is largely based on perceptions rather than on objective facts, and often the perceptions they have of their parents were of necessity limited and partial. Nevertheless, at a very early age, children *do* make decisions on the information they have, and these decisions often continue to determine the way they live their lives into adulthood. The reason for our Scripts being so indelibly etched in our psyche can be explained by the way our inner thoughts and beliefs are formed through the interaction with our parents, and with the wider environment. In the next chapter, we will see how our thinking, feeling and behaviour is influenced by the memories we have of our childhood, and by the way we experienced our parents or caregivers.

Exercises

1. Place Brothers Anthony, John and Michael in their respective life-positions.

2. Can you identify people you know (not in your community) whom you can place in each of the quadrants? Share these with your community, while respecting the identity of these people. Describe their behaviour and how this behaviour impacts on you.

3. Share with your community when and in what circumstances you find yourself in each of the life positions.

4. Draw your corralogram, which identifies how you position yourself in the normal course of the day. Share it with one of your community.

5. What practical ways could you change your principal position were you to find yourself in the Hurtful, Humble or Hopeless position?

Chapter Three

Picturing the Inner Community

"Every person is defined by the communities she belongs to."
Orson Scott Card

Imagine a community of five sisters living together in community, and interacting with each other on a daily basis. Whereas, externally their number is five, in reality there are probably hundreds of people present amongst that small group, alive and well inside the heads of the individual members. Each of us is more than a single unit, for within each person there resides an inner community of many sub-personalities. So, what we see physically in the person may hide a very different reality! Shakespeare when he said, 'there is not art to find the mind's construction in the face.' had a real insight into how we can hide behind our masks!

Borrowing the title of this chapter from Betty Badenoch (2008), the focus here is the structure of personality, and particularly the concept of ego states that Eric Berne developed to explain the inner workings of the person (Berne, 1961:30). Ego states can be defined as various sub-personalities of the person, which have developed from earliest childhood, and which impact on the way we see life and how we behave. By identifying the various ego states in a person, we come to understand the thoughts, feelings and behaviours of people, and learn how to respond to them in ways that are helpful and compassionate.

Berne said that a person exhibited three different ego states, which he called the Parent, the Adult and the Child. To distinguish the ego states from the ordinary category of parents, adults and children, he wrote the ego states in capital letters, a custom we will follow here. Berne defined an ego state as 'a consistent pattern of feeling and experience, directly related to a corresponding consistent pattern of behaviour' (Berne 1966:364).

What he meant by his definition was that each ego state can be distinguished by the thoughts, feelings and behaviours of the Parent, the Adult and the Child. The Parent thinks, feels and behaves. The Adult thinks, feels and behaves. The Child thinks, feels and behaves. Feelings and thoughts impact on behaviours creating a pattern that can be recognised. Berne illustrated the concept of ego states by forming three circles, one on top of the other, as in Fig. 3. He used the letters PAC as an abbreviation for Parent, Adult and Child (Berne, 1961:31).

Of course people are more than their ego states! In a way, the model of ego states is just that – a model or a metaphor of reality (Gobes, 1990:163). But Berne's identification of ego states has proved very valuable in being able to describe the inner reality of the person. Gobes describes ego states as 'an elegant metaphor, a richly significant representation of an inner experience' (*Ibid:*163).

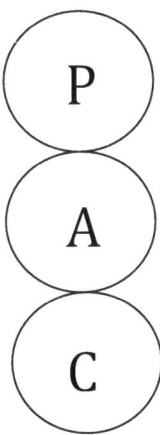

Fig. 3 The Ego State Model (Berne, 1961)

Berne, when he defined ego states as consistent patterns of feeling and experience directly related to a corresponding pattern of behaviour, understood clearly the interconnectedness of cognition, affect and behaviour. The way we behave, he discovered, is often impacted by the way we think and/or feel. This can be diagrammed as in Fig. 4 below.

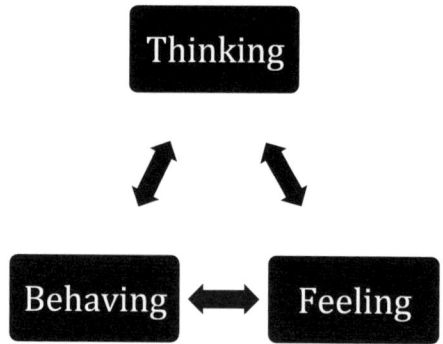

Fig. 4 Consistent Pattern of Thinking, Feeling and Behaving

This interconnectedness of thinking, feeling and behaviour is not unlike the approach of cognitive-behaviour therapy that stresses the connection between these three aspects of a person's way of being (Beck, 1975).

The Parent Ego State

The Parent ego state is created from the memories that a person has of their own parents. Thomas Harris calls these memories, recordings that continue to be played like tape recordings in the head of a person (Harris, 1967). So, in a sense, the parents of a person are alive and well inside their heads, even when the person is an adult. The person has memories of how their parents acted, spoke, behaved in the past, and now in adulthood, the person is still influenced in the present by the way their parents interacted with them in the past. To some extent, they have 'swallowed' or introjected their parents in their Parent ego state, and now they feel, think and behave under the influence of their parents as if the person was back in childhood.

There is no generic Parent ego state. It is not like the *Superego* of Freud that is a theoretical construct to describe how the *ego* is safeguarded by the *Superego*_from the uncontrollable impulses of the *id.*

The Parent ego state refers rather to specific parents in a particular moment in history. So, the Parent ego state is different for each person, because each person had his or her own unique parent. Consequently, two people could be acting from their Parent ego state, and thinking, feeling and behaving very differently because the parents of the two people were very different personalities.

The Adult Ego State

The Adult ego state is that part of the person that is busy, in the words of Berne, 'marshalling and processing data and perceptions concerning her immediate situation' (Berne, 1961: 30). In other words, the Adult ego state deals with the present, whereas the Parent and Child ego states are creations from the past that impact on the person in the present. The Adult thinks, feels and behaves in response to people and situations in the here and now. In this sense, the Adult is more rational in that it has the ability to test reality and respond accordingly. By stating that it is more rational, I do not mean that it cannot feel. Rather, the Adult feels as a result of current events instead of being overcome by ancient influences from the Parent, or by the fears or memories from the archaic Child.

The Child Ego State

The Child ego state replays the thoughts, feelings and behaviours that people experienced in childhood. The Child ego state consists of what Berne describes as a situation where 'the relics of childhood survive into later life' (Berne, 1961; 36). In the Child ego state are the various memories that people have of their childhood, and how they reacted to their parents and to various situations that took place over the course of their childhood. So, when an adult is in situations that remind them of similar situations from their childhood, they begin to react like they reacted when they were young. Hence, despite the fact that they have grown and become more 'rational' people, they can find themselves feeling and thinking like they did when they were children. When they behave in this manner, we say that they are in their Child ego state.

At the beginning of this chapter, we said that the 'inner community' consists of many members, and by this we mean that a person forms ego states from the very moment of birth and continues to do so throughout their life. The ego state model could appear to be something static that is laid down once and for all. This would reify the concept of ego states and objectify the person as a 'thing' rather than a living entity (Loria, 1990:152ff). It is important to stress, therefore, that at each stage of development, the person forms ego states and that the fully developed person not only uses their current ego states of Parent, Adult and Child, but is also impacted by the various ego states that were formed in the past. So, we will briefly outline the key stages in the development of the person to demonstrate how early formation influences significantly the way a person will live in community and indeed in society in general.

Infancy

Taking therefore the very beginning of life, we can imagine the baby who is just born and is totally dependent on the parent or caregiver for its survival. Viewing the ego state model at that stage, we could show it as drawn in Fig. 5

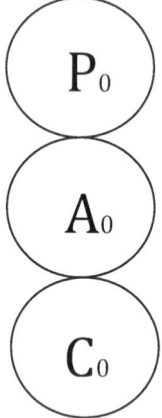

Fig. 5 The Ego State Model of an infant

I have numbered the ego states here as P_0, A_0 and C_0 to distinguish them from the earlier generic model shown in Fig.3 The reasons for this will become clearer later on. The infant at this early stage is not conscious of self, but rather is reacting to its environment. In the words of Daniel Stern this is the moment of the 'emergent self' where the infant is in a state of what he calls 'alert inactivity' (Stern, 1985:44). So, C_0 is the emergent self that is experiencing the surrounding environment and particularly the mother (P_0), who is not viewed initially as a person but rather as the source of food and comfort. The interaction between the parent (P_0) and the infant (C_0) is instinctive. The infant turns its head toward the breast and sucks, and moves its feet and hands (palmar reflex) instinctively. This interaction between the parent and the child is the work of A_0, an out-of-conscious reflex response by the infant to the environment (Schiff, 1975).

This period of pre-verbal interaction between the parent and the child is vital for the healthy formation of the emotional life of the child. The work of Allan Schore highlights the impact of the parent-child interaction on the formation of the right hemisphere of the child's cortex, and subsequently on the capacity of the child to regulate affect (Schore, 2003:215). The recent study of the mirror neurons in the brain further confirm that the interaction between the parent and her child sparks corresponding neurons in mother and infant, creating a duet of harmony between parent and child (Iacoboni & Siegel, 2004). In other words, not only is the infant responding autonomically to the parent, but also the emotional life of the child is beginning to be formed through the loving gaze of the parent, and in the primal yearnings of the child for love and affection (Hargaden & Sills, 2002: 55ff).

When a parent, therefore, even unconsciously, has negative reactions to their infant, this will be picked up somatically in the very tissue of the infant, and will ultimately impact on the infant's sense of self, and on their ability to regulate their emotions. We will see in Chapter 7 how this early parent-child interaction or implicit relational knowing influences the way the adult will eventually deal with their self-image, and how the parent's unconscious messages are transmitted to the child at this early stage of their development (*Ibid:* 60). Needless to say, it is at this stage that the ground is being prepared for the formation of the *protocol* (Chapter 1).

In Community

When a member of a community is expressing or demonstrating feelings that seem to defy rational explanation, it may well be that they are connecting with the very early unconscious messages that they received from their parents in infancy (P_0, A_0 & A_0). Hence, despite much effort on the part of the other community members to deal with the negative feelings of their sister or brother, they may find it very difficult to counter these early unconscious messages that are shaping the life of the individual. Unless we appreciate how the very early life experience of a religious impacts on their current sense of self, our response to them will be one of impatience instead of compassion. And without compassion, there is very little hope that the person will be able to change.

Childhood

With the onset of speech on the part of the child, Stern describes this stage as the 'verbal self' where children gradually begin to share their experience with others, and construct a narrative for their life (Stern, 1985:150). This is the time when children interact verbally with their parents or caregivers and begin to form an inter-subjective self. At this stage, children will begin to express themselves, and also interpret the verbal messages of the parents.

In terms of ego states, the following diagram demonstrates the move from the unconscious, somatic interaction with the environment as shown in infancy (Fig. 5) to a more conscious albeit limited self-knowledge (Fig. 6). Again, for clarity sake, and to distinguish this stage from the infancy stage, we notate the Parent, Adult and Child with the number 1.

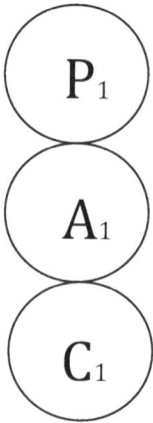

Fig. 6 The Ego State Model of a child

The Parent (P1) in the child at this stage of development is the introjected parent that the child has incorporated into his or her self (Erskine, 1988:17). The child is growing and developing, and exploring its environment. This stage occurs around the age of two to three, where language is developing, and the child is receiving verbal messages from parents, and expressing its thoughts and feelings about the world around. It is a time of curiosity and of wonder. In a sense, it is also a time of omnipotence, where the child feels that it can control its environment, and make the parents do what the child wants the parent to do for them. And yet, the child has limited knowledge and consequently does not understand fully the adult world.

When, therefore, the child sees its parents and hears their messages, he or she may not fully comprehend what is being said, or may misinterpret what is meant by the parental messages. When the parent, for example, tells the child to 'be careful' as the child leaves the house to play, the child may interpret this command as 'the world is not safe and so I better be careful' or 'I'm not capable of taking care of myself' or even ' don't trust the people you will meet'. Such messages then become incorporated or introjected into the Parent (P1) of the child and then when the parent is not present, the (P1) sends the message to the Child (C1) in the three or four-year old child (Fig.7). These messages begin to form the Script that will impact on the life of the child into adulthood. This Parent in the child has been called the 'Witch Parent' or the 'Pig Parent', or the Fairy Godmother when the P1 is benign (Steiner, 1974:42), highlighting the negative or positive messages that this Parent can communicate to the child.

The Child (C1) in the child is that part of the young person that is influenced by the messages that come from the introjected Parent (P1) in the child. This is the beginning of an internal dialogue between the Parent (P1) ego state and the Child (C1) ego state. The Child hears the introjected voices of the Parent (P1) even when away from their parents, and responds to these voices accordingly. Hence, if the child has introjected the message of its parents that the world is not safe, or that the child will not be able to manage the challenges of the world, then the child will be frightened, suspicious and unsure of itself (Fig. 7).

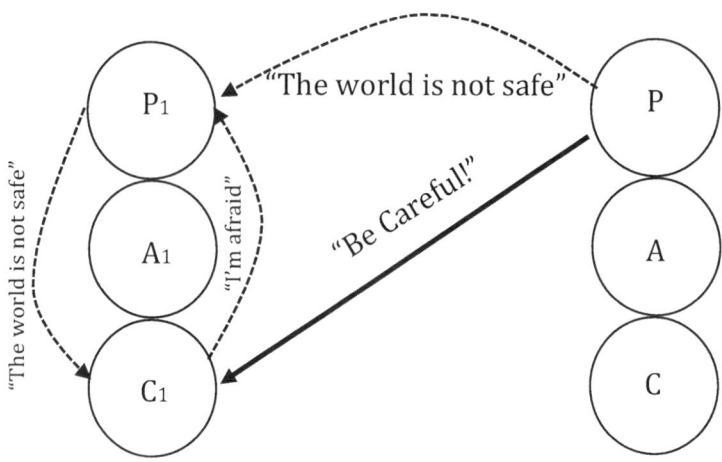

Fig. 7 Introjection of the message of the Parent of the adult
to the Parent of the child

The Child (C_1) in the child is often called the Somatic Child because, like the infant (P_0, A_0, C_0) many of the messages are stored in the very tissue of the muscles of the child, and may not always be available to conscious memory.

The Adult (A_1) in the child is often called the 'Little Professor' because the Adult has to make sense of the messages flying from the Parent (P_1) to the Child (C_1), and has to find a way to manage the fright that the Child is often experiencing in the face of the messages from the Parent (P_1) in the child. The Adult (A_1) ego state is the intuitive part of the child that seeks to work things out albeit with limited knowledge, or in the light of mistaken communication. So, when the introjected message of the Parent (P_1) is ' be careful', the Adult (A_1) finds ingenious ways of taking care of itself, and even managing the Child's (C_1) reaction to the 'Witch Parent'. This is the clever Little Professor (A_1) who works how to survive in the face of threats from the introjected Parent (P_1).

It is at this stage that the *protocol,* the *palimpsest* and the Script proper are being formed. Between childhood and adolescence the Script is being formulated in the light of the interaction between the young people, their parents, and the wider environment.

In Community

It is surprising how frequently we find ourselves working out of the childhood ego states when we are living in community! When we harbour resentments, and keep quiet when we feel slighted or misunderstood, we are in our Child ego state (C_1). We feel a mixture of emotions inside, but are afraid to express them for fear that people will dismiss us. So, our Parent ego state (P_1) warns us to stay silent, and forget the incident because of the fear or rejection or isolation. But, of course, we don't forget, and we don't forgive! At other times, we may have some fantasies about how another member of the community did something to offend us, but instead of checking this out in an adult way, again we keep the fantasy to ourselves for the sake of peace – an uncertain peace at that, and then let the resentment grow. Most of the time that we avoid conflict in community, it is from this early Child ego state stage that we are behaving.

Adulthood

In adulthood, the Script is established, and under moments of stress we find ourselves 'in Script' replying to those early messages that we incorporated in the face of the challenges of growing up. At times, we may be able to remain free of Script, but at different moments in the day, and in differing circumstances, we revert to Script beliefs and behaviours.

In Fig. 8 below, we have the ego state model of the adult, where we annotate the ego states with the number 2 to distinguish them from the infant (P_0, A_0 & A_0) and child ego states (P_1, A_1 & A_1). The sub-personalities of the grown adult (P_2, A_2 and C_2) represent ego states that are characterised by the thinking, feeling and behaviour appropriate to the mature adult.

The Parent (P_2) in the adult person is made up of the introjected parent in all its fullness. Unlike the introjection of the Parent (P_1) in the young child of between three years of age and adolescence, who introjects more their *impressions* of their parents than all aspects of the parent, P_2 is more an incorporation of all aspects of the parent, and of various adults that the grown person has allowed to influence them.

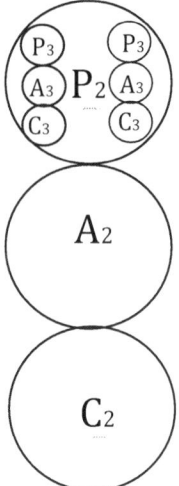

Fig. 8   Ego states of an adult

I am reminded of the quotation attributed to Mark Twain that goes like, "When I was a boy of fourteen, my father was so ignorant I could hardly stand to have the old man around. But when I got to be twenty-one, I was astonished at how much he had learned in seven years." In adulthood, the person has introjected all aspects of their parents both positive and negative, and finds him or herself under the influence of the beliefs and prejudices of their parents and formative adults.

In Fig. 8 above, I have placed various introjections (P3, A3, C3) in the Parent (P2) of the adult of the ego state model to show that others impact each of us with their own ego states. So, as adults, we have the content of the thinking, feeling and behaviour of our own parents and other influential people who go to form our own Parent (P2) ego state. Sometimes this influence is from the Parent (P3) of these introjects where their beliefs and prejudices are implanted in our Parent (P2). At other times it is their Child (C3) ego state that perpetuates Child fears and anxieties in our Parent, while again at other times, they pass on their Adult (A3) capacity to deal with life as they experienced it.

The Child (C2) in the adult refers to the thoughts, feelings and behaviours that are replayed from the various stages of childhood, from infancy right up to adolescence, when the brain is more or less fully developed (Siegel, 2014, 89ff). We all have memories from our childhood, and these memories impact on the way we think, feel and behave in the present. When we are conscious of the childhood memories, we have the opportunity to choose whether we will act according to the way we did in childhood, but often the memories may be hidden in the unconscious, and therefore we are acting from Child when we think we are being Adult.

The Adult (A2) is what Berne called 'one ego state characterized by reasonably adequate reality testing and rational reckoning' (Berne, 1961:31). The Adult ego state is the function that deals with the current reality from a stance of present action. The Adult is not contaminated by the prejudice of the Parent ego state messages from the past, or from the archaic reactions of the Child ego state. In a sense, the Adult is more conscious, aware and capable of being in the moment without the baggage from childhood. This is not to say that the Adult ego state does not feel emotion. Rather, the emotions of the Adult ego state are those that are appropriate to the situation. When people feel anger, they are justified in expressing an emotion that reacts to a current situation that he or she wants changed. When they feel fear, they are facing a real threat, and when they are sad, they have suffered a real loss. In other words, their emotions are authentic responses to current events (Thomson, 1983: 20-24).

In Community

The religious who live as adults in community will be those who work from an I'm OK- You're OK position. They are most of the time in Adult (A2), where they interact with the community members in a mature and healthy way. If there are misunderstandings, they bring them out into the open, and help resolve the issues underlying the problem. If they feel resentment, they share it with the relevant persons, and if they have fantasies about how a person has behaved, they check it out in a calm and measured way. They feel free to disagree with other people's ideas, and do not take it personally when others are not of the same opinion. They accept that people are different, and they are willing and able to recognise these differences. Overall, these religious live in harmony and have a sense of humour. They play their part in the community, and actively work to deepen the bonds of the communal spirit. In summary, they create a spirit of love, joy and peace that influences the overall tenor of the community.

An Organic View

So far, we have dealt with three levels of ego state development: infancy, childhood/adolescence and adulthood. It is now possible to bring these stages together and to view them organically. In Fig. 9 below we see how each ego exists within the whole life of the person. Thus, in the course of a day, we have access to every level of ego state, and frequently when we imagine we are thinking, feeling and behaving in the here-and-now, we may, in fact, be responding to the current reality from an introjected Parent or archaic Child ego state.

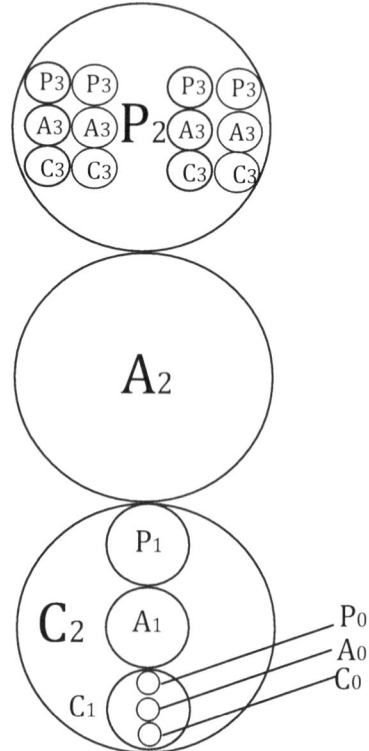

Fig. 9 The Inner Community of Ego States

So, were we to chart the various ego states, we could display them as follows:

Parent		Adult		Child	
P2	Introjected Parent	A2	Intelligent self	C2	Archaic Child
P1	Witch Parent	A1	Intuitive self (Little Professor)	C1	Somatic Child
P0	Caregiver	A0	Instinctive self	C0	Reflexive Child

Table 1   Different levels of ego states

In Community

When people, therefore, come together to live in community, it is important to recognise that each one brings with them a history, a story from the past that will impact on the present.

We cannot presume that people will always be working out of their Adult ego state when they are being influenced by many historical memories and situations. Events in the present will trigger memories from the past, and people can find themselves rubberbanded back into the past (Kupfer & Haimowitz, 1971: 10). So, like an elastic band that gets caught in a hook and stretched to the limit, there comes a time when the band is released and suddenly contracts back to its original shape. Likewise, an event in the present can suddenly 'stretch' the psyche of the person, and then equally suddenly jump them back to an event in the past that has caused them to be stressed in the present. This is a form of transference where the past and present come together behaviourally, cognitively, emotionally and even somatically (Novellino, 1984:64).

People, therefore, in community can be reacting in the present to events that have occurred in their past, which are impacting on them currently. It might be a word that someone says, or something a community member does, that reminds the person of a similar event in their past, and they automatically respond in the way they did formerly. Freud uses the term *transference* to describe this phenomenon (see Chapter 16). We transfer the past into the present and act as if we were responding to what happened ages ago (Shmukler, 1991:128ff).

Conclusion

The idea that we are comprised of various sub-personalities offers us the opportunity to identify how our past experiences are impacting on our current reality. Historical ego states take myriad forms, and it is in remembering our personal history that we begin to understand our thinking, feeling and behaviours that we experience in the present. It is also important to remember that the ego state model is simply a model to help this process. Ego states do not have an existence outside of ourselves. They are part and parcel of our lives, and offer us a way of explaining our often-confused feelings, thoughts and ways of acting in the present.

Exercises

1. Take a single page, dividing the page vertically with a line, and write down five positive qualities of one of your parents on one side of the line and five not so positive qualities on the other column. Next, turn to a new page and do the same exercise for the other parent. Then on a third page do the same exercise for yourself, writing down your positive qualities in one column and the not so good qualities in the other column without looking back at the qualities of your parents. When you have done this exercise, place the letter M or F to represent you mother or father after each of the qualities you have that you may have inherited from a particular parent. With qualities that you have *not* inherited from your parents, think of how you got this quality.

2. Share your family story in good detail with the community. By so doing, they come to know and understand you better and see how your present way of being is often influenced by your past.

3. Describe moments when you think you are in your Parent, Adult and Child ego states.

Chapter Four

How We Function

"An ounce of action is worth a ton of theory."
Ralph Waldo Emerson

In the previous chapter, we examined the structure of our ego states that were formed from our earliest years, and that impacted on the formation of our Script. We noted that the structure of ego states refers to the content of our minds and contains many memories of our past that influence the present. When Berne talked about ego states, he identified three aspects: thinking, feeling and behaviour. Somewhat simplistically speaking, the *structure* of ego states includes the thinking and feeling dimensions without an indication of behaviour. It is only when a person acts that we can be sure about what ego state he or she is employing. In analysing ego states, we therefore use behavioural analysis to identify the ego state that is currently functioning (Berne, 1961:154). Hence, this chapter will deal with the *function* of ego states, how they work, as opposed to what we discussed in the previous chapter: the *structure* or content of the ego states.

In Community

In a community of religious brothers or sisters, we see interactions at every moment of the day. At times, we can observe someone trying to control the agenda, and this may not be the community leader. Someone in the community may decide to side with the strongest personality for the sake of peace. Others refuse to agree to anything. Even when the ideas suggested are valid and positive, some will refuse to go along with the idea simply because it is the community leader that has suggested it. Community dynamics can be dynamite until we come to understand what is happening, or how, in the language of TA, the various ego states are functioning as people adapt to various individuals and situations (Berne, 1972:32).

Because I want to focus on the two types of Child adaptation in the functional ego state model, I will diagram them slightly differently from Berne's model, but include each element he uses (Fig. 10). Many writers simply refer to the Adapted Child as the function of the person who responds to the Controlling Parent, but this fails to distinguish the various forms of adaptation that can result from the over-Controlling Parent. It is especially important for religious in formation to be aware of how religious can respond to external pressure either by conforming or by rebelling, the latter being the more honest of the two reactions.

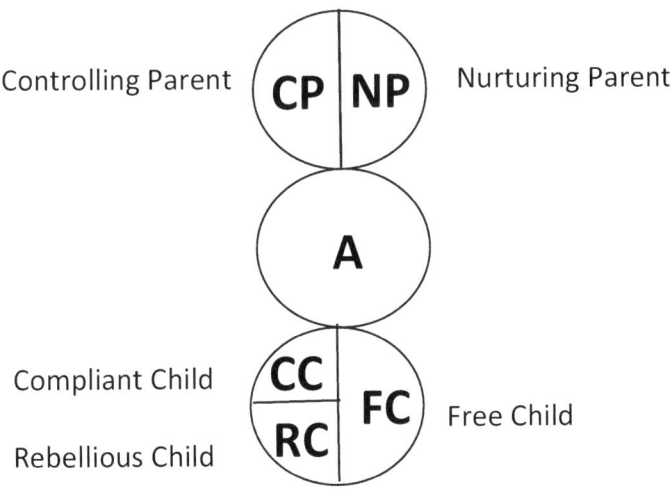

Fig. 10   The Functional Model of Ego States

The Nurturing Parent

The image of the loving gaze of a mother for her child best encapsulates what the Nurturing Parent means. It is the parent (mother and father) who unconditionally loves and accepts his or her child, and who provides everything that is needed for its healthy growth and development. From the very earliest moment of the birth of the child, the parents rejoice in the arrival of the newly born. As the child grows and develops, the parents enjoy the various stages of the child's growth, encouraging the child to achieve all the various skills a child needs to acquire, celebrating the successes of the child and reassuring the child in moments of failure or difficulty. As the child leaves home to attend school, the parents offer encouragement to their child, and then to their growing adolescent to relate with their peers, and become ultimately independent and free. The behaviour of the Nurturing Parent is gentle, and their gestures are smooth and embracing. They speak softly and quietly to their children, even when they have to correct them. Their faces are more often smiling than frowning, and their words are characterised by support and concern rather than any suggestion of rebuke.

Of course, there could also be a negative Nurturing Parent that is over-permissive, or that over-nurtures by doing things for their children when the children could well do them for themselves (Woollams & Brown, 1978:23). Often the reason for the negative Nurturing Parent is because the parents lack confidence to offer the necessary boundaries to the child for fear of losing their affection.

In Community

When we talk about the Nurturing Parent function of the ego states in religious life, we are referring to the way that we as adults treat other people in a positive and encouraging way. This is the I'm OK, You're OK life position as outlined in Chapter 2. The Nurturing Parent function responds empathically to others, and especially to those who struggle with life, or suffer from low self-esteem. It regards people as equals, and shows respect and reverence for the sacredness of the other person. So, in a community of religious, the Nurturing Parent function is a vital element in creating an atmosphere of unconditional support and encouragement to one another.

The Controlling Parent

Here again, we can imagine how the Controlling Parent behaves towards their child. They seem to see only the problems that their child creates. The child is considered more of a nuisance that has to be managed. The parent is constantly on guard in case their child is in danger, and the parent is often filled with anxiety that their child will fall or be hurt, or experience some other catastrophe. In many ways, the Controlling Parents are struggling with their own demons, and play out their need for inner control by trying to control the behaviour of their child (Holloway, 1972: 32-34). Or, some parents may feel great anxiety in managing their child. They simply don't feel competent to provide all the supports the child naturally demands from an early age, and so they seek to control the child, or punish them for expressing dependency. More often than not, the Controlling Parents are anxiously aware of how people may be viewing their parenting skills, and so they insist that the children behave so that the parent can be viewed as a 'good' parent.

Just as we saw that there can be a negative Nurturing Parent, we can also see the need for a positive Controlling Parent who is not afraid to offer direction to their child (Woollams & Brown, 1978: 23). When the child is in danger of hurting itself, the positive Controlling Parent cries 'Stop!' Control is so necessary for young children so that they learn the value of boundaries and safety.

In Community

Controlling Parent behaviour in religious life can be seen at any level of the organisation. It can be a temptation for the community leader to 'control' the members of the community, and it is not necessarily the designated leaders that can be controlling. Berne talks about responsible, effective and psychological leaders (see Chapter 22), and any one of these types of leaders could fall into the trap of trying to control the members of the community in obvious or subtler ways (Berne, 1963:143). Domination in religious communities leads to an atmosphere of tension, resentment and uncomfortable silences on the part of those who feel controlled.

The Free Child

Woollams and Brown well describe the Free Child as one who 'expresses directly what is on his mind, has fun, gets close, and does not hurt anyone in the process' (Woollams & Brown, 1978: 23) When we view an infant in the early months of life, we see the Free Child in all its glory. The infant laughs when happy, cries when uncomfortable, and screams when its needs are not being met. As the child grows and develops, the Free Child continues to express its feelings and wants in the knowledge that its parents will respond positively. And into adulthood, the Free Child is ready to speak its mind at any moment and in any circumstance. Spontaneity is the main characteristic of the Free Child where it responds to life without any fear or hesitation. The Free Child says, 'yes' when it wants to say 'yes' and then says 'no' when it wants to say 'no'. And it is ready to change its mind when the circumstances change (Joines, 2002). At the base of the Free Child is the belief that they are in a healthy life-position (I'm Ok – You're OK).

Needless to say, there can be the negative side of the Free Child 'where she hurts others or herself while expressing herself or having fun' (Woollams & Brown, 1978:23). Imagine the unruly teenager on the public transport who decides to sing and dance and play-act in public. We could say that they are only expressing youthful exuberance, and yet looking at the passengers in the bus, it is obvious that no one is comfortable with this unrestrained expression of fun.

In Community

The expression of Free Child in community is generally a sign of the healthy community, where adults can express themselves in total liberty, and are free to agree and disagree without fear of recriminations. They can also share hurts and resentments in the knowledge that they will be taken seriously, and that their concerns will be treated with respect and openness. They are free to check with others if they have hurt them, and are open in turn to receive positive and negative feedback. Creativity, spontaneity and energy are in abundance in a community that has good Free Child energy.

The Adapted Child

The functional ego state diagram (Fig. 10) as shown above is different from the Adapted Child that Woollams & Brown show in their diagram of the functional ego state diagram (*Ibid*:8). I prefer to indicate separately the *specific* ways a child adapts to the Controlling Parent, *viz.* by conforming or by rebelling, because both aspects of the child's response to the parent are adaptations and need to be treated separately (Drye, 1974: 23ff). This approach of indicating conformity and rebellion could give the impression that all adaptation is pathological or at least imperfect. Naturally enough, we all need to adapt to situations and people, and these adaptations do not necessarily become conforming or rebelling (*Ibid*:23). The normal 'give-and-take' in any interaction highlights the necessity to adapt. So, with that caveat, we will examine how the Conforming Child and the Rebellious Child behaves in the face of the Controlling Parent.

The Conforming Child

In the face of real dependency on the support of parents for very survival, the child naturally needs to be able to recruit their parents to ensure that they get their needs met. This capacity of 'recruitability' will naturally mean that the child has to maintain a connection with the parents, which may involve adapting to their demands and wishes (Barr, 1987:135ff). This is especially the case when the parents are in the Controlling Parent mode. In the face of a Controlling Parent, the child is torn between a longing for connection, and a fear and rage that its very needs are not being responded to (Fowlie, 2009:192ff). When the child experiences these strong visceral emotions of fear, rage and longing, the child cannot remain in this state, and so has to control longing, rage and fear. Rather than blaming the parents for lack of support, the child assumes responsibility for the rupture, and seeks to repair it by conforming to the wishes of the parent (Blackstone, 1993:216ff). As a result, the child creates a false self that it assumes will be more acceptable to the parent. So, the tension is between longing and belonging, and in order to maintain the belonging, the longing is controlled and even suppressed. Hence, the Conforming Child will hide feelings of resentment, hurt and abandonment, and respond obediently to the wishes and demands of the Controlling Parent.

In Community

The same type of dynamic can occur in religious life, and especially when the authority is of a Controlling Parent style. In addition, the vow of obedience tended in the past to make religious conform to the wishes and demands of the community leader as this person was seen as representing the will of God. Even today, there can be much passive conformity within religious life in order to avoid conflict be it with the community leader, or indeed with the community itself. The tension between the need to belong, and the desire for freedom can result in some religious conforming externally, but never internalising the values that should underpin their external behaviour. This can be especially true during the years of formation. The junior professed Sister or Brother knows that they will only be accepted for Final Vows if they adhere to the norms and behaviours that have been promoted during the Novitiate. They can, therefore, do and say all the right things in order to present the acceptable face of a Religious, but fail to fully internalise the values that go with being a Religious. Not that this lack of internalisation may be fully conscious; the young Religious may simply focus on how to please their formation directors in order to gain acceptance. It will only be when the young religious is Finally Professed, and when there is not the same level of guidance and supervision, that the religious may drop the façade of observance, and begin to ignore the values inherent in their early formation.

The Rebellious Child

The rage of the young baby when it does not get what it wants can be a sight to be seen. It screams, cries and thrashes around in its cot until the mother comes to give her what she wants. In the novel by Lionel Shriver, *We Need to Talk about Kevin,* we see a good example of the rage of the child when he does not immediately get what he needs. As Kevin grows into childhood and then into adolescence, this rebellion grows in intensity. Nothing that the mother does will assuage the rage Kevin feels until the rage erupts eventually into terrible violence and mayhem. Often the Rebellious Child is reacting to over-control by the parent. A Controlling Parent runs the danger of creating a child that resists any form of control. It is like Newton's third law of motion that states when one body exerts a force on a second body, the second body simultaneously exerts a force equal in magnitude and opposite in direction to that of the first body. And although the child is much smaller than the adult, it is amazing how tenacious the resistance can be! The rage, of course, can be expressed passively where the child resists complying with the desires of the parent at the moment of toilet training. Or in adolescence, the resistance can be passive where the young person 'forgets' to do what the parent wishes, or drops the dishes instead of washing them so as not to be asked to do the wash-up again.

In Community

In religious life, much of the resistance is in the form of passive aggression. Instead of open rebellion, the religious will procrastinate in doing a job they feel obliged or forced to do. They will forget to bring along their agenda to the meeting that they wish to avoid, and thereby delay the proceedings. Or they may continually disagree with the leader of the community, but instead of openly stating their objections, they will grumble with a small group of discontented companions and enjoy the company of 'begrudgers'. I think it was Thomas Merton who said that the greatest danger in religious life is passivity, where religious can simply sit back, and still get their food and shelter without having to make an effort! I was at a meeting some time ago when the facilitator in sheer exasperation said to the group that they were like five lumps on a log – a good description of passive aggression.

The Way We Function

John M. Dusay in a book entitled *Egograms. How I see You and You See* (1977), described a simple method by which an individual can see himself/herself and others in the way they function. He coined this method, the 'Egogram'. The Egogram is simply a bar graph showing, as he said, the measurement or the amount of psychological energy that people use in each of their ego states (Dusay, 1977: 3). In his book, he lists five ego states: Controlling Parent, Nurturing Parent, Adult, Free Child and Adapted Child, and he uses the histogram to chart the level of energy that a person may have in each ego state. I will slightly modify his model by sub-dividing the Adapted Child into Compliant Child and Rebellious Child, thus having six instead of five ego states. So, in Fig. 11 below we have one example of an egogram.

Sister Susan's profile points to a more mature and responsible religious. The Adult is to the fore, with a good amount of Nurturing Parent that seeks to work for the benefit of others. She adapts by way of compliance so that she goes along with most aspects of life without too much trouble.

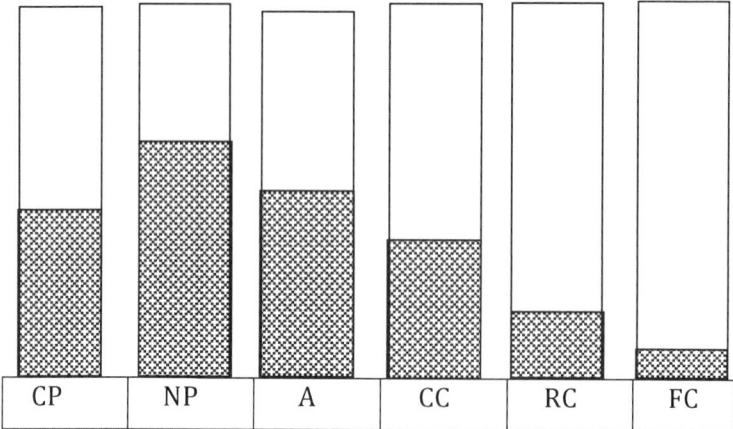

Fig. 11 The Egogram of J. Dusay (1977) - adapted
Key: CP=Controlling Parent; NP=Nurturing Parent;
A=Adult; CC=Conforming Child; RC=Rebellious Child;
FR= FreeChild

There seems to be little passive aggression in Sr Susan, although occasionally she does resist when faced with overbearing members of the community. Because she is so responsible and hard working, one of the things she is inclined to neglect is the Free Child energy that would allow her to spontaneously take the day off, or do something enjoyable as a break from her high sense of responsibility.

The Constancy Hypothesis

Dusay also applied what he called 'the constancy hypothesis' that offered an ingenious insight into the possibility of changing a person's behaviour (*Ibid*:122ff). In working with Mary, a client of his, he discovered that when the energy in one ego state increased, there was a corresponding decrease in another ego state. It is as if we are supplied with a finite amount of psychic energy that did not increase or decrease (the constancy hypothesis). He declared that the energy could be distributed from one ego state to the other, without changing the overall amount of energy. I like to use the image of the street balloon man who takes a long sausage-like balloon, blows it up and then proceeds to twist the balloon into varying sizes until he can make the shape of a dog with the various pieces. So, the same amount of air is in the balloon but the distribution of air is different in each section. So, it is with the Egogram; the psychic energy is constant but can move from one ego state to the other.

In looking at the Egogram in Fig. 11 we see that Sister Susan has fairly low energy in the Free Child. She recognises that she is very responsible, but feels the need to allow herself some time for herself so that she can enjoy life. When Dusay talks about change, he emphasises that a person gets better or develops not by *getting rid* of an ego state, but by focussing on the ego state the person *wants more* of. So, by focusing on Free Child, Susan may discover that her Compliant Child may go down. By taking the day off, and going for a picnic, she is doing something for herself and thereby avoiding the temptation to comply with the wishes of other people. So she moves *towards* what she wants to change rather than *away* from what she wants to avoid.

Behaviour is Not Everything

In the second edition of *TA Today,* Stewart and Joines make the point that the functional ego states can be observed while the structural model can only be inferred (Stewart & Joines, 2012:43). In other words, we can view the behaviour of the functional model, but in the structural model, which deals with the content of ego states within our heads, we can only guess what is going on. Therefore, at times, it is very valuable to simply observe the behaviour of other people without judging what is going on in their head. People may be acting as a Controlling Parent, whereas in reality they are feeling like a child that is scared and unsure of themselves. Their actions show the controlling part, but the inner structure of the ego state may be of a Child ego state. Complicated? It makes for more interesting exploration! In Chapter 6 we will examine the importance of accurate analysis of ego states that needs to be based on behavioural, historical, social and subjective grounds.

Conclusion

Within each of us we have many sub-personalities that affect the way we think, feel and behave. Our earliest life experiences are filed away in our unconscious and impact on the way we live and act. TA calls these sub-personalities, *ego states,* which are consistent patterns of thinking and feeling directly related to corresponding consistent patterns of behaviour. By this understanding ego states, we come to see the importance of our early life experiences, and how these experiences become part of our basic Script at significant moments in our lives. This perspective helps us view others and ourselves with compassion.

The functional ego states identify our behaviour patterns both intrapsychically and interpersonally. Whereas, originally they referred to the interpersonal dimension only, (Cox, 1999: 49-58) we now see at within each of us, there is a continual intrapsychic or inner chatter that goes on between the various ego states, creating internal conflict that we will later on see is the basis for the our projections (Woollams & Brown, 1978:18).

Exercises

1. Can you identify people you know (present company always excluded!) who fit the title of Controlling Parent, Nurturing Parent etc.? To avoid shaming people, do not name them, but describe how they behave that would identify them principally with one ego state.

2. Draw your own egogram and don't show it to your partner for this exercise. Next, ask your partner to draw *your* egogram and then compare the two egograms, exploring how you see yourself and how your partner sees you. Then reverse the process where you draw up your partner's egogram and compare it with the one they have drawn.

3. Describe to another partner in your group, the moments or situations when you find yourself in each individual ego state. E.g. 'I remember when I was in a Critical Parent ego state... etc.

4. In your community assign one of the 6 ego states to each member by drawing lots so that people do not know what ego state the other person is. Then ask each person to act as if they were in that ego state and begin a discussion with each of the ego states being represented. It makes for a very amusing session!

5. How does your egogram fit in with your Script that you discovered in Chapter One?

Chapter Five

When All is not Well

"My surface may be smooth, but my surface is my mask."
Charles C. Finn

It is commonplace to presume that religious men and women are mature and responsible people who have dedicated themselves to God for the service of humanity. Taking vows of poverty, chastity and obedience highlights the level of commitment that they have made, and witnesses to a dedicated life that is both fulfilling and worthwhile.

However, various levels of dysfunction often mar such an ideal picture. Berne calls such dysfunction 'psychopathology', and describes how the ego state functions of a person can be contaminated or excluded in their day-to-day functioning (Berne, 1961:44). When a religious is 'in Script', they are automatically living and working under some form of contamination. We will look how such contamination and exclusion affects the lives of religious both in community life and in ministry.

Contamination

In Fig. 12 below we can see three types of contamination where the Adult is affected by the intrusion of either Parent or Child, or of both Parent and Child. Contamination occurs when people believe that they are acting from an Adult ego state, whereas in fact their Adult is being affected by the presence of a Parent, Child or both Parent and Child ego states together.

Parent Contamination

Br Raymond appeared to be the ideal religious. He was sure of himself in most matters, and was ever ready to give advice to those around him. 'Make sure you read Sandra Schneider. It's the best set of books on religious life ever,' he said. Instead of saying, "In my opinion, I think Sandra Schneider is the probably the best set of books on religious life", or 'I really enjoyed reading Schneider's work', Br Raymond leaves no space for other viewpoints.

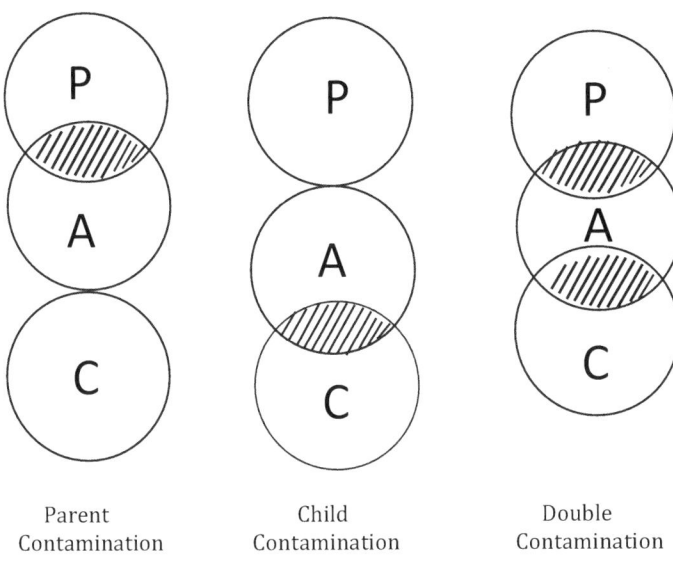

| Parent | Child | Double |
| Contamination | Contamination | Contamination |

Fig. 12 Contaminations

Then he goes on to say, "We are spending too much money on drink.' Here again he is stating his opinion as fact. He could have said that he was concerned with the level of money spent on drink, but in both cases he is assuming that he is talking from his Adult ego state, whereas he is being contaminated by his Controlling Parent. Contamination of the Adult ego state is often seen when the person practises what those in the mentalization field call 'psychic equivalence' where opinion or appearance is taken as fact (Fonagy et al., 2004:258ff). Br Raymond finds it almost impossible to imagine that others would not see things the way he does.

If Br Raymond were asked what his highest bar was in the egogram, I am sure that he would say Adult whereas, from what he says, and from the way he dominates conversations with definite opinions, it appears that the Controlling Parent has contaminated his Adult to a considerable extent.

Berne said that Parent contamination is best demonstrated by certain types of *prejudice*, and various sorts of *delusions*

(Berne, 1961: 47). The sort of prejudice one would expect from the mouth of Br Raymond would be phrases like, 'Young Brothers have no sense' or 'These theologians who don't agree with the Catholic Catechism are being unfaithful to the Church'. Delusions can be seen in the way Br Raymond imagines himself as the future leader of the Congregation of which he is a member. Such delusions are based on what the field of mentalization describes as the 'pretend mode' where there is no real connection between what the person imagines and what is the reality outside of the mind of the person (Fonagy et al. 2004: 261ff).

Child Contamination

Sister Sinead has been asked to take over the running of the school where she has worked for the last ten years. Suddenly, she begins to suffer from headaches and colds. She explains to her superiors that she cannot undertake the job because she finds it very difficult to meet the parents when they come to discuss the progress of the child she teaches. Sister Sinead is a religious who has spent over thirty years in religious life, and has taught for over twenty-five years. She qualified as a teacher, gaining good results in both the theory and practice of education. This is a case where her Adult is contaminated by beliefs that are not based on any real substance. However, she honestly feels insecure, frightened and lacks any real belief in her ability to undertake a position of responsibility, but she does not link these feelings to her Child ego state.

Child contamination occurs where the Adult feels more a child than an adult despite the outward appearance of a mature person; the main emotions that dominate in their world are fear, and inferiority. At the same time, this contamination is not viewed as coming from the Child. Sister Sinead believes that she is making a wise decision in refusing the request, and offers the above justifications for doing so. She believes that she is in Adult, but in reality her Adult is being contaminated by her Child ego state. Just as a child responds to the world using rather primitive processes, these same processes still continue to occupy a place in us as adults (Little, 2005:133).

Double Contamination

Some theorists hold that if there is any contamination from either the Parent or the Child, there is, in fact a double contamination. This concept is further reinforced by the idea of the *relational unit* where Parent and Child ego state are linked by an emotional bond (Little, 2006:7ff). So, when in the case of Br Raymond's Parent contamination which is predominantly characterised by 'shoulds' and 'oughts', it is more than likely that his Child contamination is full of fear of disobeying his inner Controlling Parent who is laying down the law. The Parent and Child are in a struggle without the presence of an active Adult. And when Sister Joan is contaminated by her Child ego state that frightens her and robs her of any sense of confidence, she will probably have a Parent ego state that tells her that she is stupid, incompetent, or that she cannot cope with stress. And again, her Adult seems to remain silent in this impasse.

Exclusion

Berne describes the phenomenon of *exclusion* as an attitude that is maintained in the face of any threat (Berne, 1961:44). The Parent, the Adult or the Child can be excluded by the other two ego states, or indeed the reverse can happen where one of the ego states can exclude the other two ego states. We can have therefore an *excluded* ego state with the other two ego states in full flow, or we can have one ego state *excluding* the other two ego states.

The diagrams (figs. 13 &14) below will clarify the difference and I wish to acknowledge Stewart and Joines for the way they made the difference so understandable (Stewart & Joines, 2012: 60-61).

The Excluded Ego State

Were a religious to *exclude* their Parent ego state, they would be living a life at odds with the spirit and values of religious life. By definition, a religious is a person who lives according to a constitution, and who professes to live the gospel values in a radical way. In recent years, I have come across situations where religious have been found to have abused children, or have been involved in sexual relationships with vulnerable adults.

In other cases, some religious have been found to have embezzled money from their Congregation while appearing to be models of commitment to ministry. How can this happen? It happens by the process of *excluding* the voice of the Parent, whose voice is the voice of morality.

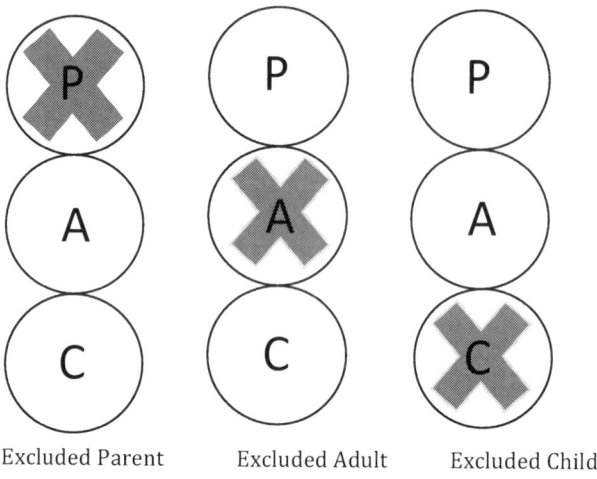

Fig. 13   Exclusion of Ego States

By excluding the voice of what should be done, a religious allows the desires of the Child to predominate. When desire blocks out duty, then anything is possible. Their life-position will be I'm OK and I don't care how others are as long as I'm OK!

When a religious *excludes* the Child ego state, they seem to forget that they were ever children with the thoughts, feelings and behaviour of the child, with the memories of growing up, and having to learn, and make mistakes along the way. They will have *excluded* the somatic Child (C1) that seeks to be supported and comforted. They come across as the dutiful religious with a strong element of the 'tyranny of the ought'. They often 'should' people in a very directive manner, with little understanding or empathy for those who are weak, and who struggle to live up to the ideals of religious life. So, the religious with such a Script will often have the life-position of I'm OK-You're Not Ok, a position of moral superiority.

In *excluding* the Adult ego state, a religious is at the mercy of an internal battle between a persecuting Parent and either a Compliant or Rebellious Child. This intrapsychic or inner war leaves the person confused and in turmoil with no real ability to stand back and take an objective view of what is happening. They may suffer from scruples, where a punishing Parent persecutes the frightened Child with images of damnation and punishment for the slightest infringement of the law. The religious with the excluded Adult becomes terrified of a punitive God with no real understanding of the God of love. In some extreme cases, when the Adult is totally excluded, the person loses all ability to reality-test, and slips into some form of psychosis, thereby needing hospitalisation. The person in this situation moves from a life-position of I'm Not OK-You're Ok to eventually permanently stay in the confused position of I'm Not Ok-You're Not Ok.

The Excluding Ego State (Constant)

Another type of pathology involves the situation where *one* ego state dominates the life of the religious (Berne, 1961: 46; Woollams & Brown, 1978:38). When a single ego state dominates to the exclusion of the other two ego states, we have a *constant* or *excluding* ego state (Fig. 14).

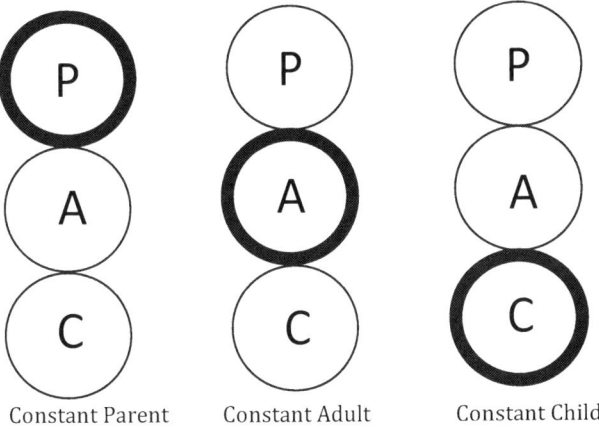

| Constant Parent | Constant Adult | Constant Child |

Fig. 14 Constant ego states

A religious who has a constant Parent will be very preachy and authoritarian with little sense of humour. He or she will find it difficult to smile! Life for them is something that is serious and sacred, to be treated with due reverence and sobriety! There is a Calvinistic dimension to these types of people who seem to like quoting the law and making everything of prime importance.

The constant Adult religious is like Dr Spock from Star Trek, who functions like a computer with little space for doubt, and who has excluded any trace of emotions or of empathy. They want to know how people think, but have no interest in how people feel!

The constant Child religious seems incapable of being serious even in moments when it is totally inappropriate to have fun and games. They cannot hold a serious conversation without telling jokes or punning, and they want to be always distracted from work by entertainment of any sort. While likeable at times, they can be rather trying in the long term.

Conclusion

In the normal run of a day, we can find ourselves in situations that trigger various forms of contamination. For some people it will be the Parent contamination that seems to intrude on the Adult, making the person rather opinionated and dogmatic. For others, the Child ego state is the culprit, creating feelings of scare, or rebellion in the face of everyday events. The challenge for each of us is to be aware of when the contaminations kick in, and to discover the patterns of events that cause such contaminations. Thus, we can begin to access our Adult more, and work to prevent further contamination by the rigidity of the Parent or the confusion of the Child.

Exercises

1. Share with your community the situations when you are more in each of the ego states, when you are in a *constant* or *excluding* ego state, and when you *exclude* an ego state. Check this out with the community if they see you as you see yourself!

2. Offer suggestions yourself and seek suggestions from others as to how you can correct the balance to avoid any form of exclusion.

3. Examine your community life and see does the community as a group fit into one of the *excluding* or *excluded* ego states. How would the community structure or timetable need to change in order to have a more balanced lifestyle?

Chapter Six

The Identification Parade

"You can't judge people and touch their souls at the same time."
Tama Kieves

Judging people and still remaining in relationship with them is quite a challenge: the gospels warn us *not* to judge, or we will be judged ourselves! (Mt.7: 1). Berne, however, offers another slant to the analysis of human behaviour when he suggests that to have a clear understanding of how an individual is behaving in a group, there is need for an accurate diagnosis (Berne, 1963:181ff).

Berne was interested in how a person moves from one ego state to the other, and how this movement can be explained (*Ibid:*37ff). We will deal with this matter further on in this chapter, but for now, we want to examine how we can identify or diagnose the ego states of a person at any one moment and in any situation.

Berne goes on to note that such diagnosis should not be dependent simply on the opinion of the observer, but should include a diagnosis based on behavioural, social, historical and subjective grounds. Simply to judge from one of these criteria alone will not necessarily provide an accurate picture of the person under scrutiny. Berne stresses that a complete diagnosis of an ego state requires that all four aspects (behavioural, social, historical and subjective) be examined, and that any diagnosis should always be tentative rather than definitive. Berne's recommendation that we be careful in our assessment of people's ego states is a salutary one that avoids premature rash judgement. (Berne, 1961:75).

Needless to say, one of the dangers of diagnosis is that we put people into boxes. Instruments like the enneagram, the Myers-Briggs Personality Inventory and other personality tests run the danger of describing the whole personality of someone within very confining limits. A person gets labelled as a number 1 in the enneagram, or an INFJ in Myers-Briggs, and people then mistakenly treat them according to this narrow classification. The same behaviour could happen as we study ego states and personality adaptations (Joines & Stewart, 2002). That said, we *do* judge people. We want to understand how they work, and how they are different one from the other, and why these differences exist. Every day we are assessing people, reacting to how they are and behave, and responding internally and externally to their interactions with us. Hence, it is useful to have a means of accurate assessment that can give a more rounded view of the people we judge. Once we have a clear picture of the person under review, we then have the responsibility to treat them with dignity and compassion.

When a person is in Script and working from either a humble, hurtful or hopeless life-position – to name the Not-OK positions – they will be working out of various levels of contamination and coming from one or other ego state. A look at the four aspects of analysis or diagnosis should prove useful.

The behavioural and social types of diagnoses of ego states deal with *external* behaviour and its impact on us, while the historical and subjective diagnoses refer more to what is happening *within* the person. In addition, the historical and subjective diagnoses connect us to the past, whereas the social and behavioural diagnoses deal with what is going on in the present (Novey, 1991:123).

A brief look at each of these types of diagnosis provides us with a useful way of understanding the behaviour of people and can also offer ourselves some insight into our own personality. Whereas it is much easier to diagnose other people, the challenge facing each of us is to begin to understand ourselves from the four dimensions that Berne offers us.

Behavioural Diagnosis

As the title suggests, the observer who sees the way a person is acting, and who judges them accordingly makes a behavioural diagnosis. So, when we see someone who is controlled, calm and with little exaggerated expression of emotion, we may presume that they are in their Adult ego state. Or we may see another person ranting and raving over what appears to be an insignificant detail, and decide that they are back in their childhood, reliving an early trauma, and in their

Child ego state. Berne suggests that we look at the demeanour, gestures, voice and vocabulary of the person in order to make an accurate behavioural diagnosis (Berne, 1963: 182ff).

Demeanour

When we notice someone standing rigidly, and looking tense with lips pursed and eyes blazing, we can assume that the person is in Parent. Or we may observe people with their heads bowed and a cute look of embarrassment on their face, giving the impression of a person in Child. Or again, we may come across a person standing in a straight but relaxed fashion with very little movement and no sign of tension, giving the impression that here we have someone in Adult. Desmond Morris in his book *Peoplewatching* gives us a detailed study of how people behave be they in Adult, Parent or Child (Morris: 2002). Berne cites the findings of Darwin who offered illustrations of emotional expressions of people and animals, and the more recent work of Ekman (1980) focuses on the face as a way of accessing emotional states.

Gestures

The classic wagging of the finger in front of someone else points to the Parent ego state where admonitions usually accompany this gesture. On the other hand, when people use their fingers to count the points they are making, or who often steeple their hands, they are very often in Adult, demonstrating a certain confidence and calm. The Child ego state can often be seen when a person appears to be washing their hands with no sign of water, and moving their head from side to side, showing a certain level of nervousness.

Voice

Berne describes how people can have two or three types of voices depending on the ego state from which they are coming (Berne, 1963:183). For example, a person may speak with a strong and strident voice, giving great emphasis to each word and putting great force into the voice. They come across as the controlling and critical Parent that has no hesitation in expressing their annoyance or impatience with another member of their community, especially with someone they consider inferior to themselves. That same person, in the presence of a major superior, loses all their power and becomes a 'nice and gentle' voice, giving the impression that they are the most humble of creatures. At that moment, they have moved into Child in the face of another they perceive as Parent. Yet again, this same person could, theoretically, have an Adult voice in their professional capacity, where they feel competent and on top of things, and regard their colleagues as equals. That voice is carefully modulated with no element of force, and no indication of inappropriate gentleness.

Vocabulary

Words can betray the ego states also. The Parent often uses words like 'must', 'should' and will often use 'you' language when indicating disapproval. A person in Parent also employs 'one' language when referring to themselves instead of using an 'I' message. They also use words like, ridiculous, stupid, unbecoming, and other judgemental words when expressing their opinions. The Adult is very obvious when they speak, for they qualify each element of the sentence (adding parenthesis all over the place) and making sure (as much as they can) that they have covered all the bases of their argument for fear (or anxiety) that they omit anything! And the Child ego state betrays itself with more sounds than actual words as in "gee!", "gosh" "Mmmmm!" and so on. Usually, the Child uses simple words, afraid that they will not be able to use more grown up ones!

Social Diagnosis

In many ways, the social diagnosis is probably the most accurate of all four diagnoses, because it impacts immediately on us personally as we interact with another person. Social diagnosis refers to the way the behaviours, words, gestures and voice of the other person affects the way we think, feel and behave in response. When a person is curt and critical with us, and we feel small and inferior, we can be very sure that the other person is in Parent while we are in Child. We know they are in Parent specifically because of our emotional reaction to them. Being in Child presupposes that the other person is in Parent.

If we find ourselves responding to someone without any real feelings at all other than one of ease, we can safely assume that they are in Adult because we find ourselves likewise in Adult.

Likewise, if we find that the person we are speaking to simply will not cooperate with us, and seems to be putting obstacles at every stage of the work, we need to pay attention to the likelihood that we are in Controlling Parent, and the other person is in Rebellious Child. They are reacting to us, and providing us with an indication as to how we are coming across to them.

In summary, the mechanism of the social diagnosis works where one ego state directly invites the other into the complementary ego state. We will see more clearly how this plays out when we discuss the analysis of transactions proper in Chapter 10.

Historical Diagnosis

The historical diagnosis is gained from a member of a religious community as he or she begins to disclose information about himself or herself that otherwise would not be known by the rest of the community. Many communities now have introduced the idea of telling their family story, their faith story, their vocation story and their ministry story. As members of the community share their life-story, they offer to the rest of the community a window into their life. Such sharing can lead to developing a great level of trust and intimacy among the Sisters or Brothers. Telling one's personal story can help explain why a person behaves the way they do. If the religious comes from a troubled background, they will no doubt show the effects of this negative experience. In telling their story, the narrator may gain fresh insight into her or himself, and come to a level of compassion for his or her current ways of behaving, as well as inviting similar compassion on the part of the rest of the community. There can, of course, be a danger in telling one's story over and over again; the Script at the basis of the story could be reinforced, leaving the person trapped in an old story that does not change. Part of the work of therapy involves telling the old story, and then gradually seeking to reinterpret events from the past in a new light. Historical diagnosis can therefore lead to putting a new show on the road.

Subjective Diagnosis

It was Francis Bacon, who said, 'It is a sad fate for a man to die too well known to everybody else, and still unknown to himself' (Bacon, 2001:XI). Subjective diagnosis offers a person the opportunity to know him or herself and allow this knowledge to shape their present and their future. Berne held that subjective diagnosis comes from self-observation, where the individual comes to realise that he or she is acting from a specific ego state, and recognises that he or she has the choice to move from one ego state another one in full consciousness (Berne, 1963: 181). This internal monitoring is an essential element in the current practice of the examen of consciousness that many religious undertake on a daily basis.

Moving from One Ego State to the Other

Diagnosing a particular ego state implies that people move from one ego state to another one depending on the circumstances that one encounters. Ego state diagnosis is an attempt to track the changes or shifts in ego states, and understand when and why a person changes ego states.

When we discussed the egogram of John Dusay in Chapter 2, we talked about a given amount of energy that was available to all the ego states, and that could be moved around, increasing the energy in one ego state, and thereby reducing the energy in another ego state. Berne very early on in his career talked about the charge of 'psychic energy' or cathexis that enabled the person to move from one ego state to the desired one (Berne, 1977:146ff). He classified the energy under three categories: *bound, unbound and free* (Berne, 1961: 37ff). His concept of energy is simply a theoretical concept that cannot be verified physiologically. However, it is interesting to explore how the energy shifts from one ego state to the other, if in fact that is what happens!

The *bound* energy that Berne talks about is the amount of energy that is present in each ego state. We all know people with high energy levels and those with lower energy. This difference in energy levels may refer to Berne's bound energy theory. Berne talks about the energy being *bound* in the sense that it is *potential* energy, available for use when the need is there.

Unbound energy is the type of energy that moves from one ego state to the other. So, from my understanding of Berne, this is a different type of energy that kicks in when there is movement from one ego state to another due to certain circumstances. It is brought about by external events that release the energy so that it is *unbound*.

And finally, he describes *free* energy, which is the consciously created energy that people can muster when they need to move from one ego state to another ego state. This is the energy of the 'real self' according to Berne, the part of the personality that is 'me', the part that is the authentic person as they truly feel in the moment.

At times, people have to decide to present a side of themselves that is not their self. When standing before a class of thirty students, the teacher has to marshal an 'executive self' that will function in a professional manner. To do that he or she will have to use the free energy to unbind a certain amount of energy (*unbound* energy) to manage the situation. The teacher may not be feeling his or her 'real self' at the time but circumstances require that an 'executive self' is more appropriate.

Conclusion

By diagnosing the ego state a person currently employs, we understand them better, and can interact with them more appropriately. By employing the various levels of diagnosis, we have a good chance that we will see the person in their 'real self' when they are being authentic, or recognise when they have their 'executive self' on display. With this greater understanding of how people 'work', we can respond to them in a way that is both more respectful and compassionate.

Exercises:

1. Begin to study the gestures, demeanour, voice and words of characters on the television and see if you can identify what ego state is in action as you watch.

2. Historical diagnosis involves people talking about their past in order to understand how and why we reside in various ego states. Maybe at community meetings you could begin to share moments from the past that have impacted on you, and that could explain why you stay more of the time in a particular ego state.

3. Share incidents when you felt that people were either in their Parent or Child ego states, and how you reacted to them at the time.

Chapter Seven

How Parents Influence

"Parentage is a very important profession, but no test of fitness
for it is ever imposed in the interest of the children."
George Bernard Shaw

When people enter religious life, it is important to realize
that they come from a family background where their Script has
been well established. Formation needs to take into account the
fact that life-positions, and various levels of contamination may
make it difficult to influence the way a person thinks, feels and
behaves, thereby making formation a challenging process. In
addition, the more we understand how religious people have
already been formed in their original family, the more we can
have a more compassionate approach to members of our
communities who may display various levels of dysfunctional
behaviour.

In the next three chapters I outline how parents influence
their children in very powerful ways, and show how the early
family formation needs to be acknowledged and managed.

Back in Chapter 1, I said that Script was an unconscious life
plan, based on decisions in childhood, which were reinforced by
parents. When I say 'decisions made in childhood', I may be
placing too much responsibility on the child. Children are
greatly influenced by the words and actions of their parents, and
although the child *does* ultimately decide what they will do, the
power of influence that a parent has cannot be overestimated.
The Script that the young child eventually forms is very much
shaped by the Script messages that the parent sends to him or
her very early in life (Woollams & Brown, 1978:155 ff).

When I was explaining the structure of ego states in Chapter
3, I noted that especially in early childhood, the response of the
child to its parents is the result of his or her *perception* of what
the parent did or said. These perceptions are what go to
influence the child, and at times the perceptions may be very
inaccurate. At other times, perceptions may be very clear

memories, but without a full understanding of the motivations for the way the parents acted. Nevertheless, the words and actions of the parents are powerful influencers in the life of the child even when they may be perceived inaccurately.

Messages

Messages sent from the parent to their child can be verbal and non-verbal. The verbal messages include suggestions and attributions transmitted by the parents, and the non-verbal messages refer to the *process* of imitation where the parents model what they want their child to do (*Ibid:* 156). In other words, the verbal messages refer to the content or the *what* of the messages that the parent wants to communicate with their child, and the non-verbal messages deal with the *how* of what the parent wants their child to do.

Modelling

The child picks up the non-verbal messages as he sees his parents modelling behaviour (*Ibid:*155). Parents may want their children to do what they say, and not to do what they do, but in reality, it is the example of the parents that is the most powerful influencer on the child. Parents can tell their children to join the library, and read a book instead of wasting time, but if the child does not see the parent reading a book, it is very unlikely that their child will join the library. On the other hand, a parent who always shows kindness and respect to the beggar who comes to the door, is giving a powerful message to the child to help and respect those less fortunate than they are. Someone said, 'We teach by what we say, more by what we do, but most of all by the things we love.' Modelling is a powerful way of passing on values and beliefs in a non-verbal way.

Attributions

Phrases like, 'There's a right way and a wrong way to do things, and you always choose the wrong way', attributes to the child the label of always messing things up. The result of such a message is that the child begins to believe that it can do nothing right, and therefore decides not to try. Often with the attribution comes a belief on the part of the child, followed by a decision. Or the more direct message, 'Why can't you be like your brother?' attributes a quality of inferiority to the child who then comes to believe that she can never measure up, or else decides that at all costs she will compete with her brother, or indeed with everyone so that she is better than the next person. And yet, no matter how much she succeeds, the voice inside her head is, 'Why can't you be like…"

Suggestions

Suggestions by the parents can also become powerful motivators for their children to behave in certain ways. "Why don't you?" phrases give strong motivations for the child to act accordingly. "Why don't you go out to play?" can be picked up by the child as a message that the child is a nuisance and not wanted. So, the child decides either to avoid any form of showing affection to the parents, or becomes clingy and whinging, never satisfied with the amount of affection he or she gets. Even phrases like, "Would you think of sharing that with your sister?" could mistakenly be understood as 'You are really a selfish and heartless child' leading to the child feeling shame and guilt.

Modelling, attributions and suggestions will have a greater or lesser impact on the child depending on the way such messages are received. Even when these messages are sent with the best of intentions on the part of the parents, the perception of the child can turn the best motives into the most negative of outcomes. Hence, parents will never know with certainty how their actions impact on the lives of their children, and can never be fully in control of how their behaviours affect their children.

The Script Matrix

Berne rightly attributed to Claude Steiner the design of a diagram to analyse and illustrate the messages handed down from parents to their children (Berne, 1972:315ff). Steiner, a close follower of Berne, drew what he termed 'the Script matrix' to chart the way parents communicated with their children from the moment of the child's birth and throughout their entire childhood (Steiner, 1966:133-135). This diagram succinctly examines the verbal and non-verbal messages that the parents transmitted to their offspring.

The diagram drawn by Steiner has the two parents sending verbal and non-verbal messages to their child (Fig. 15).

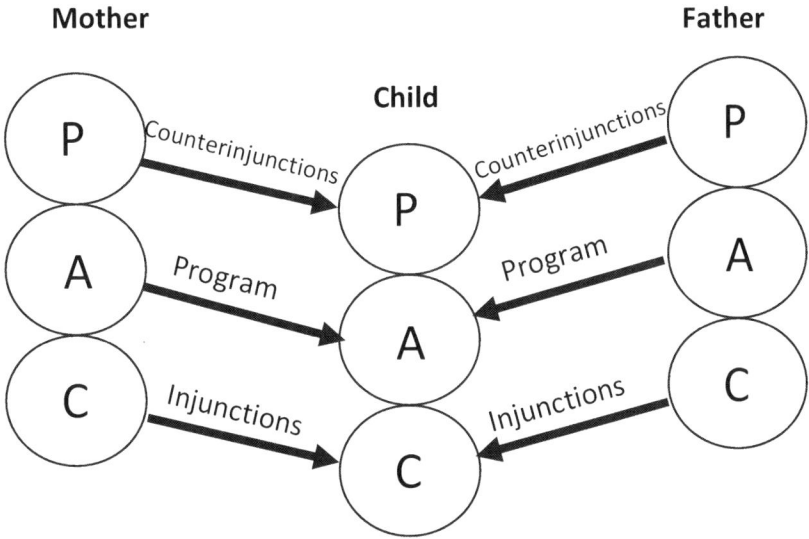

Fig. 15   The Script Matrix (Steiner, 1966; Stewart & Joines, 2012)

The mother and father have their own Parent, Adult and Child, and from the way the arrows are pointed, we understand that messages are being send from each of the ego states of the parents to the equivalent ego states of the child. From the top we have the counterinjunctions from the Parent of each of the parents to the Parent of the child. The term 'counterinjunctions' could mistakenly imply that these messages sent from the Parent of the parent run counter to the injunctions. In fact, they do not necessarily contradict the injunctions, but unlike the injunctions, the counterinjunctions are more verbal messages from the Parent in the parent, whereas the injunctions are usually non-verbal messages that come from the Child in the parent (see Chapter 8).

Steiner holds that the main injunctions 'tend to come from one of the parents, and the parent of the *opposite* sex is often the source. The parent of the same sex then teaches the youngster how to comply with these injunctions and attributions' (Steiner, 1974:85). For example, if the mother sends an injunction of 'don't be close' to her son, the father then shows how to remain aloof from people. The program is the 'how to' way the parent (in this case the father) demonstrates the way to carry out the injunction of the other parent (the mother).

Counterinjunctions

Counterinjunctions include messages and suggestions that the parents give verbally to their children right from the very time that the children learn to speak. Much of the time the messages aim to keep the children safe, and make sure they behave in society. Messages like: "Don't touch the oven!" "Look left and right!" "Sit up straight!" "Watch your manners!" are constantly directed to children in the hope that they will internalise good behaviour that will keep them safe, and make them good citizens.

In response to these messages, the child makes certain decisions, which in TA are called the *counterscript,* which is 'a set of decisions made by the child in compliance with the counterinjunctions' (Stewart & Joines, 2012:135). Often the counterscript becomes part of the Script or unconscious life plan that shapes the way we live our lives. In response to the messages given by the parent as cited in the previous paragraph, the counterscript of the child could include decisions like: "I better be careful because the world is not safe" or "I mustn't let my family down by not observing the rules". Such a counterscript could describe the behaviour of someone who is very careful to the point of being paralysed, and who is so guarded to avoid breaches in etiquette that they are constantly anxious.

Very specific types of counterinjunctions are what Taibi Kahler described as *drivers* (Kahler, 1975:280ff). Drivers are sorts of behaviour that result from counterinjunction messages directed by the parent to the child in the form of commands. The word 'driver' is used by Kahler to indicate how compulsively driven the person is with regard to a particular behaviour. The *driver behaviours* are therefore compulsive behaviours that respond to the *driver messages* that children pick up from their parents. These driver behaviours are very identifiable, and just like we were able to diagnose ego states by the gestures, demeanour, voice and vocabulary, we will also be able to identify driver behaviour by careful observation. Kahler identifies five drivers: *Be Perfect, Be Strong, Try Hard, Please Others,* and *Hurry Up.*

Driver behaviours are in response to the parent whom the child believes will only love or accept the child *if* his or her behaviour lives up to the parents' expectations. The child does not experience the parents as unconditionally loving and, in order to gain their conditional love, the child feels driven to behave in specific ways. The child believes "I'm Ok as long as...I'm perfect, I'm strong, I please others, I Try Hard, or I Hurry Up". Hence the child adopts behaviours that he or she believes will make him or her acceptable to the caregiver or parent (Fowlie, 2005). This is the beginning of the formation of what Winnicott calls, 'the false self '(Winnicott, 1965:140ff). Since the true self of the child seems to him or her to be unacceptable, the child adopts a more 'acceptable' persona – a false self.

The *Be Perfect* Driver

Br Sean dresses immaculately with nothing out of place. He wears a suit at all times, and on the odd occasion he wears a pair of jeans, they are perfectly pressed. His bedroom and his office are in pristine condition with 'a place for everything, and everything in its place'. He is very careful of his diet and only eats those things that are healthy and nourishing. He examines the content of any packet to ensure that it does not contain high levels of sugar. He works very long hours, and on usually six if not seven days a week, and when asked how he found a particular day, he will describe how much he got done as a measure of the satisfaction level he experienced. He seems unable to 'take it easy', and begins to feel anxious if he finds himself with nothing to do. At times, he feels exhausted, but continues working because he feels he must. When he is criticised, Br Sean becomes very defensive, very quick to defend himself, and takes to heart any hint of negativity. Very often he is asked to do extra jobs because people know that he will do them perfectly. In general, his demeanour is carefully controlled and his gestures kept to the minimum. He often speaks long and complicated sentences with many parentheses, and yet keeping the train of thought intact. It is as if he is afraid to leave a detail out when he speaks. His vocabulary is frequently sprinkled with 'shoulds' and 'musts', and he is inclined to lack a sense of humour.

Br Sean grew up in a household where doing things properly was demanded of him. He would be frequently criticised if he did a sloppy job, and he soon learned that if he wanted to be loved, he had to do everything right. He would be OK as long as he was perfect.

The Be Strong Driver.

Sister Rose is not seen as a very emotional person. She seems to maintain an even keel without often showing how she feels. You would never know from her face how she is feeling, as she seldom shows any expression other than one of calm. Rather than accept responsibility for her feelings, Sister Rose points to people and events that cause her to feel a particular emotion. A favourite phrase of hers is 'He makes me really angry,' instead of saying that she is angry with him. Or she says 'That is boring,' rather than say that she is bored. Her posture is also quite immobile hardly using any gestures when she speaks. This is not to say that Sister Rose does not have feelings; it simply means that she finds it difficult to express them.

The reason for Sister Rose 'hiding' her emotions is that as a child, she found that her parents could not manage her strong feelings. She realized, therefore, that she would be OK as long as she contained her feelings when in their presence. She retreated into her own world, and found that she could manage once she was strong and in control of her emotions.

The Try Hard Driver

Sister Philomena has a *Try Hard* driver. Everything seems to be a bit of a struggle. She has to *try hard* to finish anything. When faced with a job to do, Sister Philomena frowns a lot, gives the impression that she did not understand what she was meant to do, and seldom finishes the job. By the way she cocks her ear to listen to instructions, she gives the impression that she is hard of hearing. "I don't know what you mean," is a phrase frequently on her lips, as is "I'll try!" when asked to complete a task. St Philomena tries a lot, but seldom delivers. Procrastination and forgetfulness characterise the way she conducts her life. Often she 'completes' a job, only to find one or two mistakes that ruin the overall effect of the work. She seems bewildered at times, and just finds life too much of a struggle.

Sister Philomena came from a home where there was too much control over her. She resisted having to go along with the demands of strong parent direction, but did so in a covert fashion. She discovered that she was OK as long as she tried hard. It seemed she did not have to succeed; she did not have to 'do it'. And so, she continues to resist passively, maintaining control of her own life, but often infuriating others by her lack of action.

The Please Others Driver

Br Joseph smiles a lot, but it seems like a forced smile as he looks coyly when meeting someone and shows his teeth in a grimace. He appears shy as he attempts to ingratiate himself with others, and yet he is simply attempting to come across as a friendly person. He uses phrases like: 'do you see?' 'Sort of...like...uhuh...' seeking to make the other person understand, and not come across as too powerful, too knowledgeable. He is afraid of showing his strength in case that would make others feel inferior. Frequently, he shows his 'inability' in order to please the other person or to put them at ease. Br Joseph rushes to help out when no help is needed, and can be infuriating in the way he constantly offers to do jobs when he already has enough to do.

Br Joseph was the 'favourite' son of his mother, and loved the attention he received. When, however, he felt that some of the affection was not flowing freely, he sought to please his mother in order to maintain the supply of love. He felt that he was OK as long as he pleased her, and became stressed and overreacted when he felt he was not pleasing enough.

The Hurry Up Driver

Sister Elizabeth speaks incredibly quickly and rushes around like a whirlwind making those around her wanting to avoid the tornado. Agitation characterises her way of behaving where she is seen tapping her fingers on the table as she listens to someone speaking. It appears as if she wants them to hurry up and conclude what they are saying. She sits with her legs crossed, shaking one leg continually in a kicking fashion as if she wants to jump up and go somewhere. Time is her enemy where she is constantly racing to complete jobs in the shortest possible time. She often uses phrases like, 'Lets go...we haven't time...we'll be late' pushing herself and others to run instead of walk. Often she will rush a job simply to get it done, ignoring the fact that the job is only half-done.

Sister Elizabeth came from a family 'in a hurry'. She was encouraged not to waste time and not to drag things out. Her parents were in a hurry and everything in the household was done in fast-forward motion. So, she understood that she would be Ok as long as she hurried up.

We have them All!

As we read about the drivers, we may identify with each of them. In truth, we may indeed have elements of each driver, but generally we will have a *primary* driver that we automatically assume in moments of stress or in reaction to an unexpected situation (Stewart & Joines, 2012:162). The *primary* driver will of course be linked to our Script and our life-position where it is used to maintain the Script decisions. The primary driver also gives a clue to our general personality type, the study of which is outside of the scope of this book, but which can be a very useful study to deepen our understanding of self and others.

Implications for Formation

Formators who are attentive to the various drivers that young religious in formation display, can adjust their approach to each person so that their driver behaviour can be attenuated. We will see, however, that the approach to modifying driver behaviours is not by directly seeking to change them, but rather to understand the circumstances for the person assuming a particular driver, and focusing on changing the circumstances. How this is done will be made clearer in the following chapter.

The Antiscript

In Chapters 7 and 8 we show the power of parents to influence how their children come to form their script. However, I should point out that often children will rebel against the injunctions and counterinjunctions of the parents and act by way of opposition to the messages that the parents transmit. So if, for instance, a parent sends a counterinjunction of *Be Perfect*, the child may decide that it is going to be anything but perfect. Or if the parent sends an injunction *Don't Succeed,* the child will decide that it is going to succeed at all costs. Berne calls this 'rebellion' the antiscript where "people who rebel against their scripts, apparently doing the opposite of what they are 'supposed to do" (Berne, 1972:160). The fact is, of course, that when people are working by way of antiscript, they are in fact in their script because they are not acting freely, but in opposition to their parents' messages.

Conclusion

The idea of driver behaviour offers us a valuable instrument for analysing our own behaviour and that of other members of the community. As stated elsewhere, there is always the danger when we begin to analyse other people, that we limit them by our categories. The challenge is always to seek to understand with an empathic eye the ways people act as a result of their early life decisions. Once we focus on the fact that people made the best possible decisions in their childhood, with the limited knowledge they had, then we can be more understanding when these same decisions are obviously not serving them well in the present.

Exercises:

1. As you think back on your childhood, remember some of the sayings that your parents used frequently. List as many of them as you can. What message did they give you?

2. What sorts of behaviour did your parents model for you? What influence had this modelling on how you live your life today?

3. The main exercise in this chapter is to observe! The thing about observing driver behaviour is to remember that *no one* characteristic is sufficient to classify the driver behaviour. A person may say, "I'll try to get that done by tomorrow but this does not necessarily mean he or she is working from a *try hard* driver. They may have a *Be Perfect* driver, and simply do not want to promise something they may not be able to deliver. And so, we need to look at the gestures, demeanour, voice and vocabulary in order to get a complete picture. A great way of observing driver behaviour is to watch some television programmes and begin to identify the drivers. Even more effective, is to record a programme and replay slowly, pointing out the characteristics you see in the driver behaviour of the characters.

4. Needless to say, another way of getting to know driver behaviour is to begin to notice the drivers in the members of your community. However, a word of warning! Be careful not to persecute each other as you begin the process. Pointing out other's drivers can become annoying and shaming. It is preferable for you to do the observing of yourself, and to share that with others, instead of having people pointing out your drivers to you.

Chapter Eight

Unspeakable Thoughts

"Man hands on misery to man. It deepens like a coastal shelf.
Get out as early as you can. And don't have any kids yourself."
Philip Larkin

Berne described various levels of contamination in the person as psychopathology, and in this chapter I will discuss some of the more serious effects of the messages from parents that create serious dysfunction in their adult children (Berne, 1961:44ff). These adult 'children' can become members of a religious Congregation, and create tensions and difficulties due to their high level of dysfunctional behaviour. Communities are made up of individuals, and often the quality of community life is as good as the most dysfunctional member of the community. Hence, there is need to understand the various pathological expressions of the Script of an individual religious, and to appreciate how this impacts on community life. It is only when such pathological dysfunctions are acknowledged that positive action can be taken to ameliorate the situation.

From the Script matrix described in the previous chapter, we have dealt with the verbal messages or counterinjunctions that are directed from the Parent in the parent to the Parent in the child. This chapter deals with the very early negative non-verbal messages that are transmitted this time from the Child in the parent to the Child in the child. These are unconscious messages from the parent that lead to the child decisions that go to form the early protocol as explained in Chapter 1. Philip Larkin's lines from his rather grim poem on parents reflect the impact that the injunctions have on the formation of Script (Larkin, 1991). We will see how negative the impact of the parents' messages have on the quality of a person's presence in their community.

Bob and Mary Goulding were friends of both Eric Berne and Fritz Perls, the founder of Gestalt Theory. In the Gouldings' work as therapists, they combined some of the insights from both Berne and Perls to create what they called *Redecision Therapy* (Goulding & Goulding, 1979). They identified twelve negative pre-verbal messages that the parent can send to their child, influencing the sort of decisions that children make as they respond to the unconscious parental messages they receive. These unconscious pre-verbal messages are what we call 'injunctions'.

As the word implies, injunctions are negative messages that are directed to children to prevent them from engaging in certain ways of thinking, feeling and behaving. Each injunction begins with the phrase 'Don't', sending a negative command to the child so that the child is prevented from thinking, feeling and behaving in a particular way. Whereas the counterinjunctions present a conditional message of acceptance (You are OK as long as you are perfect, strong...etc.), all the injunctions point to indications that the parents reject some or all aspects of their child. Berne says that the parent sends the injunctions to their offspring of the opposite sex (Berne, 1972: 134). So, the mother sends injunctions to her son, and the father sends injunctions to the daughter.

At first sight, it may be difficult to accept that a parent would send negative messages to their newly born infant. Why would the parent be so negative? The usual image of the parent is one where the parent loves and protects their child. However, the reality is often less positive and, at times, as dark as the Philip Larkin poem on the previous page and at the beginning of the Chapter.

Often the reason for the rejection by the parent lies in the very Script of the parent that 'kicks in' at some stage when the parent interacts with their child. Or else, there can be some aspect of the child that triggers a problem in the parent, and which the parent tries to deal with by sending a message to the child to stop creating this disturbance (Holloway, 1972: 32ff).

We will now discuss the twelve injunctions as proposed by the Gouldings, outlining the elements of each one, and showing how each injunction could impact on a member of a community in the way they behave. We will also suggest reasons to explain why a parent would send such injunctions to their children and how such messages impact on the way the child develops.

Don't Exist

This is probably the most damning of injunctions, where the parents communicate to their child that he or she is not wanted. This message comes from the Child ego state in the parent, and is picked up by the Child ego state in the child. In other words, this is not a fully conscious command – Don't exist - on the part of the parent, but may express itself in a feeling that results from the fact that the parent does not bond with the child, or that the parent cannot cope with the new arrival. The mother may feel overwhelmed in having to manage all the things that need to be done to satisfy the needs of her child. Or the father may not have wanted a child in the first place, or feels now that the affection he received prior to the child's birth is now being given to the child, leaving him lonely and unloved. Sometimes, financial considerations enter into this area where the parents already have a number of children, and were managing to provide for them. Now, an extra child appears and this puts a strain on the finances, leaving both parents harried and resentful at the new arrival.

Initially, this injunction is a non-verbal message, communicated from the right brain of the mother to the right brain of the child. Such a negative message can impact on the very physical development of the neocortex of the developing child, stunting its growth and eventually forcing the premature development of the left 'thinking' side of the child's neocortex. This premature development of the left side of the brain leads to the underdevelopment of the emotional right side of the brain (Wallin, 2007).

Sometimes, the parents may eventually verbalise such negative implicit or covert message, letting the child know that he or she is not wanted. Some mothers talk to other adults in the presence of her child, about how difficult the child's birth was on the mother, thereby giving what Berne called, 'The Torn Mother Script' (Berne, 1972:101). Or, in moments of frustration, one parent might say, 'Things were fine until you came along,' giving the verbal expression to the pre-conscious Child feelings that either one or both parents felt about their child.

The result of this Don't Exist injunction can lead the child to feel unwanted, and could go to explain feelings of suicide in the grown-up son or daughter. This is not to say that all suicides can be explained in this way. A child can react in many ways to this injunction, and another reaction could be, 'It's OK for me to exist as long as I work hard, please others or engage in using the *drivers* already mentioned in the previous chapter. In other words, the drivers can be used to counter the preverbal messages of the injunctions.

A religious Sister of Brother can show various indications of having a *Don't Exist* injunction. Very often, the workaholic person has an unconscious belief that they only a right to live if they work non-stop, and never give themselves a break. In fact, when they do take some time off, or go on holidays, they can begin to feel anxious, because the very thing that justifies their existence (work) is now on hold. Hence, their very existence is under threat. Religious who are also addicted to drink, drugs or food may also be acting out in response to the *Don't Exist.* The way they abuse their bodies may be an indication that they are unconsciously obeying the early parent injunction against existence.

Don't Be You

Children can be a disappointment to their parents even at the outset. Franz Kafka in *Letter to My Father* expressed how he felt when his father was disappointed with him almost from birth (Kafka, 2008). Some parents want a girl and then, much to their chagrin, a boy arrives. This disappointment will be picked up by the child who does not experience the loving expression of a delighted parent, but rather feels the dutiful acceptance of the parent for the child who is either the wrong sex, the wrong temperament or the wrong size. And as the boy grows up and begins to speak and understand what his parents are saying, he gets subtle messages that the child – a girl – next door is simply beautiful and the pride of her parents. By inference, the boy understands he is the wrong sex.

The Religious who feels that they are not accepted as they are could be re-living the *Don't Be You* injunction. This may not refer necessarily to their sexual identity, but may include a sense that they are not good enough, not intelligent enough, not religious enough, and so on. They feel they are not acceptable as they are, and will therefore work to conform and become what is expected of them, or rebel at the lack of acceptance.

Don't Be a Child

Referring again to Franz Kafka's *Letter to My Father*, he recalled how his father could not accept him the way he was, and wanted him to be like the father himself:

> "You can treat a child only in the way you yourself are constituted, with vigour, noise, and hot temper, and in this case such behaviour seemed to you to be also most appropriate because you wanted to bring me up to be a strong, brave boy." (Kafka, 208:22)

Kafka's father seems to have sent him the injunction, *Don't be a Child*. Probably from the very moment of the child's birth, the father felt incapable of seeing the child as someone weak and dependent. He could not wait until his son was a grown man when he could talk to him man-to-man.

Some parents find it difficult to communicate with young children and are more comfortable with grown ups. As a result, some children find that they cannot relate to their parents because the parents appear distant and aloof to them, incapable of getting on their wavelength. At times, children also feel that they have to grow up and be sensible if they are to be accepted, when all they want to do is to play. So, they feel pressurised to be a man or woman albeit in children's clothes. Time for play, such a necessary aspect in the development of the child, is somewhat foreshortened before the injunction: *Don't Be a Child.*

There are some religious who find it difficult to access their child energy, feeling most uncomfortable when they attend parties and social gatherings. They feel foolish in such settings, and want to escape to have a 'serious' adult conversation with like-minded people. In community, they are inclined to view any form of levity as an indication of immaturity and inappropriate for religious. They probably are living the injunction *Don't Be a Child* and seeing it as a virtue instead of realising that they have lost out on the ludic aspect of life.

Don't Grow Up

In the generation born in the late 1980s and 1990s it seems that these children did not develop a sense of responsibility as early as children did in earlier times. The Peter Pan Syndrome refers to the younger generation's apparent unwillingness to grow up, and to leave behind their alleged immature behaviour. This phenomenon may be due to the injunction *Don't Grow Up* that parents communicate nonverbally especially to their last born child. When parents are approaching the time when the children will be leaving home, the arrival of an 'unexpected' child can put off the day when the parents will be on their own. And so, the parents, rather than encourage their child to grow and develop to take their place in the world, they send the *Don't Grow Up* message, so that the parents put off the time when they will inevitably have an 'empty nest'.

Stewart and Joines also suggest that the *Don't Grow Up* injunction arises especially for fathers with regard to their daughters (Stewart & Joines, 2012:141). They enjoy the daughter when she is his 'princess' but are not so confident when she grows into a queen. As the father sees his daughter developing physically, he may become uneasy or scared of his sexual responses to her, and withdraw, giving the message that it is not OK to grow up.

When a religious has a *Don't Grow Up* injunction, he or she comes across as never serious, unwilling to take responsibility, and often over-dependent on other members of the community to support them. So, they will frequently express their inability to complete tasks on their own. In many ways, they give the impression of people who have little confidence in themselves, demonstrating that they have a young head on old shoulders! Despite their years, they seem immature on many levels.

They associate with younger people, even imitating teenage dress, imagining that they can connect with adolescents and therefore be effective youth ministers. In reality, they fail to maintain healthy boundaries, not recognizing that they are no longer teenagers. Such behaviour could well be the result of the *Don't Grow Up* injunction.

Don't Succeed

Philip Larkin, quoted at the head of this chapter, says of parents in the same poem:

> "They fill you with the faults they had
> And add some extra, just for you" (*Ibid:*1991).

Again, the question is, why would parents not want their children to succeed? As the child comes into the world, it may appear strange that the parents somehow would not want their child to be the best they can be. The *Don't Succeed* injunction seems to emerge from the parents' own poor self-image. The poor self-image foments in the Child of the parent, creating a mixture of low self-esteem and resentment. The parents feel so badly about themselves, and resentful that they have not succeeded in life, that they find it difficult to wish for success in others, even for their own child. For these parents, they fear that were the child to succeed, the parents' failures would be all the more obvious and painful. And so, they do exactly what Larkin says: "They fill you with the faults they had," criticising their children, and putting them down so as not to have to compete with them.

The impact on the child can be most devastating. In order to gain the affection of the parents, and to maintain the connection with them, the child will often underachieve so as not to be a threat to the parents. The child will fail just to 'please' the parents who on a conscious level may reprimand their child for failing, but at an unconscious level may feel satisfaction that their child is not superior to them.

The *Don't Succeed* injunction can show its face very frequently in community. Because of the competence and confidence of some religious, other members of the community may feel resentment and jealousy. A religious who has experienced the *Don't Succeed* injunction from their parents, will be highly sensitive to the danger of being isolated, alienated and excluded. And so, the religious can hide their metaphorical light under a bushel, and remain hidden amongst the lowest common denominator. Instead of developing their talents to the full, they profess a sufficient level ignorance, incompetence and banality to find acceptance within the group. In this regard the words of Marianne Williamson are so relevant (1992:190-191):

> Our deepest fear is not that we are inadequate.
> Our deepest fear is that we are powerful beyond
> measure. It is our light, not our darkness that
> most frightens us. We ask ourselves, who am I to
> be brilliant, gorgeous, talented, fabulous?

In these cases, false humility dominates, preventing the religious from achieving their fullest potential for fear those who do not have the same gifts and capabilities will reject them.

Don't

Fear and anxiety in parents arise from beliefs that the world is dangerous, and that 'bad' things will almost certainly happen. The impact of fear and anxiety is felt in the sympathetic nervous system, causing increased heart rate, dilation of pupils, sweat glands being activated, and the suppression of the immune system to name but a few of the internal physiological changes that take place in the body. When a parent feels such fear and anxiety as she looks at her newly born infant, the unconscious message is transmitted to the child, and anxiety and fear can become part of the child's physiological make-up. Fear makes the parent hyper-vigilant with regard to the safety of the child, and causes her to overreact when she sees her child in possible danger. So, when the infant begins to crawl, the mother is constantly on edge in the certainty that the child will come to harm. The injunction *Don't* feels like the only solution for the parents in order to avoid the fear and anxiety they are experiencing.

As the child learns to speak and listen to the mother, the word 'Don't ' appears often in the dialogue between them. The mother continues to be afraid that the child will cross the road and be killed, or will fall in the garden and break her leg or meet with an even greater tragedy. This anxiety can create in the child an equal level of fear that something terrible will happen. The child, as a result, will become anxious about the future, and hence prevent him or herself from any real level of adventure and curiosity.

Br John can be very difficult to manage, as he is always

imagining that things will go wrong. In discussions, he is frequently looking at the negative side of things, afraid that he or the community will make a mistake that could have serious consequences. The result is paralysis by analysis where plans are shelved, and ideas abandoned because of the fear of failure. No doubt, Br John picked up the injunction *Don't* and this has prevented him from achieving many positive projects. And so, Br John builds a wall of protection around himself that, while apparently keeping him safe, in reality, prevents him from experiencing the challenges of a fully involved life.

Don't Be Important

Max Ehramm's (1920) inspirational tract, *Desiderata*, has the line,

> You are a child of the universe no less than the
> trees and the stars; you have a right to be here.

Such sentiments are in direct opposition to the injunction, *Don't Be Important*, which is not unrelated to the injunction *Don't Succeed.* Parents who have a poor self-image avoid any possibility that they could be important, and consequently they avoid promoting themselves or their children in society. Their dictum is "It is better to keep quiet and give the impression that you know nothing, than to open your mouth and remove all doubt!" So, the parents (in their Child ego state) communicate to their child the message that they are not to be important, and should avoid being the centre of attention. They put this injunction into practice by often ignoring any display of drama or exuberance on the part of the newly born, in the belief that giving the child attention will only make them want more attention.

The result of this injunction is that the child grows up with the belief that they should not get a 'swelled head', and should be humble and unassuming, 'fitting in' wherever they find themselves, and avoiding any display of importance.

For religious in community, the injunction *Don't be Important* can be observed in some Congregations where there is a very strong ethos of 'common life', and where everyone dresses the same, observes the same rules and regulations, and treats everyone the same. Aristotle's dictum that 'it is as unjust to treat equals unequally, as it is to treat unequals equally' is often ignored. This happens when the injunction *Don't be Important* pervades a community (Irwin, 1991:73). When everyone must be treated in exactly the same way as the next person, individual needs are ignored because it seems individual differences are not considered important.

Don't Belong

John O'Donohue in his book *Eternal Echoes*, said about belonging: 'Belonging will always be fractured and temporary. Our longing will be permanent and full' (O'Donohue, 1998: 126). In this he points to the reality that often people feel they don't belong. August Wilson, the American playwright, experienced this dissociation from his family when he reflected: "I've been with strangers all day and they treated me like family. I come in here to family and you treat me like a stranger" (Wilson, 1990). How and why would parents transmit the injunction *Don't Belong* to their children? Again, the main reason for this Child in the parent prohibition is that the parents themselves do not feel connected with others, and find emotional attachment difficult if not impossible. Hence, they do not form a close attachment with their children, and thereby give the message *"Don't Belong"*.

Wallin in *Attachment in Psychotherapy* describes the work of Mary Ainsworth that charts the impact on children of the parents lack of emotional attachment to their children (Wallin: 2007:39ff). The child picks up the message *Don't Belong,* and consequently lacks any sense of belonging, resorting to what Ainsworth calls 'avoidant attachment'.

We will see later on how religious structure their time in order to achieve or avoid levels of connectedness in a community. Br Sean finds it very difficult to 'belong' to a community, and when he is transferred from one place to another, he seems to make the transition without any difficulty. This is mainly because he has never felt any real sense of belonging, Because of the way he experienced his parents, who transmitted the message *Don't belong* from the earliest time he can remember, Br Sean seems incapable of maintaining any long-term friendships. As a result, he finds that he often feels alone and isolated.

Don't Be Close

In Susan Kay's novel, *The Phantom,* she has Erik saying:

> *"They kiss on meeting, they kiss on parting, that simple touching of flesh that is taken entirely for granted as a basic human right. I've lived on this earth half a century without knowing what it is to be kissed"* (Kay, 2005).

Some children have never seen their parents being physically close or expressing their affection demonstratively. The likelihood is that the parents avoided any real closeness to their children from a very early age because of their Child ego state fear of closeness. Human contact – flesh-to-flesh – between the baby and mother is so important. African mothers can be seen carrying their babies close to their bodies by wrapping a cloth containing their child around themselves so that the child is literally attached to the mother most of the day. *The Scientific American* (Harman, 2010) reported that particularly in the new-born period, flesh to flesh contact helps calm babies: they cry less and it helps them sleep better. Harman also said that some studies show babies' brain development is facilitated by close contact with the mother— probably because they are calmer and sleep better.

In the formation period of young people in religious life, there used to be a dictum *Noli me tangere,* (Jn. 20:17) meaning 'do not touch me', to warn the young religious to refrain from physical expressions of affection. No doubt, the injunction *Don't be close* must have had its impact on the formators at the time when they coined this phrase. While the formators may have feared any homosexual tendencies on the part of the novices, the result of this injunction, probably dating back to the parental injunction and reinforced by religious practice, is that some religious find it difficult to express affection in a physical way.

Don't Be Well (Don't Be Sane)

With parents who have mental illness, the arrival of a child can be a moment of stress and resentment. Potentially, their child could be normal and sane, thereby highlighting the problems that the parents have. At an unconscious level, therefore, the parents may communicate the message *Don't be Sane* to their child. Schizophrenia has both genetic as well as environmental factors that influence its occurrence in young people. Could it be that the injunction *Don't be Sane* may be a causal factor in its appearance in young people?

The Munchausen Syndrome involves the person feigning illness or exaggerating illness in order to gain attention. This attention-seeking behaviour could be established early on in a child's development when they perceive that they get more attention from their parents when they are ill than when they are well. By being ill, the child experiences the care and concern of the parents, while no attention seems to be given when the children are well.

Br Tom has always some medical complaint that necessitates many visits to the doctor. Daily, he discusses some aches or pains he is experiencing, and much of his conversation revolves around illness and medicine. It could be that Br Tom internalised the *Don't be Well* from an early age, and is still living out this Script.

Don't Think

Parents who are anxious often have difficulty in thinking straight. Their emotions block their capacity to think matters through, and they frequently believe that it is better not to think too deeply about things in order to ward off fears and uncertainties. With this approach to life, these parents can often appear confused by the flood of emotions that drown their thinking capacity. When their child is beginning to learn to speak and make sense of the world, these parents are inclined to send a *Don't Think* injunction. They are anxious, and mistakenly think they can protect the child from a confused world by avoiding too much mental activity. So, when the child asks many questions, the parents may respond in ways that discount clear thinking, leaving the child equally confused and not prepared to think clearly for themselves.

Br Andrew comes across as highly emotional and over-reactive. He seems incapable of stepping back and thinking before he speaks. Consequently, he can say things that are both hurtful and imprudent, creating misunderstanding and tension in the community. He is often so overcome with his feelings, that what emerges from his mouth are a series of *non-sequiturs* that leave the rest of the community equally confused and annoyed. In addition, when he tries to explain the reasons for some of the choices he makes, he only succeeds in confusing people with an avalanche of muddled thoughts and words.

Don't Feel

John Powell, the Jesuit popular psychologist, somewhere in one of his best-selling books, tells of his father whose main advice to his son was, "Keep your bowels open and your mouth shut!" By this advice he wanted to warn his son about letting his feelings be known to anyone. Many men have this injunction from an early age. Some of it is culturally determined. Parents often discourage their sons at an early age from expressing such emotions as sadness, hurt, and disappointment – those emotions that would make people cry. The dictum 'boys don't cry' can result in the *Don't Feel* injunction being transmitted both verbally and non-verbally early in the life of the child. Parents who find it difficult to express their own feelings find it more comfortable if their children are likewise inclined.

One of the dangers of community life is that the expression of feelings is not always appreciated, because it can disturb the even tenor of the group. Some religious, coming from a home where the *Don't Feel* injunction was frequently passed on to them, prefer to live a 'quiet' life where emotions do not emerge, and where thinking is preferred to feeling. The result of such a lifestyle is that many religious lead lonely isolated lives, and have to face their difficulties alone, without the support of their community.

Parents and Injunctions

Some find it difficult to blame their parents for the non-verbal, unconscious injunctions that they send to their children. The phrase, "They did the best they could" is often used in refusing to examine the possible injunctions that they received from their parents. Needless to say, it is not a matter of blame, but a matter of understanding. In our desire to understand ourselves and the way we live and are, we look back at our early childhood to begin to understand what has shaped us. Naturally, we cannot remember the very early years – the pre-verbal years – but we do know ourselves to some extent and when, for example, we notice that we have difficulty in expressing our feelings or thinking, a possible reason for this may be that some of the injunctions stunted our growth in one or more areas of development.

Program

We have covered two of the three elements in the Script matrix: counterinjunctions in Chapter 7, and injunctions in this Chapter. The remaining element is the program. Steiner defines the program as 'the manner in which the parent of the same sex demonstrates how attributions and injunctions can be followed...'(Steiner, 1974:87). So, for instance, if a mother transmits the injunction, *Don't Feel,* to her son, it is the father who will show his son how to avoid feelings by being withdrawn and unemotional. Or if the Father transmits the injunction to his daughter, *Don't be Close,* then the mother will show her daughter how to avoid closeness in her relationships, by never showing physical closeness either to her husband or to her children. The program, therefore, is linked to the modelling referred to earlier, where the child learns how to implement the injunction and counterinjuction messages of the parents (Chapter 7).

The Drowning Man

The idea of the 'drowning man' diagram (Fig. 16) is a clever way of explaining how best to approach people with a view to modifying their driver behaviour. As we have seen, the driver behaviours are the observable behaviours that a person displays in order for them to feel OK. Because the message from the parents was one of conditional acceptance, people assume that as long as they behave with the driver behaviour, they will remain without major stress.

However, each of the drivers creates their own problems. The *Be Perfect* driver, for example, puts great pressure on the person to get things right, and to work until they almost drop. The *Be Strong* driver prevents the person from being in touch with their feelings. The *Try Hard* driver traps the person in a cycle of straining to get things done without ever succeeding. The *Hurry Up* driver causes the person to rush around without getting things done properly. And the *Please Others* driver, traps the person in seeking to obtain the approval of others at every possible moment.

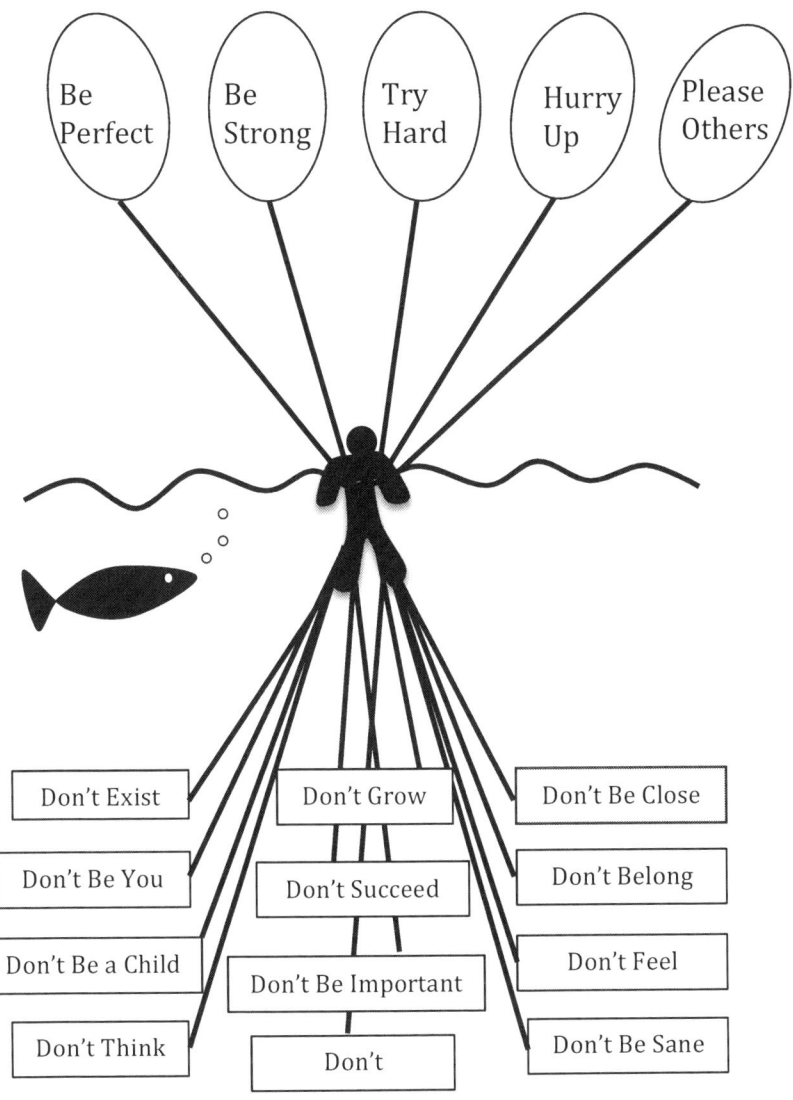

Fig. 16 The Drowning Man (Lee, 1998)

We see in Fig. 16 the image of a man in the sea, weighed down with cement blocks (the injunctions). He should be drowning, except for the fact that he is being kept afloat by the very powerful helium balloons (the drivers or counterinjuctions). The lesson here is that people cannot get rid of the drivers *before* they unshackle the injunctions that are pulling them down. So, if a Be Strong driver, for example, controls someone, we need to explore with him or her the various injunctions that force him to hang on to the driver. Such injunctions as: *Don't Feel; Don't be Close; Don't Belong; Don't be a Child* are some of the issues that the person has to face *before* they begin to allow themselves to let the *Be Strong* balloon go!

The implications for members of a community is that they should be careful not to focus exclusively on the *behaviour* of their fellow religious, but should try instead to understand *why* they have the driver in the first place, and be willing to tolerate the behaviour while seeking to understand what injunctions lie beneath the drivers. Then they can focus on how to help their community member to deal with those negative messages.

Trying to change the driver behaviour of another person, will ultimately fail, because the driver behaviour is what keeps him or her afloat. Without the 'safety blanket' of the drivers, people will feel great stress. So, it is at this juncture that we are challenged to be tolerant of the driver behaviours of others, and begin to be curious as to the reason for such ways of behaving. As we come to appreciate the motivation for the driver behaviour, we can replace resentment with compassion, and work at the injunctions in order to replace them with positive permissions to exist, to feel, to think, and so on. When, therefore, people begin to feel the permissions to be themselves, the necessity for driver behaviour gives way to a sense of OKness that no longer requires the person to adapt to the requirements of the Controlling Parent. Consequently, they give themselves the permission to express their potency in all aspects of their lives. They also will feel more accepting of others.

Transgenerational Scripts

The important thing to remember with regard to the role of parents in the communication of injunctions is that these same parents in turn probably received the same injunctions from their own parents (Berne, 1972:320). This means that injunctions are passed on from generation to generation until some member of the family works to break 'the bind that ties'.

Fanita English coined the phrase 'episcript' or the 'hot potato' to describe the phenomenon of the passing on of the Script from one generation to the next (English, 1969:77ff). When parents cannot handle their Script, they hold it like a hot potato, and they pass it on to the next generation so as to avoid burning their own hands! In passing on the unresolved trauma, the parents continue to almost hypnotise their children to fulfil the obligations that the Script had imposed on the parents by previous generations (English, 2010: 227).

How the Script is passed on from generation to generation is beyond the scope of this book. The work of Gloria Noriega, however, is worth studying to understand the various mechanisms for the transgenerational transmission of Script and how the transmission of Script can be interrupted (Noriega, 2012: 269ff).

Conclusion

The fact that the injunctions are preverbal unconscious messages transmitted from parents to children highlights the challenge of uncovering these early influences and counteracting their power of influence. As we will see in the exercises below, probably the best way to have a glimpse of the unconscious is to reflect on how we think, feel and behave in the present moment. As we engage in some level of introspection, we can begin to analyse how we view ourselves, others and our future. The extent to which we experience some level of discomfort, unease or inner conflict may be an indication of the types of injunctions that our parents may have communicated to us. The challenge then facing us is how to move from injunctions that stunt growth to permissions that enhance life (see Chapter 24).

Exercises

1. Since it is almost impossible to remember when you were an infant, you will not be sure of what injunctions your parents might have communicated to you. One way of accessing what injunctions they *might* have communicated is to reflect on how you think, feel and act now. By answering the following questions, you may gain insight into the injunctions that you may have experienced. By identifying the injunctions, the challenge will be to work toward the permissions that will counter the injunctions. These will be discussed later. Each question is linked to an injunction.

2.
   a) Do you find it easy to take a break when you have not finished the work you are supposed to get done? (Don't Exist)
   b) Are you content as you are – gender, size, features, etc.? (Don't be You)
   c) Can you have fun and enjoy parties and social events? (Don't be a Child)
   d) Do you always feel mature and grown-up? (Don't Grow Up)
   e) Have you accomplished what you are capable of? (Don't Make it)
   f) Are you often ready to take a risk in taking on something new? (Don't)
   g) Do you feel important and valued? (Don't be Important)
   h) Have you a wide circle of good friends? (Don't Belong)
   i) Do you feel close to people? (Don't be Close)
   j) Are you often concerned with you health? (Don't be Well)
   k) Can you think clearly and express your ideas with ease? (Don't Think)
   l) Can you easily express your feelings? (Don't Feel)

Share your responses with the community or with one other person in the community

Chapter Nine

Scripts and Time

"I wish it need not have happened in my time," said Frodo.
"So do I," said Gandalf, "and so do all who live to see such times.
But that is not for them to decide.
All we have to decide is what to do
with the time that is given us."
J.R.R. Tolkien

So far we have described the nature of Script, and the life-positions that form the basis of Script. We explained the structure and function of ego states, and identified the various contaminations of ego states that go to make up the Script. We also identified the elements of the Script Matrix, which charts the way parents transmit verbal and non-verbal messages that go to make up the Script.

As we look at ourselves, and the members of our communities, it is hoped that our understanding of Script - ours and others - will contribute to a better understanding of community dynamics, and result in an increased acceptance of the differences that exist between community members. When we come to realise that much behaviour is due to an unconscious life plan, we hopefully will appreciate that a lot of the dynamics of the community arises from unconscious processes that often elude inspection.

This chapter examines how the Script plays out in time, and how we structure our time with regard to the process of the Script (Berne, 1970: 150ff). We will also link driver behaviour with the Script process to better understand how we can diagnose some characteristics of the Script (Table 2).

Taibi Kahler uses the term 'process Script' to explain how the Script plays out in the day-to-day life of a person, combining the process of the Script with *driver behaviour* already discussed in Chapter 7 (Kahler, 1978: 205ff; 2008: 103ff; 147ff; 181ff).

Drivers	Process Scripts	The Gods
Be Perfect	Until	Jason
Be Strong	Never	Tantalus
Try Hard	Always	Arachne
Please Others	After	Damocles
Try Hard /Please Others	Almost 1	Sisyphus
Please Others / Be Perfect	Almost 2	
Please Me	Open – ended	Baucis & Philemon

Table 2. Drivers, Process Scripts and the Gods

Berne lists the types of Scripts that are connected to time structure as: *the Never, the Always, the Until, the After,* the *Over and Over,* and the *Open Ended Scripts* (Berne, 1970:151ff). He links these Scripts with characters in Greek mythology to better portray how the Script works. We will follow his example and add some examples of religious who live out these process Scripts in their daily lives, showing how Script limits people's lives.

The Never Script

The Never Script is represented by the Greek hero Tantalus who was made to stand in a pool of water beneath a fruit tree with low branches, with the fruit ever eluding his grasp, and the water always receding before he could take a drink. So, Tantalus was never satisfied, and felt eternally frustrated with life. When he wanted to eat or drink, he was never able to get what he wanted. It seemed it never occurred to him that he could shift his position and get to the water or the fruit!

Br David felt that he could *never* get what he wanted. He often had many wishes and plans, but he always felt that he could never achieve his deepest desires. Often he blamed the situations he found himself in, thinking that life was cheating him. Like Tantalus, opportunities seemed to elude him and he *never* felt that he could do anything about the situation. So, he felt frustrated with life and, at the same time, too readily resigned to the fact that the environment was working against him. Br David frequently complained about the situation he found himself in, but *never* could imagine that life could be different. His resignation was more a type of passivity, where life seemed to be passing him by without any change. Willy Loman in Arthur Miller's *Death of a Salesman* is a good example of the person with the *Never* Script.

The driver *Be Strong* is linked to the *Never* Script because the only way to deal with the belief that the person can *never* get what they want is to dampen all strong feelings of disappointment and accept fate (Kahler, 1975:280ff). Br David seldom showed real authentic emotions. He seemed to be 'in control' avoiding expressions of anger, sadness and fear, and remaining stoical before a reality that he felt he could *never* change. Low-level depression seemed to stalk him, leaving him in a state of annoying resignation with his lot. For many years now, Br David has 'battled' with the depression without making any real progress. He passes a lot of his time watching television, and is inclined to overeat and, at times, drinks too much.

The Always Script

In Greco-Roman mythology, the mortal Arachne was a great weaver who boasted that her skill was greater than that of Athena, goddess of wisdom, weaving, and strategy. When Arachne refused to acknowledge that her skill came, in part at least, from the goddess Athena, Athena took offense and set up a contest between the two. Athena saw that Arachne had insulted the gods, and so she ripped Arachne's work into shreds. Arachne hanged herself. Moved to mercy, Athena brought Arachne back to life, but sprinkled her with Hecate's potion, turning her into a spider, and cursing her and her descendants to *always* weave her webs.

Looking at the life of Br Malachy we can see that he seldom stays in any community for more than two years. He has been in religious life for the last thirty years, and has moved almost twenty times. It seems that after the initial settling in period, he *always* begins to find fault with everything and everyone. The ministry is not what he wanted, the superior does not understand, and the community is unconcerned with his needs and wants. And so, he applies for a change and moves on. In some other cases, the community had requested that he try another community that may better suit him. The cycle seems to continue forever. 'It is *always* the same,' he complains.

The *Try Hard* driver is very much connected to the *Always* Script. It seems that Br Malachy tries hard to 'fit in' in each community he joins, but he never succeeds! He tries hard in his ministry, but again never actually makes a fist of it. He seems to feel that nothing will change, that it will *always* be thus. Like Arachne, he feels condemned to a repeating cycle of frustrated attempts to achieve something worthwhile, but finds himself trapped, and moves on in the hope that the next community and ministry will be better. Because, at an unconscious level, Br Malachy believes that things will *always* be the same, his attempts are only attempts, but he never succeeds despite trying hard.

The Until Script

The Greek hero Jason, went in search of the Golden Fleece in order to win back the kingdom for his father. He could not return *until* he overcame many obstacles in his search for the Golden Fleece.

Sister Michael works herself to the bone. She never seems to take a break and when invited to, she says she cannot go away *until* she has finished the work at hand. The problem is that she never finishes the work. It appears that she is continually busy, and keeps postponing the time when she can relax. She often talks about her plans when she retires, but it seems that *until* then she will continue unrelentingly, going from one job to the next. Even in the course of the day, she will frequently miss her meals, having become engrossed in a job, and feeling that she can't stop *until* she has finished. It is even difficult to get her to celebrate her birthday, because very often she will be away at a workshop, and she frequently postpones the party *until* she returns, by which time, the moment is lost and she continues on regardless.

The *Until* Script is very much linked to the *Be Perfect* driver. Sister Michael is never satisfied *until* the job is perfectly done. She is a stickler for detail, and never rests *until* every 't' is crossed and 'i' dotted. She has never enough time to complete a job, and is frequently late for appointments because of her need to finish the current job perfectly. Sister Michael never has enough time in the day, and is always struggling to get her work done before she can feel relaxed and satisfied, two feelings that are often struggling to emerge because of her Script process.

The After Script

In the Greek legend, Damocles used to make comments to the king about his wealth and luxurious life. One day when Damocles complimented the tyrant on his abundance and power, Dionysius turned to Damocles and said, "If you think I'm so lucky, how would you like to try out my life?" Damocles readily agreed, and so Dionysius ordered everything to be prepared for Damocles to experience what life as Dionysius was like. Damocles was enjoying himself immensely until he noticed a sharp sword hovering over his head that was suspended from the ceiling by a strand of horsehair. This, the tyrant explained to Damocles, was what life as a ruler was like. He may have the power and wealth, but afterwards he will pay for it.

And so, the *After Script* refers to the idea that while power and wealth and happiness may appear attractive, *afterwards* is the realization that any of the three elements of power is not as attractive as they initially appear. The motto of this Script is, according to Berne: 'You can enjoy yourself for a while, but *after that* your troubles begin' (Berne, 1970: 151).

This Script applies very much to Br John, who never seems to be able to enjoy himself fully. When he takes Sunday off to go walking in the hills, he tells his companions that he is going to regret having taken the day off to exercise because of the pile of work that is still on his desk. Or when he is socializing and having a drink, his comment often is, 'I'll pay for this in the morning!' He is torn between enjoying himself in the moment, and feeling an impending negative result in the future for his momentary lapse in taking life seriously.

The *After* Script can be linked to the *Please Others* driver. The relationship between the two can be explained by the two parts in the frequent statements of the *After* Script: 'I'm enjoying such and such, but I'll regret...' The person is doing something to please himself in the first part of the sentence, and in the second part is the idea that the negative results of the behaviour will somehow displease others. So, in the case of Br John, the pleasure of walking in the hills is offset by the thought that *afterwards* he will not get his work done and therefore displease his superior.

The Almost (over and over) Script

Albert Camus wrote a famous philosophical work on the myth of Sisyphus, the Greek hero (Camus, 2005:115ff). He describes the story thus:

> The gods had condemned Sisyphus to ceaselessly rolling a rock to the top of a mountain, whence the stone would fall back of its own weight. They had thought with some reason that there is no more dreadful punishment than futile and hopeless labour.

Camus goes on to say that the real torture for Sisyphus was that he was conscious of the futility of his efforts. Sisyphus *almost* completes his task, and at the last moment he slips, and the stone rolls back down to the bottom of the hill. And so, he has to begin again pushing the stone back up the hill until the weight of it causes him to let it roll back again! He *almost* succeeds.

Sister Frances has an *Almost* Script where she *almost* completes whatever she attempts to do. She will prepare a prayer sheet for the community, and discover that she has left out a line in the hymn for the community to sing. Or, she will have dressed well for the social event, forgetting however to have her shoes repaired, and resorting to a pair of shoes that clashes with her outfit. She is *almost* well turned out but not quite! Sr Frances also procrastinates, and so for Christmas she wrote all her cards for posting, but only realized after Christmas that she forgot to post them!

The driver *Try Hard* fits well with the *Almost* Script. Instead of succeeding, the person will *Try Hard* and almost achieve what he or she wanted to achieve. They will push the stone up the hill, but at the last moment, they will let it fall down again. Frustration and passive aggression characterize this type of

Script. By being passive, they also cause considerable frustration and aggression in others. Hence passive aggression!

Taibi Kahler identifies two types of the *Almost* Script (Kahler, 1978:216). The first one we have already described which he calls *Almost* Type 1. In the *Almost* Type 2, we would have Sisyphus pushing the stone up the hill, and reaching the top with great effort. Then, when Sisyphus has reached the top, instead of sitting back and taking a rest to enjoy the view, he sees that the top of the hill is also the beginning of another hill that had been hidden on the way up. And so, he begins again to push the stone up the next hill, unaware that there could be yet a third hill awaiting him.

Br Bart has the *Almost* Type 2 Script. He suffers from what his companions call 'course-itis', where he addicted to pursuing more and more courses! Having completed his primary degree, Br Bart went on to do his Masters, and now he is contemplating doing a doctorate. Some say he is killing himself by degrees! It seems that no sooner has he finished a job, than he feels a certain compulsion to begin again. It seems that someone like Br Bart, is more under the influence of the *Please Other* and the *Be Perfect* drivers. The *Try Hard* does not really feature in his make-up. The desire to continue studying and not to give himself a rest is the result of the driven nature of a *Be Perfect* driver.

The Open Ended Script

The Greek legend of Baucis and Philemon refers to the hospitality that this old couple gave to Jupiter, and as a reward were promised that they would live forever. Consequently, they were turned into laurel trees that intertwined and offered shelter to passers-by. Berne interprets this story by saying that the couple lived forever and, having carried out their parental duties, spent 'the rest of their lives growing vegetables, or gossiping like leaves rustling in the wind' (Berne, 1972:237).

Brother Frank had recently retired from his teaching post, and was settling into a slower pace of life. Months later when he was asked how he felt about being retired, he replied, 'It's strange but now that I have nothing to do, I find I don't have time to do anything!' In fact, while some of the retired Brothers in the community were quite active in helping out in the parish, there were a few retired Brothers who, like Baucis and Philemon, were living out their retirement by passing the time doing the crosswords, reading the daily paper, and spending hours in front of the television. Somehow the spark had gone out of their lives.

The driver that seems best suited to this process Script is *Please Me*, which is a version of *Please Others* (Kahler: 1978:220). Although most seem to add the *Be Perfect* driver onto this process Script, I am inclined to limit the driver to the *Please Me* driver.

Conclusion

The combination of process Script and driver behaviour helps give an accurate picture of Script behaviour on a day-to-day basis. It is worth spending time alone in order to allow ourselves to reflect deeply on our behaviour patterns. Self-reflection is a powerful door to self-understanding, and combined with gentle feedback from the people who know us best, this personal scrutiny will provide us with a more complete picture of our way of being in the world.

Exercises

1. As you review the various process Scripts, can you identify people you know who have one or more of these Scripts? Describe their behaviour without necessarily naming the people.
2. Which of the process Scripts would you apply to yourself? Describe what it is like to have to deal with this Script?
3. What would you do differently were you liberated from the Script/s you identified in question 2?
4. How could some of your community members support you as you make these changes?

PART TWO

How We Communicate

"The single biggest problem in communication
is the illusion that it has taken place."
George Bernard Shaw

We communicate out of our Script, and in this section we examine transactional analysis proper to explore the dynamics of communication, and to understand how knowledge of our Script and our Life positions will impact on interpersonal communication (Chapter 10). An understanding of these dynamics can assist in resolving conflicts in community. Chapter 11 introduces a technique of conflict management that flows from an appreciation of the analysis of transactions, and should prove very useful in resolving misunderstandings, resentments and fantasies that can pollute the atmosphere of a community.

Berne's idea of *strokes* as 'units of recognition' suggests a way of improving the effectiveness of communication in the community (Chapter 12), and affirming the qualities of the community members. How community members structure their time to gain or avoid strokes (Chapter 13) offers a valuable insight into the way a community structures its time to facilitate or prevent levels of intimacy between people who live in community. Chapter 14 examines how people play psychological games in order to confirm their Script decision, and receive strokes albeit negative ones. In Chapter 15 we see how *racketeering* and *stamp collecting* lead us to express inauthentic feelings, which prevent members of the community from being authentic in the way they interact with each other. In the final chapter of Part 2 we discuss some of the unconscious processes that explain our strong reactions to people, showing how transference and projection prevents us from effectively communicating with the other members of our community.

Chapter Ten

How to Say 'Hello'

"A different language is a different vision of life."
Federico Fellini

Community is all about communication, and often the challenge of community living is the manner in which the members of the community interact with each other. TA has a valuable contribution to make in analysing the ways people communicate, and how they can change their communication style to improve interpersonal relationships in community. Transactional Analysis (TA), the very name of Berne's theory, involves the analysing of transactions between people.

Berne defined a transaction as 'the unit of social action', which consists of one person sending a message or stimulus (S) to another person, and the other person replying or returning a response (R) (Berne, 1963:328). 'Hi there!' could be the stimulus sent from one person with the response from the other person being, 'How are things?' Thus begins a conversation with a stimulus followed by a response, and continuing on for a series of transactions between two or more people. In analysing the transactions, we use the ego state model to identify the nature of the communication. A conversation consists of a series of transactions linked together, and coming from the ego states of each person (Woollams and Brown, 1978:65). There are three types of transactions: complementary, crossed and ulterior transactions, and three corresponding rules of communication. A clear understanding of the specific type of transaction that takes place in a conversation will offer people a variety of options in the way they interact with other people (Karpman, 1971: 79ff).

Complementary Transactions

Complementary transactions (sometimes also called *parallel transactions*) are those transactions where the stimulus and response arrows are parallel, creating a communication path between two people (Woollams & Brown, 1978: 65). In Fig. 17a &17b we have some examples of complementary transactions.

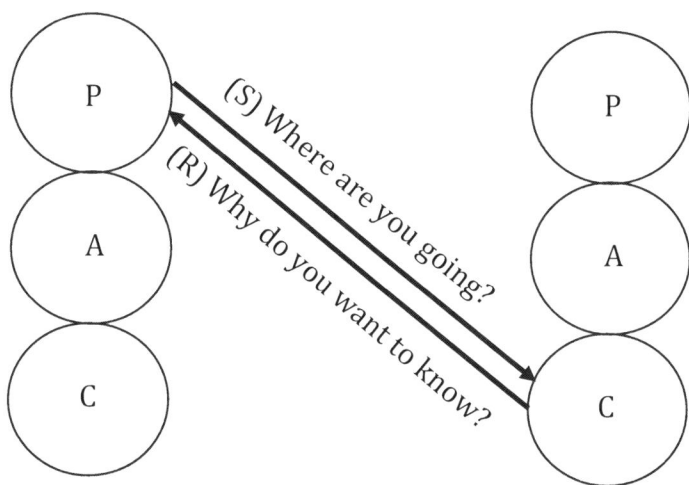

Fig. 17a   Complementary Transactions

In Fig. 17a above, it is clear that the stimulus is directed from the Parent ego state to the Child ego state, and the response is returned to the source of the stimulus i.e. from the Child ego state to the Parent ego state. The arrows between the two people in diagram 17a are parallel and therefore the transaction is considered to be *complementary*. The first rule of communication is: *As long as the transactions remain complementary, communication may continue indefinitely* (quoted in Woollams and Brown, 1978:65). We notice in this first complementary transaction, that the message is coming from what is perceived as a Controlling Parent and the response is coming from a Rebellious Child. Since the transactions are complementary, we would expect this series of transactions to lead to a nasty confrontation. The Controlling Parent could respond to the Rebellious Child, 'Don't be so rude!' to which the Rebellious Child ego state could reply, 'Would you shut up!' and so on until both parties metaphorically murder each other.

In community life, where there is tension and bad feelings about a situation, there will be complementary messages continuing indefinitely between two people, and often escalating into a full-blown war of resentment, fuelled by fantasies and misunderstandings. We will see that in the third rule of communication, the reason for such difficulty in the community is that beneath the level of verbal communication, there is another conversation going on at the psychological level, and this is not being addressed. And it is the psychological level that determines everything!

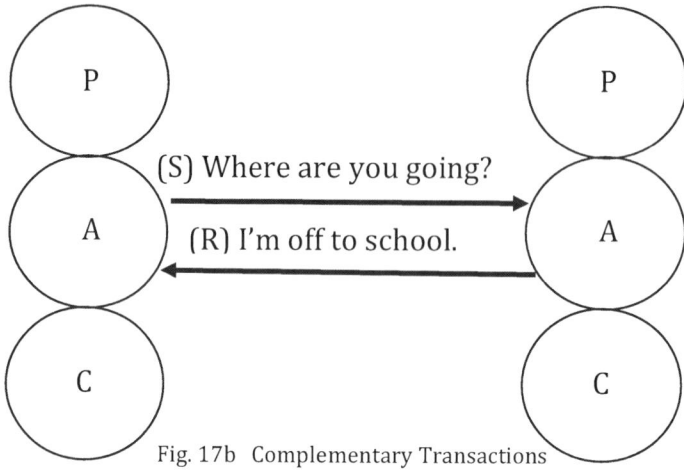

Fig. 17b Complementary Transactions

In Fig. 17b above, the same message that came from the Parent in Fig. 17a now comes from the Adult, and the response is a parallel complementary transaction, coming also from Adult. One could imagine, this conversation, which began with 'Where are you going?' and followed with 'I'm off to school', continuing in Adult fashion with: 'Best of luck!' To which the Adult replies, 'Thanks!' In this case, we have peace and harmony with each person respecting the other, and the conversation continuing at an Adult-to-Adult level.

Crossed Transactions

In figs. 18a and 18b below we see an example of crossed transactions where the lines of communication are not parallel. In this diagram we see that the arrows are crossed, and the ego state that is targeted is not the one that responds.

In Fig.18a we see the Controlling Parent sending a message to the Child of the other person. However, the other person decides not to respond from the Child ego state and so avoids a complementary transaction. Instead, she decides to respond from Adult, thus crossing the transaction.

In Fig. 18b overleaf, we have the stimulus coming from the Adult ego state of one person directed to the Adult ego state of the other person. But in this case, the other person responds from Parent to Parent. Although it looks like a parallel transaction (the arrows are parallel), this is also a crossed transaction since the ego state that is targeted (the Adult) is not the one that responds (the Parent responds).

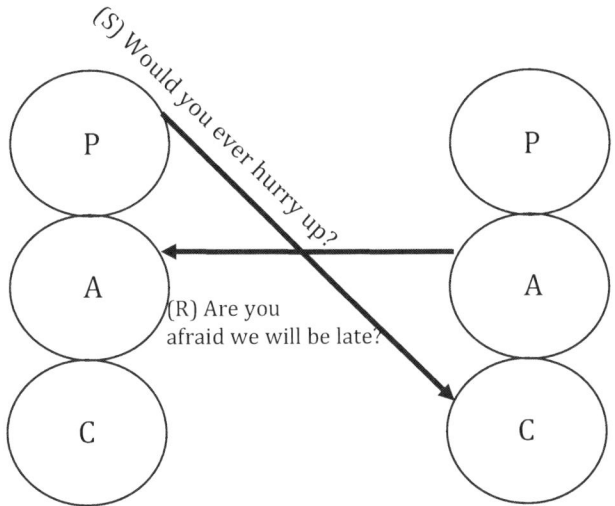

Fig. 18a Crossed Transactions

This gives us the second rule of communication: *Whenever the transaction is crossed, a breakdown in communication results and something different is likely to follow* (quoted in Woollams & Brown, 1978:68). When one person changes their ego state position, they invite the other person to move to a complementary transaction. So, in Fig. 18a the response of the Adult to the Controlling Parent, invites the Controlling Parent to move to Adult. In Fig. 18b, what appears as a complementary transaction (the arrows are parallel) is in fact a crossed transaction because the ego state addressed (Adult) is responded to by the Controlling or Critical Parent.

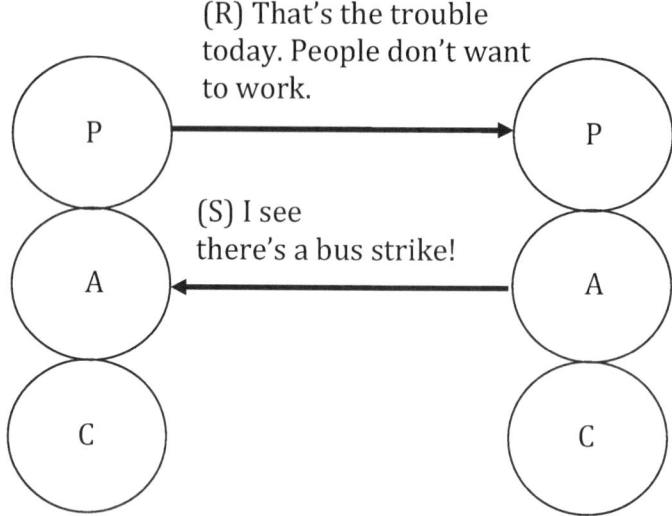

Fig. 18b Crossed Transactions

What could, therefore, have been an Adult to Adult conversation degenerates into a Parent to Parent critique of society, and invites the other Adult to join the Controlling parent into the Controlling or Critical Parent ego state.

We will see later on that the ability to move from ego state to ego state and to create crossed transactions, forms the basis for conflict resolution, and offers possibilities for mending broken relationships in a community setting. This is by no means an easy task, but with practice there is hope that impasses can be resolved.

Ulterior Transactions

Ulterior transactions contain a social message and a psychological unspoken message. By ulterior transactions we mean that the person says something verbally (unbroken line), but, beneath the words, there is another non-verbal message (dotted line), a psychological message, being transmitted. Two examples we have in Figs. 19 a & b.

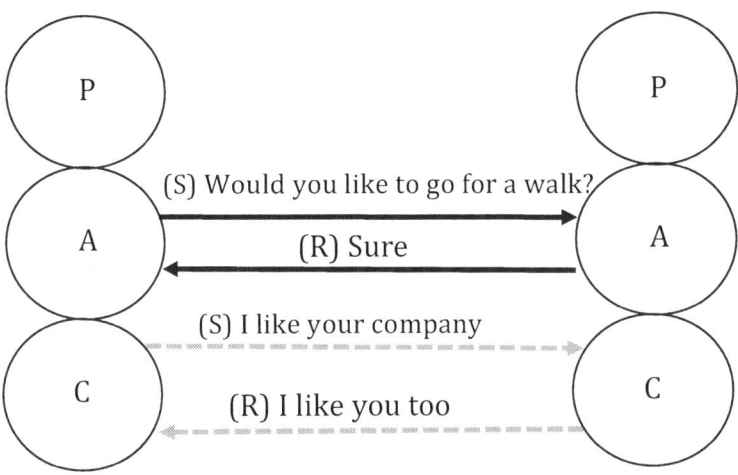

Fig. 19a Ulterior Transactions

In example 19a, we have a social and verbal message at an Adult level between two people, with one person inviting the other to go for a walk, and the other person replying in the affirmative. At the same time, and with the same people, there is a non-verbal and psychological message at the Child level where another message about the quality of the relationship between the two people is being expressed. So, in fact with an ulterior transaction, there are four ego states involved, and two sets of complementary transactions (the arrows are parallel)

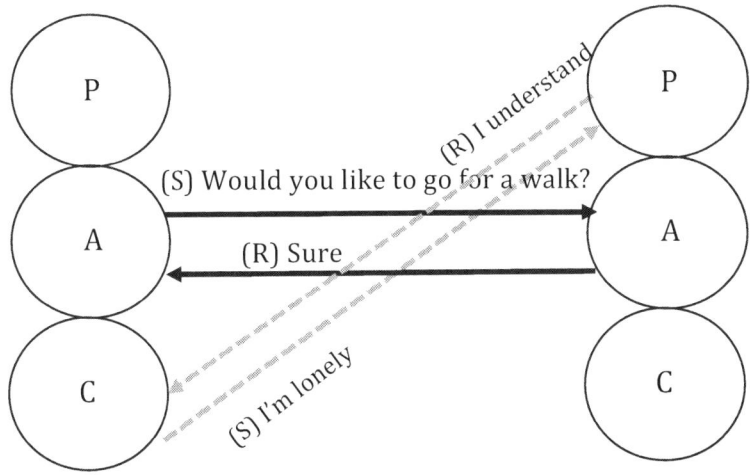

Fig. 19b Ulterior Transactions

occurring simultaneously, with one set on the social level and the other on the psychological level (Woollams & Brown, 1978: 70).

In Fig. 19b, we have the same words being used on a social level, with the same person requesting the company of the other person, and the other person accepting the invitation, just as we had in example 19a. However, at a psychological and non-verbal level, we have very different psychological messages being played out. Here in example 19b, the psychological message is being directed from the Child to the Parent, seeking to express a sense of isolation and a need for comfort. This message is not verbalised and could well be missed by the other person. At the social level, all we have are the words of invitation which the other person can accept or reject, but the psychological level sends a completely different message, which in this case, the other person picks up, and responds to in a complementary Parent to Child psychological transaction.

The third rule of communication refers to the ulterior transactions and goes like this: *The behavioural outcome of an ulterior transaction is determined at the psychological and not at the social level* (Berne, 1966:227).

Most difficulties of communication in a community involve ulterior transactions, where the real agenda is at the psychological level, and where the psychological level is being ignored. This is the basis of psychological games that stunt the growth in community. Eric Berne in his book *Games People Play*, focussed especially on the complementary ulterior transactions, which he defined as games (Berne, 1964: 44).

As long as the psychological level is being ignored, there is little chance that the conflict will be resolved. The challenge in conflict resolution is to bring out the psychological messages and make the implicit explicit. Then, the real issues can be dealt with from an Adult-to-Adult position.

Communication is in Our Hands

You will remember that in Chapter 6 we discussed various levels of diagnosis to determine which ego states were in actions at any particular time. Social diagnosis involves becoming aware within ourselves which ego state we are experiencing, and thereby becoming aware of the ego state being employed by the other person. If we feel we are in our Rebellious Child, we can be very sure that the other person is in their Controlling Parent. Or, if we feel like we are in our Controlling Parent, we may be experiencing the other person either in their Rebellious or Compliant Child.

Once we realise what is going on in any communication with another person, we have the power to influence the outcome of the process. Steve Karpman, in his article *Options,* highlighted the fact that we have the choice to respond to another person in whatever way we choose to (Karpman, 1971: 79ff). The trigger for changing our transactional stance is the level of discomfort that we are undergoing at the time.

Often what happens in community conflict is that the level of discomfort is ignored because the psychological level is being discounted, and the people involved seek to solve the problem on the social level. In this case, what happens is that a series of complementary transactions continues indefinitely, and the conflict persists unabated.

Karpman proposes that the only way to resolve the discomfort is for one of the people to change position. So, if one person is in the Child ego state, and feeling oppressed by the Controlling Parent of the other person, the option open is for the first person to move either to Adult or to Free Child, or even to Nurturing Parent; the choices are multiple. What needs to happen is for the complementary transaction to be crossed, and the person to move from one ego state to an alternative one. When the change happens, Karpman's thesis is, the topic of conversation will change and the previous topic will be forgotten.

We can imagine the following conversation happening between Br Michael and Br Kevin:

Michael: We need to make three copies of the document. (Scared Free Child ego state but perceived by Br Kevin as a Controlling Parent)

Kevin: No, one copy will be fine. (Rebellious Child)

Michael: What happens if we lose the one copy? (Controlling Parent)

Kevin: Why would we lose it? We're not incompetent. (Rebellious Child becoming Critical/Controlling Parent)

Michael: Didn't you lose that other document last week? (Critical Parent)

Kevin: Are you still going on about that? For God sake, let it go. One copy will be enough. (Rebellious Child)

Michael: There you go again, getting angry for no reason. (Critical Parent)

Kevin: I'm not angry. You're the one getting obsessive about losing documents. (Rebellious Child/Critical Parent)

Thus the conversation could continue indefinitely where each party is trapped into a cycle of confrontation, and with no real awareness of what is going on. What started as a moment of anxiety from the Free Child of Michael becomes a battle between the Critical/Controlling Parent confronting a Rebellious Child. It seems that neither party was aware of the psychological messages that were going on below the social and verbal level. Both seemed stuck in an I'm OK – You're Not OK positions.

The conversation could have gone in different fashion with a much healthier outcome:

Michael: We need to make three copies of the document. (Free Child ego state)

Kevin: Three copies? What's your thinking here? (Adult)

Michael: I'm feeling anxious that we may lose the one copy (Adult awareness of being anxious)

Kevin: I can understand your anxiety. Do you remember I lost a document last week? (Adult)

Michael: Yes, I suppose that thought probably made me over-anxious (Adult)

Kevin: So, maybe it is a good idea to make three copies. (Adult)

Michael: Great. I can do that. (Adult/Free Child)

Kevin: Thanks; I appreciate you offering to help out. You are so helpful.

(Nurturing Parent/Adult).

In this second conversation, Michael was experiencing an authentic feeling of fear similar to his position in the first conversation. However, this time Kevin recognises in the second conversation the psychological level of fear beneath what was perceived as a Controlling Parent in the first conversation. Kevin remains in Adult, inviting Michael to access his Adult awareness of his Free Child natural fear. This moves Michael into his Adult, and eventually there is a moment of resolution where the Free Child of Michael interacts with the Adult/Nurturing Parent of Kevin in an I'm OK- You're OK position.

The point Karpman makes is that we have a choice, an option to employ any series of transactions, and we can invite the other to change by changing first what ego state *we* want to use (Karpman, 1971). Often, people resent the idea that *they* have to change ego states instead of expecting the other person to move first. Such a position is the stance of the Rebellious Child, and will only compound the impasse. What Karpman is inviting us to do, is to move into our Adult and recognise that *we* can influence the outcome of any dialogue by being flexible to move into whichever ego state is appropriate at the time. Sometimes, it will be useful to be in the Controlling Parent ego state, while at other times, that is the most inappropriate ego state to employ. It depends on the situation, and on the awareness that we have as to what is going on in the interaction between people. Awareness is vital for us to become conscious of the psychological level that lies behind the mere words that are spoken.

Conclusion

It is worth pointing out that the transactions between people especially in moments of conflict often defy analysis. What usually happens in any form of confrontation between people is that both dissociate, and enter into a series of enactments or complementary transactions that simply escalate (Stern, 2010:83ff). Once any form of conflict occurs, and the various levels of enactments ensue, it becomes far more difficult to extricate both parties from the impasse. Therefore, there is need for much practice in order for people to manage the times when the interactions between people become argumentative, aggressive, and potentially violent.

Exercises

1. In your group or community, share a time when you were in conflict with someone. Remember the sort of dialogue that went on and the feelings you had during the conflict. Now, using the language of TA, identify the various ego states that were in action during the conflict. Get in touch with the psychological level of both you and the person with whom you were in conflict. Next, imagine how the conversation could have gone were you to have responded differently. The group might have suggestions that they want to contribute to your analysis. Each member of the community is invited to share a personal incident.

2. Look back at your egogram (Chapter 4) and discuss with the community the various moments when you felt more in Controlling Parent, Adult or Free Child, linking your ego state with various events when you managed, or failed to manage moments of conflict in community.

Chapter Eleven

Peace Not War

"Peace is not merely a distant goal we seek,
but a means by which we arrive at that goal."
Martin Luther King Jr

Jean-Paul Sartre in his play *Huis Clos* (No Exit) has Garcin, one of the characters in the play, say 'L'enfer, c'est les autres,' (Hell is other people). Sometimes, religious communities can be like the hell that Sartre describes in *Huis Clos*. There may not be fire and brimstone in the convent or monastery; instead, there are community members who make life a hell on earth for the rest of the group. Or if there is not hell in the community, there may be a type of limbo, where people co-exist in an atmosphere of spiritualised tolerance that masks underlying discord, and avoids open conflict. Instead of war, there is discontent, feelings of resentment and buried hurts. Communities can experience this situation to a greater or lesser extent.

Many religious communities struggle with the management of conflict, and often resort to promoting 'peace and any price', settling into a type of life that is not a battle but certainly not a peaceful place to live. Douglas William Jerrold, an English nineteenth century dramatist commented: 'Not peace at any price! Chains are worse than bayonets.' (Quoted in Wood, 1899/2012). But for many, the chains seem the only option, for the idea of bayonets is terrifying.

In the previous chapter, we saw how various transactions can lead to differing levels of conflict, which may be overt and recurring (complementary transactions), or covert and pervasive (ulterior transactions). We also learned that people have options in crossing transactions and changing the dynamic of the interchanges. It is this process that we want to discuss in this chapter.

Doctors Ellyn Bader and Peter Pearson, Directors of *The Couples Institute,* have proposed a method for conflict resolution, which I have adapted somewhat in various workshops I have run. Dr Bader is a Transactional Analyst as well as someone who has specialised with her husband in the area of couple therapy. What I intend to do in this chapter is to take the approach they designed for conflict resolution, and apply the concepts of TA to the roles of the *Inquirer* and the *Initiator*, which they suggest are the two roles necessary for managing conflict. The Inquirer is the one role that is a *sine qua non* for conflict resolution; the Initiator's role can only fully come into play when the role of the Inquirer has first been mastered (http://www.couplesinstitute.com).

The Inquirer

We have seen in the previous chapter how conflict ensues when attention is not given to the psychological level in any communication. By focusing simply on the social and verbal messages, both people miss the heart of the communication, and what results is a situation where the dialogue continues between two 'deaf' people. Peter Drucker, the management guru, said, 'The most important thing in communication is hearing what isn't said' (BrainyQuote.com). The role of inquirer is to be the effective listener in the transactions between two or more people, and especially to pay attention to the psychological level behind the social level.

In order to become that effective listener, the Inquirer has to accomplish four tasks, which I have slightly modified from the Bader and Pearson model by giving the process the title: 'The 2Cs and the 2Es", naming each task with easy-to-remember names: The 2Cs are: Be Calm and Be Curious. The 2Es are: Be Empathic and Be an Echo. We will take each in turn.

Be Calm

When we are faced with the power of a Critical or Controlling Parent, we are automatically pulled towards either the Compliant Child or the Rebellious Child. In both cases, the sympathetic nervous system is activated and we become agitated, tense and somewhat out of control. The functional model of ego states kicks in where the internal Child begins to feel anxious, and physiologically we are inclined to move towards flight, fight or freeze as a response. Many messages from the internal Controlling or Critical Parent speak to the internal Child. Messages like, "Keep quiet! It's not safe to say anything." or "Look at you, you little wimp! Can you not stand up for yourself?' cause the Child ego state to experience a growing tension that builds up, and leads to explosion or silent implosion. Dissociation and enactments are in full flight (Stern: 2010).

Because of such tension, the ability to think clearly is compromised, and we only react to the message from the other person in a reactive and uncontrolled manner. The result is a series of complementary transactions that potentially escalate. Either we feel Not OK with the other person OK – in the victim role – and we 'flee'; or *we* feel OK, and begin to persecute the other person whom we consider not OK, and so we fight.

Either reaction prevents the possibility of carefully listening, and potentially makes the situation worse. The challenge therefore is to remain calm. This means that we need to seek first to understand the other person before even trying to respond with our own ideas (Covey, 1989). We need to avoid defending ourselves, arguing, or taking things personally. In a word, we need to STOP, be SILENT, SENSE what is happening inside us, and SEE the big picture, especially from the other's point of view. These 4Ss are helpful reminders that may keep us grounded when the storms are gathering!

Be Curious

Curiosity can come either from the Free Child or the integrated Adult. When we are curious, we are focussed on the world beyond us. We move from my world to your world, from my point of view to your viewpoint. Being curious involves asking questions that show we are keen to understand the other's experience. It is important not to assume that we immediately understand what the other person is saying, but seek clarification all along the way (Erskine, 1996:316ff).

The Adult in us has the ability to gather the psychic forces, bound, unbound and free (see Chapter 6), and to engage the skills of the Adult to deal with the current situation. The Adult in us is able to remind ourselves that the problem is not ours, and that we do not need to be upset. The Free Child in us can become more curious and 'playful' as we begin to enjoy the challenge of listening carefully to the other person. Even the Nurturing Parent at an intrapsychic or inner mind level can soothe any stress and anxiety that may be lurking in our Child ego state, and allow us to ask open questions.

The asking of questions is a real art, and requires considerable practice. Often, for instance, the 'Why?' question needs to be considered carefully as it can give the impression of an aggressive confrontation (Strachan, 2007: 24). The 'Why?' question is especially dangerous when feelings are running high, as it appears that people are being accused or blamed. So, instead of asking, 'Why did you do that?' and alternative could be, "What was your thinking when you decided to take that plan of action?' Somehow, this alternative question does not have the same edge as the 'Why?'

When we are curious, we invite the person to be open and without defences, and in touch with their real needs. The person then begins to grow in self-esteem, and increases their ability to relate on an Adult-Adult basis (Erskine, 1996:320).

Be Empathic

The first E of this Inquirer process is: *Be Empathic.* Empathic transactions involve the sending of an emphatic message to another person, with the other experiencing the message as empathic or otherwise (Clark, 1991:312ff). The message is empathic when the other person experiences being understood and accepted.

The process has two parts whereon, we express understanding of the other person's viewpoint, while, at the same time, the other person feels that he or she has been understood. Our capacity to mentalize involves the ability to perceive and respond to the people's emotional state, mirroring them, while becoming aware of our own emotional states, which may be very different from the other person's (Allen & Fonagy, 2006:12). The phrase 'stand in the shoes of your brother or sister for a mile' is a challenging reminder of the need to see things from the other's point of view. When people feel that they have been heard, some of their defences drop, and they become more open to be self-reflective instead of being oppositional or reactive.

This level of attunement moves beyond empathy where the person enters into a process of communion and unity of interpersonal contact (Erskine, 1996: 316ff). It involves being aware both of the boundary between the other person and the self, and of the affect that one person has on the other person. This attunement is both affective and cognitive, involving feelings and thinking as we recognise the relational needs of the other person (*Ibid:*320). Such attunement validates the other person's thinking, feelings and behaviours in a way that the person recognises a presence that is supportive of their current state of mind. It is as if the person feels totally understood and accepted for who they are, and how they are in the moment. The result of such attunement is that the person feels free to lower their defences, and reveal even more of their reality.

We mentioned in Chapter 1 the discovery of mirror neurons where the mother experiences in herself what her child is feeling. This discovery of the intersubjective connection between people lays the foundation for empathy and attunement. When we are in attunement with others, we experience the other *as if* we were executing the same action, feeling the same emotions, making the same vocalisations, or being touched as they are touched (Stern, 2004:79). And in this intersubjective moment, we experience empathy, sympathy and identification with the other person. Such empathic moments are moments of real meeting (*Ibid:*151).

Be an Echo

The second E of the Inquirer process is: *Be an Echo.* This technique requires the listener simply to 'play back' what they have heard from the other person. In a way, what we feedback is a replay of what the person said, which lets the other person know that they have been heard accurately, both at a social level and especially at a psychological level. Berne uses the word, *specification,* to describe this same process where the listener is non-directive, and simply repeats what they have understood (Berne, 1966:234). Sometimes the re-echoing may involve some level of *advanced* empathy where we name the emotion that we are picking up (even though the person has not named their emotion), and check with the person if our interpretation is correct (Egan, 1994). So, having listened to someone describing the struggles they are having in community, we might offer an interpretation, "So, you were feeling annoyed and frustrated..." which goes beyond what the person said, and interprets the feelings behind the events. The person can then agree with our interpretation of the emotion, or state more accurately what they felt in the first place.

The main challenge at this stage is to be attuned to the person, and to enter into the world of the other person without our own agenda running. This is a very Adult ego state position, where we concentrate on the here-and-now as we listen to what is being communicated (Erskine, 1996: 321). Often the person may present their experiences in some coded form, and the challenge often is to decode what is being said and get to the heart of what lies behind the social message (Berne, 1966:243).

Practice! Practice! Practice!

Because of the tradition in religious life to be charitable and tolerant, the managing of conflict is something that is almost foreign to us. Arnold Mindell in his book *Sitting in the Fire*, says:

> Creating freedom, community and viable relationships has its price. It costs time and courage to learn how to sit in the fire of diversity (Mindell, 1995:17).

He goes on to say that the world depends on how we deal with the terrorism in ourselves and others (*Ibid*:99). As community members, we have the opportunity to model coping with violent or less violent tensions, and when we can embrace the 'terrorist' within and without, we will transform our communities into places of energy and life. But this approach takes a lot of practice. The exercise at the end of this chapter could begin the process of learning the skill of 'Sitting in the Fire'!

We see in Fig. 20 over, that the process of conflict resolution invites us to move from being calm to being curious, to the empathic and echo stage. This is not a linear process. Depending on the circumstances, we may move from one skill to the other in no particular order. However, the most important element in the role of the Inquirer is the Be Calm, for without it, our access to the other three elements is significantly compromised. Once we can stay in Adult, and have the option to move to each of the ego states, then we can be curious, empathic and be an echo in the face of conflict and misunderstanding.

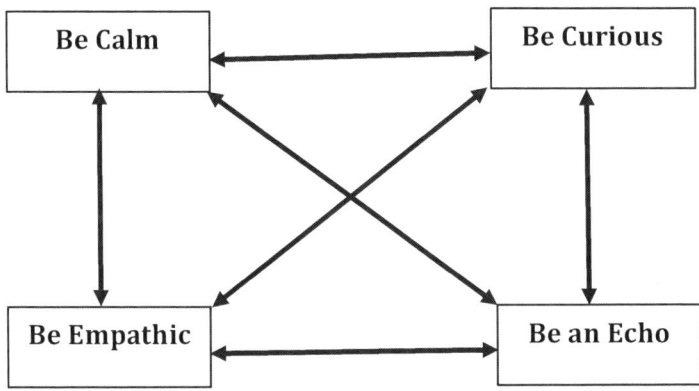

Fig. 20   The Cycle of Inquiry

In any moment of conflict, we need to practise moving through each of the four elements of the inquiry cycle so that our responses become elegant interactions that show empathy and respect for the other person.   Practice will make perfect...eventually!

The Initiator

The role of the Initiator adopts the adult ego state in the here-and-now, expressing clear messages with little or no ulterior transactions. The main transaction is an Adult-to-Adult interchange where the person engages in four moments of interaction from an I'm OK - You're OK position. The four moments can be summarised by 2 Fs and 2Bs:

1. Focus on one issue only
2. Feelings and thought together
3. Blame no one
4. Be open

Briefly, we will comment on each of these moments.

Focus on One Issue

Focusing on one issue avoids generalised ramblings, and motivates the Initiator to clearly state what he or she wants. In choosing the one issue, the Initiator gives the other person the opportunity to be clear and focused as well. One of the difficulties in moments of confrontation is when the Initiator 'drags' in other matters to back up their argument on the one issue they want to deal with. This only muddies the water, and potentially defeats our purpose.

For example, the Initiator may want to confront a practice in community where he or she is finding that the banter that goes on at the table is often hurtful both personally, and to other members of the group. The Initiator knows that it is one individual who is mainly involved in beginning the banter, and wants to bring this to their attention. The fact that the same person seems to be spending too much of the community's budget is not relevant at this time!

The focus needs especially to clarify what exactly the Initiator wants from the meeting. In this case, he or she wants the other person to stop using banter in a hurtful way. Often, in the stress of such a meeting, the Initiator may renege on what they want, and end up not getting the desired result. Someone said that we should ask for 100% of what we want 100% of the time (Joines, 2003). There is no guarantee that we will get the 100%, but unless we ask we definitely will be disappointed. So, the focus needs to have the 100% in the forefront, recognising, at the same time, that the other person may not be willing to give it.

In undertaking this dialogue, the Initiator should check that the person in question is ready to hear the matter to be discussed. It is important to choose a time that suits the other person in order for the interaction to have the greatest hope of resolution. Because also the interaction is very delicate, and could lead to unhelpful confrontation, it is also important to choose a setting that is appropriate. It is not advisable therefore to bring up the issue in the more public community room where others could enter while the meeting is taking place.

Being in Adult involves having prepared for the meeting well, and having sufficiently mastered the 2Fs and the 2Bs to feel confident that the Initiator can deal with the possible negative reactions of the other person.

Being in Adult also invites the other person to move into Adult during the interaction. Were the Initiator to be in Controlling Parent, they would only be inviting the other person into the Adapted Child ego state. A successful confrontation needs to be done in the context of an 'I'm OK-You're OK' position, where the behaviour is being confronted and not the person. The behaviour is not acceptable, while the person needs to realise that *they* are OK.

Feelings and Thoughts Together

At the outset, the Initiator may feel nervous in approaching the other person to discuss the issue of banter. It is important, therefore, that they acknowledge this level of agitation, and even share it with the other person. Not only should the feeling be expressed, but also the reason for the feeling needs to be clearly stated. Sometimes people share their feelings without giving the context. The result is that the other person begins to fill in the gaps and may often fill them in wrongly. So, the Initiator may be feeling nervous because they don't like confrontation, or because they think that bringing the issue may make matters worse. Whatever the reason, the challenge is to be honest and open. Honesty is vital in this situation.

In sharing feelings, it is also valuable to go beyond sharing only one feeling. Often there are a number of feelings lurking below the surface feeling, and it can be important to risk being vulnerable and thus getting greater clarity about the issue. In many ways, such vulnerability is opening access to the Free Child energy, and again inviting the same access for the other person. So, the Initiator could share his or her nervousness for bringing up the issue, and below the nervousness and fear might be a sadness that members of the community are suffering. Or, the real feeling may be of anger that one person is persecuting others or indeed herself or himself. One feeling might lead to uncovering others, and then the feelings might change. Feelings, someone said, are like a river that flows and meanders, accelerating or slowing down, depending on the bends of the river or the rocks and gullies it encounters! (Johnston: 2003).

In sharing feelings, it is also important to remember that feelings are an expression of who I am; they are part of my identity, my own uniqueness. Consequently, 'I messages' are very effective in sharing our feelings. The Free Child is always in touch with authentic feelings, and authentic feelings are what we need to share especially in moments of conflict.

Blame No One

Blaming comes from the paranoid life-position (see Chapter 2) of I'm OK-You're Not OK, which seeks to *get rid* of people whom we find difficult. When we blame others, according to Bader & Pearson, we begin to prevent ourselves from knowing ourselves. Projection is where we try to avoid the problem within ourselves, and see instead the same problem in other people (see Chapter 16). So, if we find ourselves blaming others, we need to be alerted to the fact that we could be projecting.

It is also important to remember that when we decide to confront someone's behaviour, we are taking a risk to speak our truth, and are taking full responsibility for our action. When we blame, on the other hand, we shift that responsibility and disempower both ourselves and the other person.

Blaming involves sending 'you messages' from the Critical Parent, and seeks to change the other person. Instead of focusing on the behaviour we dislike, we target the person, and invite them either into a sort of compliance or a rebellious denial or justification. When we blame, we may think we are in Adult, but in fact are acting out of a Parent contamination, expressing prejudice and judgements that cloud the core issue in question.

Be Open

The experience of having to confront the behaviour of someone in community is both a crisis and an opportunity. The crisis involves the possibility that the group will disband or that things will get worse. The opportunity refers to the rich learning that comes from an encounter that is challenging and risky; the risk involves being open and honest about how we feel and what we think is going on. As we face the challenge of confronting someone about his or her behaviour, we can learn an immense amount about ourselves. The invitation is to be open to what these learnings are. This is the position of the Adult ego state that honours honesty and openness.

The process of confrontation is not primarily as we said earlier about changing the behaviour of the other, but about sharing the impact that their behaviour has on the Initiator and on other members of the community. In the final analysis, we cannot *force* the other to change. Controlling Parents create Rebellious Children. All we can do is openly and honestly to make it clear what we want, and request that the other person accedes to this request. When we are in Adult, we simply risk speaking openly as we honour our truth, and invite the other person to receive it with respect.

Conclusion

The dual movement of Inquirer and Initiator can be likened to a dance where one partner leads and the other follows. Depending on the situation, we may be invited to be either the Inquirer or the Initiator, and if we are the Initiator, we need to recognise that we will also need to be the Inquirer. For example, in the incident described above where it is a matter of confronting the problematic behaviour of hurtful banter, the most appropriate role is the Initiator. This focuses on the problem, and seeks to resolve the issue without blaming, while being open to sharing feelings and thoughts about the situation. In addition, the Initiator will need also to become the Inquirer when the person being confronted decides to respond. At that moment, the dance requires the reversal of roles, with the Initiator moving into the Inquirer role. In TA language, we are talking about Karpman's Options of moving from one ego state to the other according the needs of the situation (Chapter 10).

Learning to dance takes practice, and in the case of dealing with conflict, practice is vital so that the interchanges are fluid and elegant. Hence the value of the exercises that follow.

Exercises

1. Share with the group an incident of confrontation that you experienced in the past. Analyse it using the language of the Initiator and Inquirer.

2. Take a situation (preferably a real one) where you have to initiate a confrontation and use the skills of the Initiator, and using the 2Fs and the 2 Bs. Do this with one person from the community, and allow the rest of the community to critique the proceedings.

3. Divide the community into groups of three. One person brings a problem or difficulty and the other person becomes the Inquirer, using the 2Cs and the 2Es. The third person observes, and at the end of the session, all three people give feedback as to how they experienced the interactions, beginning with the inquirer, then the initiator, and finally the observer.

Note: The more practice you do with these skills the better you will be able to dance!

Chapter Twelve

Strokes

"They didn't recognize me," I repeat.
He stops in turn, my hand still on his arm.
"It is because they have never seen you," he says.
Muriel Barbery

In the introduction to *Are We Together?* there was a quotation from the Constitutions of the Christian Brothers stating that 'Community is the principal source of companionship'. In the Presentation Sisters document *Our Way of Life* (2012), the Sisters express a similar desire 'to be, like Mary and Nano, heart-centred women, developing caring and meaningful relationships especially in community.' Indeed, most religious Congregations express the commitment to form Christian communities that will be a sign to society that community is possible.

Sometimes, however, the reality is somewhat distant from the aspirations expressed in the Rules of a Congregation. At times, communities of Sisters and Brothers can be lonely places, where men and women survive without the love and support of their fellow members. Part of the reason for the lack of love and warmth in community is probably due to the absence of the human touch in the midst of the spiritual search.

In this chapter, we explore the vital importance of human contact as an essential dimension of communication. Without human contact, people simply curl up and die.

In her autobiography *Life and Death in Shanghai*, Nien Cheng describes how, when she was in prison in solitary confinement, she used to goad her prison warders until they eventually entered her cell to punish her physically (Cheng, 1995). She reflected on this strategy, saying that it was better to be hit by the guards than to remain isolated from day to day. We all need human contact.

Berne recognised the need of human touch, or what he called 'stroking', in order for the human person to survive (Berne, 1964:13). He cited the work of Spitz that 'demonstrates that sensory deprivation in the infant may result not only in psychic changes, but also in organic deterioration' (Berne, 1961: 83). This need of the infant for touch he called *stimulus-hunger,* which is very evident when babies are born. Infants need to be in physical contact with the mother in order to grow and develop. Without contact with the mothers, the baby suffers serious physiological and psychological damage. Schore cites the work of Tronick who studied the effect on the newly born when the mother fails to respond to her child, and instead shows no facial expression; the child becomes dissociated, and could suffer major psychological difficulties were the mother to continue such behaviour (Schore, 2012:270).

As children grow and develop, they can no longer remain in physical contact with the mother, and yet they still need the connection with the caregiver. As they begin to crawl and later walk, they need to know that the mother is not far away and is there to support the child. This need for this more distant connection, Berne called, *'recognition hunger'*, and a stroke is the mechanism that satisfies this hunger. For Berne, therefore, a 'stroke' can 'denote any act implying recognition of another's presence'. He defines a stroke as 'the fundamental unit of social action' where two people interact by some form of recognition. (Berne, 1964:15). I prefer to call a stroke 'a unit of recognition' or what Woollams and Brown call, 'a unit of attention' (Woollams & Brown, 1978:45). Whatever the definition, the experience of stroking and being stroked offers a valuable way of promoting good healthy growth in community.

Types of Strokes

Stewart and Joines (2012: 78) neatly classify the different types of strokes as:

- *Verbal or non-verbal*
- *Positive or negative*
- *Conditional or unconditional*

With regard to the verbal and non-verbal strokes, the latter can include such actions as a wave, a nod of the head, or a hug, or simply a pat on the shoulder. The verbal strokes when continued for any length of time become transactions, which are in fact a *series of verbal strokes.*

The positive and negative strokes refer to positive or negative comments made to another person. Often when people do not receive positive strokes, they will settle for negative ones. Anyone who has taught in a school can appreciate how a pupil who does not get enough attention for being well-behaved, will begin to cause trouble simply to get a stroke, albeit a negative one. So, it seems, *that any kind of stroke is better than no stroke.* Nien Cheng's story mentioned earlier on confirms this hypothesis.

Conditional and unconditional strokes differ in that the former refers to a stroke given to someone for *what* they do, whereas the latter is given to someone for *who* they are. So, I can stroke a person by complimenting them on a job well done (conditional stroke) or simply express my appreciation for them as a person (unconditional stroke). Telling someone I like him or her for who they are is a good example of the unconditional positive stroke.

Different Strokes for Different Folks

Whereas we all want and need strokes, it is very important to understand that each person has different needs, and therefore appreciates being stroked in particular ways. Gary Chapman in his book *The 5 Love Languages. The Secret to Love that Lasts,* shows how people differ in the types of strokes they appreciate (Chapman, 2009). For some people, words of affirmation make all the difference, while others need quality time, where they receive the stroke of a person's presence. Yet others love to receive gifts that stroke their importance and value. Others again experience being stroked by the 'little acts of kindness' or service from their partner, while others again find that physical touch is the most significant form of stroking. Each of us has our own preference for the types of strokes we need, and it requires sensitivity to stroke people in the way that answers their individual needs (Samuels, 1971: 23-24).

Stroke Filter and Discounting

When someone, therefore, gets a stroke that does not respond to their particular need, they simply reject the stroke.

Imagine a husband bringing flowers home to his wife to express his love for her, when what she wants is for him to sit down with her, and listen to her hopes and desires, her joys and sorrows. He, on the other hand, feels hurt that she does not appreciate the thoughtful gift he has brought home. In TA language what is happening here is that she is employing a *stroke filter* that only allows those strokes in that respond to her particular need at the time.

Not everyone in a religious community wants the same sort of strokes. Some like a hug to show support and affection. Others will run a mile away from any physical contact, but appreciate it when a Sister offers to help another Sister prepare for an exam.

When we receive a stoke that does not match our need, another way of describing what we do with the unwanted stroke, is to say that we *discount* or ignore the stroke. Discounting and filtering are the ways we refuse the strokes we don't need or want.

Rules for Stroking

The following rules for stroking are based on what Claude Steiner called the *stroke economy* (Steiner, 1974: 114ff). Steiner lists these rules in the negative, whereas I prefer always to put them positively. The rules for stroking are:

1. Give strokes when you have them to give
2. Ask for strokes when you need them
3. Accept strokes if you want them
4. Reject strokes when you don't want them
5. Give yourself strokes

Give strokes when you have them to give

Thomas Fuller, a seventeenth century English churchman said, 'It is more difficult to praise rightly than to blame' (Brainy Quote.com). Indeed, what truth lies in this sentence! As I began writing this section of the chapter, I looked up the Internet to see if there was a suitable quotation that would encapsulate what this section is trying to say. Most of the quotations I found seemed to undervalue the importance of stroking people for who they are or for what they achieve. It seems that many view the desire for praise as a weakness instead of a normal human need.

There is no doubt that people grow in self-esteem as they receive positive strokes. The experience of being praised creates an atmosphere in a community where the members feel appreciated and supported.

In the community setting, there are many occasions when we have the opportunity to stroke people for their behaviour or indeed for their basic goodness. What prevents us then from giving strokes? It seems the only obstacle to being generous with our strokes is a lurking fear that such positive action could make people proud! There was a time when humility was considered a virtue, and humility implied that people should not be praised. The result of this mistaken idea is that members of communities can become starved of positive strokes, and begin to shrivel up and die psychologically.

Ask for strokes when you need them

Many people believe that if you have to ask for strokes, they are not worth getting. In some cultures, people are very reluctant to seek positive stokes and prefer to wait – sometimes in vain – until the strokes are given freely. However, if we believe in the value of strokes, the challenge may be to ask directly for positive feedback or indeed critical feedback (negative strokes) when we have completed a task. Taking the risk to ask for strokes demands an openness to both positive and negative strokes, and can be a clear sign of someone who is in an I'm OK-You're OK position.

In communities, however, there can be members who have been starved of strokes and therefore spend much of their time looking for them. Because their supply of strokes is low, they will seek to obtain strokes by any means (Capers & Holland, 1971:40). Coming from an I'm not OK-You're OK, they are highly sensitive to being ignored, and so continually draw attention to themselves in the hope of getting strokes. The challenge for the other community members is to give them a mixture of appropriate positive and negative strokes, and avoid offering what Berne called 'marshmallow' or 'plastic' strokes, which he described as 'an overly sweet or affected response of encouragement or approval' (Berne, 1976:348). The trouble with the 'marshmallow' strokes is that they do not achieve what strokes are meant to achieve – boosting the self-esteem and well being of others. Consequently, giving these artificial types of strokes is better avoided.

Accept strokes if you want them

Jess Lair, the founder of the self-help movement said, "Praise is like sunlight to the human spirit: we cannot flower and grow without it"(www.Livinglifefully.com). And yet many people find it difficult to accept a positive stroke, or allow it to penetrate their stroke filter. When some people receive praise, they can be inclined either to minimise its importance with an embarrassed mutter of acknowledgement, or they will minimise the content of the positive stroke. So, in response to the stroke by a fellow community member on the successful speech she made: 'That was a great job you did, Sheila,' her response was, 'It was nothing. I just put a few things together and it worked out well.' Sister Sheila finds it very difficult to accept the positive remarks of her community members, and yet deep down she appreciates and grows with the positive strokes. It seems, at times, there is a taboo against enjoying the strokes we get for fear that if we enjoy them too much we will be continually disappointed when they don't arrive with sufficient frequency. Another way of refusing strokes is to make them into 'counterfeit strokes'.

Counterfeit strokes are created when people distort the message of the stroke they are receiving in order to confirm their life position (Bruce & Erskine, 1974: 18-19). They may receive a positive stroke, and proceed to blemish it, changing it into a negative one. This reinforces their not-OK position where they hear an internal Critical Parent say, 'You don't deserve good strokes.' Bruce and Erskine give the example of the person getting the stroke for a speech they made, 'You did a good job', and responding by, "I forgot the main point.'

Within the rules for stroking, the most appropriate response to a positive stroke is 'Thanks!'

Reject strokes if you don't want them

Some negative strokes can be very toxic, coming from an I'm OK- You're Not OK life-position, given by someone who wants to *get rid* of the other person. When a stroke involves a discount of the person, then there is some sort of distortion of reality, and a belittling of the person (Stewart & Joines, 2012:90). The difference between a negative stroke and a discount is where a person either says, 'You made a mistake there' (negative conditional stroke), or 'I see you can't spell' (discount). With the negative conditional stroke, the person points out a real mistake, without making reference to the value of the person. In the discount, the person is devalued. When strokes become discounts, the spectre of bullying looms large.

It is very important for a person to reject any form of devaluing and bullying. Often, however, the person who is the target of the discounts may be coming from an I'm Not OK-You're OK position, and may feel they deserve the criticism. When this happens in a community setting, it will be important for the rest of the community to support the weaker member, and confront the bully. Unwelcome strokes should always be rejected.

Give yourself strokes

The chat host Oprah Winfrey once said, 'The more you praise and celebrate your life, the more there is in life to celebrate' (www.thinkexist.com). What she was highlighting was the value of self-stroking, of celebrating when we have achieved something worthwhile (positive conditional self-stroke), or when we simply look in the mirror in the morning and give ourselves a positive unconditional stroke. Giving ourselves positive strokes means we are coming from the life-position of I'm OK - You're OK. Sometimes, we may find ourselves in situations where there are not many opportunities for positive strokes from others. Imagine the person undertaking research for writing a book. They spend hours and days alone in the library, and then return home to write the next chapter of their book. They have moved out of home to give themselves the peace and quiet to finish the work. So, there is little chance that they will get many positive strokes. At those moments, it is very important that the person is able to give themselves positive strokes, so that they can continue with energy and enthusiasm. It is also important that the person has what Kupfer calls 'a credit bank' of strokes, where the person has stored up unexpected strokes in their stroke bank from the past, and that now can compensate for the temporary lack of strokes in the present (English, 1971:27-28).

A Stroking Community

A joyful community is a community that abounds with the strokes that members give to each other on a regular basis. When some member does something worthwhile, the other members celebrate with them praising their efforts in a sincere way. C.S. Lewis said "Praise is the mode of love which always has some element of joy in it" (Lewis, 1961:52). Where there are strokes that praise, there will certainly be joy that abounds.

Strokes of gratitude create a climate of warmth where people get recognition for the little acts of kindness they do, or for the thoughtful gesture they give to one another. Marcel Proust suggested, "Let us be grateful to the people who make us happy; they are the charming gardeners who make our souls blossom" (www.goodreads.com). Praise works! A community of gratitude and praise is a community that creates a spirit of gentleness and joy.

There are many other ways of stroking, including strokes that may be negative. The important aspect of stroking is that both positive and negative strokes show there is life in the body! It is the community that seems to avoid any form of stroking that is in real danger of dying out. Positive strokes are the ones that build up the community, while negative ones need to be handled in a way that minimises negative fallout. When people are positively stroked, they feel a level of potency to be themselves, feeling the protection of the group, and reassured with the permission by the community members to act freely in a stroke-plentiful environment (Crossman, 1966:153).

Conclusion

Most communities seem to be characterised by an economy of scarceness when it comes to giving and receiving strokes. A corollary of this is that the communities that seem to thrive are those who are liberal in the frequency and quality of strokes that are exchanged between members. It often seems strange that in religious communities where the gospel invitation is to love one another, there is a significant lack of real support and mutual encouragement. It is hoped that once religious begin to experience giving and receiving strokes, that they will grow in their appreciation of the power of affirmation.

Exercises

1. Share with the members of your community your answers to the following questions and check with them that your answers match the way they see you! [Based on the Stroking Profile (McKenna, 1974:20ff)]

Score each question with a number:
1. Never; 2. Seldom; 3. Often; 4. Frequently;
5. Very frequently; 6. Always.

a) How often do you give positive strokes to others?

b) How often do you give negative strokes to others?

c) How often do you accept positive strokes?

d) How often do you refuse negative strokes?

e) How often do you ask others for the positive strokes you want?

f) How often do you ask indirectly or directly for negative strokes?

g) How often do you refuse to give the positive strokes they expect from you?

h) How often do you refuse to give negative strokes?

2. Form groups of five people. Each person is given a piece of paper on which they write the names of the five people in the group (this includes their own name). Then against the other four names in the group, write a positive quality you see in them and give an example to justify your choice. Then in turns, each person reads out the positive quality of the other four people and hears in turn their own qualities from the other four. At the end you will have four qualities from the other members of

the group. An interesting addition to the exercise is to identify which positive quality surprised you, and then which one was not mentioned that you would have liked to receive.

3. Discuss how the members of the community could improve the way they stroke each other, and under which circumstances

Chapter Thirteen

Time Structuring

"I have measured out my life with coffee spoons."
T.S. Eliot

Some men's religious communities do not come together for prayer, very seldom hold community meetings, or take time to recreate together, or even sometimes to eat together. It seems that such communities have let go of many of the structures that, in the past, kept the community united. Now each member of the community 'does his own thing'. Without a definite structure, however, Berne maintained that a group could not survive in the long run. In fact, he called this need for a definite shape to our day, *'structure hunger',* and maintained that it was a 'psychological need' without which people cannot grow in a healthy way (Berne, 1963: 215).

How, then does it happen that a community ceases to become a community, and becomes instead a sort of bed and breakfast? Often, this occurs due to unresolved conflicts, smouldering resentments and unsubstantiated fantasies.

Somehow, it seems that the members of the community arrive at a stage when they find it easier to avoid any form of real contact with the other members, and prefer to manage on their own. And yet, talking to the individual members of these communities, words like 'loneliness', 'isolation' and 'hurts and resentments' often come to the surface. It appears that grudges or disappointments from the past have caused the community to practically dissolve in order to avoid further unpleasant feelings. Or simply, the community has let the structures go without any real reason other than the fact that people apparently prefer to do things on their own, avoiding any form of group activity. Such individualism seems to have developed especially in America where there seems to be a significant decline in social capital. Social capital refers generally to the collective value of all "social networks" [networks here refer to any grouping of people], and the inclinations that arise from these networks to do things for and with each other (Putman, 2001).

The problem with the strategy of doing away with community structures is that people no longer give or receive any strokes, positive or negative, and so metaphorically the members of the community 'shrivel up and die'. *Structure hunger* thus creates a psychological need for a certain level of predictability and routine, which requires some form of group activities (Berne, 1966: 230).

Time Structuring and Intimacy

Berne analysed the way people structure their time in a group, identifying certain behaviours that provide the necessary strokes for the wellbeing of the individual (Berne, 1966:230ff). When people get enough strokes, their structure hunger is satisfied. He explained that the most gratifying expression of social contact is intimacy, where people are able to reveal themselves openly and without any form of defence mechanisms thus gaining maximum strokes. Berne recognised, however, that people find it difficult to maintain any level of real intimacy for an extended period of time, and therefore people resort to other less intense activities that yield fewer strokes (Berne, 1964:18). In fact, all the ways of time structuring, he maintains, are substitutes for the real experience of intimacy (*Ibid:* 17).

Berne defines intimacy as 'a candid Child-to-Child relationship with no games and no mutual exploitation' (Berne, 1970:126). It involves, he says, a contract between two people set up from the Adult ego state, involving clear commitments with each other. Then as the mutual understanding becomes clearer, the Adult gradually retires, and if the Parent does not then interfere, the Child comes alive and more relaxed in the relationship (*Ibid:*126). The most intimate of transactions occur, therefore, on a Child-to-Child basis.

In community life, the members can organise their day in ways that facilitate or avoid levels of intimacy. Intimacy is a risky business, which can leave us exposed and hurt unless there is a high level of trust in each other. And intimacy is not a state that can be maintained forever. Each community member will, therefore, structure their time by withdrawal, rituals, pastiming, activities or games (Berne, 1966:229ff). The risk involved in each of these activities is in proportion to the amount of strokes a person receives. The higher the risk taken, the more the strokes are collected (Fig. 21).

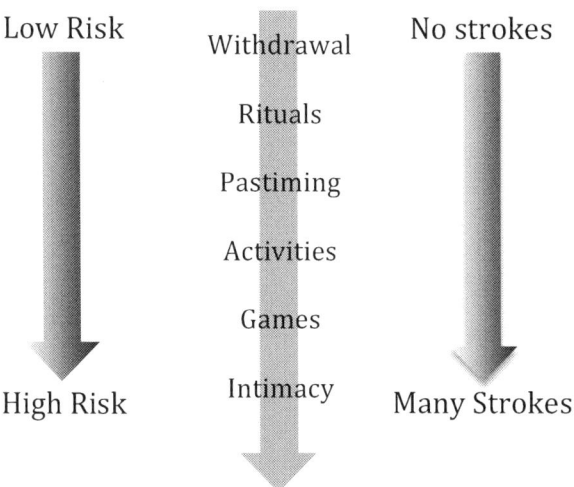

Fig. 21 Stroke and Risk Proportion

Withdrawal

Withdrawal can occur either mentally or physically (*Ibid:* 230). The former occurs when someone goes into a world of their own, and engages in an inner world of interests, fantasy, worries or other preoccupations. This form of withdrawal could be linked to the normal introverted nature of a person, who is more inclined to process things inside rather than share them with others. While an extrovert gets energy from others, and therefore potentially gets more strokes, the introvert is more inclined to give themselves strokes, which are equally valid.

Physical withdrawal can occur also when people stay in their rooms for most of the day. Others who are actively involved in ministry during the day, then keep to themselves at the end of the day, feeling they need to be alone. More and more frequently, religious have televisions in their rooms, and so the idea of a community room, where strokes used to abound, is a thing of the past for some communities.

Withdrawal is necessary for everyone from time to time;

religious need moments on their own to pray and meditate, both requiring time alone for peace and quiet. Withdrawal of itself is not something negative. What can be examined, however, is the level of withdrawal in a specific context. The more a person withdraws, the less chance the person has of getting strokes from other people. Many religious have admitted that they are lonely in their religious communities, and because they feel alone, they further withdraw thereby setting up a vicious cycle of stroke deprivation and non-involvement. Withdrawal also can be a way of escape from intimacy or indeed from any form of positive or negative strokes.

Rituals

Berne defines rituals as 'stereotyped, predictable exchanges such as greeting and farewell rituals' (*Ibid*:231). The strokes involved in rituals are not risky for either party, since the interaction is a well-rehearsed interpersonal exchange. Rituals are mainly programmed by the Parent of each member, and involve a well-established pattern of behaviour that generally remains unchanged. When one person says, 'Hello, how are you?' the ritualistic response goes something like, 'Fine, how are you?' These types of rituals can take place quite a few times a day, even with the same person. The objective for the ritual is simply to make some contact with the other person without any further intention of developing the conversation. So, the strokes that accrue are few and far between. Talking about the weather is a good example of ritual!

In community, the practice of rituals can also feature, keeping the level of contact at the bare minimum, and ensuring that no deeper connections are made. Were a community to remain at this level of interaction, it would hardly be a place for growth and development of the members.

Pastimes

While Berne calls this type of stroke 'pastiming', others call it *'pass-timing'*, which I believe well captures the essence of this type of stroking behaviour (Head, 2013). Pass-timing is literally passing the time during the waiting period before a meeting begins, or at the bus stop while awaiting transport (Berne, 1976:65). This is the 'chit-chat' that two people can do at a party when they want to 'warm up' and get connected. Many male (and some women) religious spend a lot of time discussing football or sport of all kinds. Others like to chat about what they saw on television the previous day. In many ways, pass-timing serves to assist in the selection process of our acquaintances who may eventually become friends (*Ibid:*66). We feel attracted to those who have the same interests that we have. Berne also maintains that pass-timing serves to establish a position or role for the person. For instance, if a religious headmaster talks a lot about the way he deals with parents who are complaining about how their children are being treated, then this religious is placing him or herself in the role of the strong, non-nonsense educator (the Controlling Parent). In this case, the religious is establishing with his companions, his preferred role, and hopes to get strokes for taking that position. With pass-timing, the strokes are increasing, but are still not that plentiful, nor do they particularly lead to any real form of intimacy.

Activities

By activity, Berne means the work a person is involved in with a group of fellow workers (Berne: 1966:231). The flow of strokes can vary greatly in this instance, and all the strokes are related to the work at hand. So, engaging in activities might involve collaborating in a joint-project, with the necessary Adult-to-Adult interactions required to complete the task (Berne, 1972:43). When a religious community sits down together to work out their approach to their ministry, they are engaging at a level of intimacy that will elicit an increase in strokes. The interactions in this case are no longer stereotyped, nor just 'fillers 'before an event, but create the possibility for a definite increase of strokes.

Joint activities can both unite and divide people depending on the way the group interacts. In the World Council of Churches in Geneva, this ecumenical church organisation came up with a slogan, 'Doctrines divide, but work unites!' They subsequently found that work could be as equally divisive as differences in belief. Despite the challenge of working together, however, joint activities generally garner more strokes than do withdrawal, rituals or pass-timing.

Games

When we talk about games we should use the term 'psychological games' to distinguish them from the type of pass-timing we mentioned above, which includes talking about sport. Berne defined games as 'an ongoing series of complementary ulterior transactions progressing to a well-defined, predictable outcome' (Berne, 1964:44). 'Games' is the subject of the next chapter, which will give us the chance to unpack this definition. For now we will therefore simply mention a few aspects of games that are worth noting.

Firstly, it should be said that playing psychological games provides a rich source of strokes for both parties. Secondly, the strokes will usually be negative strokes where both people feel worse off in the end. Thirdly, games are played for 'concealed motivations' that only later become obvious, and seem to recur at frequent intervals with the same people (Berne, 1961: 104). Fourthly, the stimulus and response of the ulterior transactions that make up the game involve the Child-to-Child ego states of the people involved. Fifthly, a game is coming from the Script of each person, and confirming the beliefs of the Scripts that were laid down in early childhood. And finally, it should be stressed that games are unconscious processes in which both parties find themselves embroiled before they realise what is happening.

The analysis of games provides a very valuable opportunity for understanding the types of conflicts that occur in any community or grouping. It is true that Berne talks about 'good' games that lead to the wellbeing of both parties, but on the whole, when we talk about games, we are talking about 'bad' ones (Berne, 1964:143). Games are part and parcel of life and, although they are frequent occurrences, they often escape close scrutiny, and are avoided because of the pain that is often experienced as they unfold. Most of the time people avoid games by deciding to remain at the stages of withdrawal, rituals, pastimes and activities, somewhat content with the less threatening sources of strokes.

We know that games are being played when we feel that the relationship with any member of our community suddenly takes a turn for the worst. When we feel hurt or angry, or resentful, or vindictive as a result of some misunderstanding, then a game is surely being played. The challenge is to know what sort of game is underway, but for this chapter, it is sufficient to recognise their existence.

Intimacy

Often when we think of intimacy, we associate it with the closeness of a married couple, and do not necessarily link it to religious life. Berne defines intimacy as 'a candid, game-free relationship, with mutual free giving and receiving and without exploitation' (Berne, 1972:45). For Berne, intimacy involves the Child ego state in all its openness and simplicity, living in the here and now (Berne, 1964:160). When religious are being intimate with each other, we see them without masks, without any form of defences, ready to engage with each other at the deepest level possible.

A community where there is a level of intimacy is a community where people are willing to share their vulnerability, their hopes and fears without any form of subterfuge. These religious know each other in all aspects of their personality, and have a compassionate understanding of the struggles and difficulties that each has confronted over the years. An intimate community is one where there are many positive strokes, as the group celebrates the quality of life together. There are also times when there are negative strokes due to hurts, misunderstanding, resentments and unchecked fantasies. But these communities are willing to face these situations, and work at creating peace and reconciliation when they experience difficulties.

It is in these communities that the members grow in autonomy, where the members are both aware of their real selves, and of the authentic selves of others. They have no difficulty in expressing their Free Child energy with spontaneity, and rejoice that they can reveal themselves without the need for pretence.

Conclusion

At the heart of religious life is the community, and yet so often religious find themselves settling for the less risky aspects of intimacy. Withdrawal is often seen as a virtue where it is confused with contemplation or recollection. Then activities become more important than the affective side of life. In all, the quality of community is diluted to little more than a place where people gather to get their physical needs met. This is unfortunate, and need not be the case. The challenge facing religious today is to create quality communal life that proclaims to a world torn with religious, ethnic and political strife, that brothers and sisters dwelling in unity is a possibility.

Exercises

1. Using the life wheel below, chart how you fare in the way you structure your time. Starting from the centre, identify how much time you spend in each section of Fig. 22.

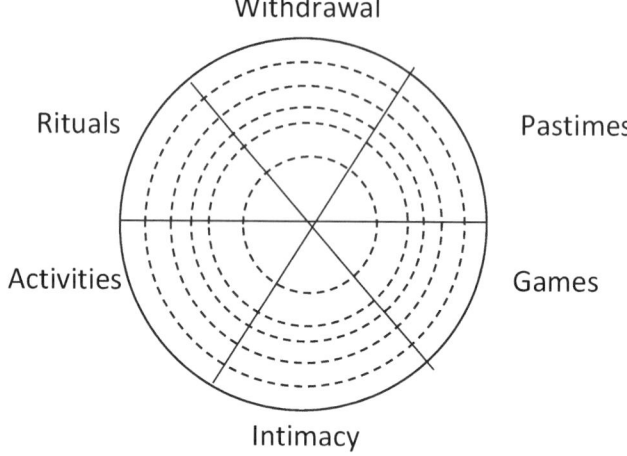

Fig. 22   Time Structuring Chart

Discuss your chart with other members of the community, (they may have a different view of how you spend your time!) and share how you would like to structure your time differently, and what difference that would make for you.

2. Identify the various situations where each of the time-structuring behaviours is evident in your community: e.g. when do we see withdrawal happening? Or pass-timing? Etc. Pick one or two of the behaviours and discuss how things could be done differently to create a greater level of intimacy among community members.

Chapter Fourteen

Games in Community

"How dreadful...to be caught up in a game
and have no idea of the rules."
Caroline Stevermer

What is a game and how do we know when games are being played? And maybe more importantly, why do people play games? These are the questions that come to mind when we talk about the psychological games that take place in a community or in any group for that matter.

What is a Game?

Berne described a game as, 'an ongoing series of ulterior complementary transactions, progressing to a well-defined predictable outcome' (Berne, 1964:44). This needs to be unpacked somewhat.

Ulterior Transactions

The 'ongoing series of ulterior complementary transactions' brings us back to Chapter 10 where we discussed how people communicate with each other by complementary, crossed and ulterior transactions. *Duplex ulterior transactions* are those interpersonal interactions that have two levels of communication: the social level of the words, and the psychological level of the unspoken meaning behind the words. So, for example, a person could say, 'I'm feeling very tired' when behind the words is the real message, 'You hurt me yesterday, and I want to be alone' or 'You hurt me yesterday, and now I am going to make you pay by giving you the silent treatment!' The problem is how do we get to the real message in any conversation? How do we get behind the words, and know what it going on? When people play games, it is difficult to work out what is happening, and how the game started in the beginning, because the real outcome is not on the social level but on the psychological level.

Complementary Transactions

The complementary aspect of the transactions that occurs in games simply means that the transactions keep going on unless one of the parties decides to shift ego states, and thereby stops the game. With complementary transactions we have a situation where a cycle of interactions seems to be happening, and nothing is changing. When two people begin to argue, it is usually the case that one of the parties is in one ego state – often the Controlling Parent, and the other person is in the Rebellious Child. Unless one of the twosome shifts ego states, and moves to Parent, Adult or Child, the interaction will continue indefinitely. With a game, therefore, both parties are locked into an unending series to exchanges, and often the only way the game ends is when both parties withdraw to lick their wounds. But the problem is not resolved.

A well-defined predictable outcome

In Chapter 1, we talked about our script, and described it as 'an unconscious life plan, based on decisions made in childhood.' By this we meant that the child at an early age decides how his or her life is going to unfold. A child may make the decision 'Nobody is going to force me to do what I don't want to do' as a result of feeling dominated by the parents, or maybe the decision could have been, 'I'll try to please everyone' as a result of getting many strokes early on in life, and feeling insecure when the strokes stop flowing.

So, a game is what we do to play out these early Script decisions. If my Script is 'Nobody is going to force me to do what I don't want', then the person is going to play games to back up or confirm that early decision. Each game I play will send the following message: 'There we go again, I knew that people were going to force me to do what I don't want to do." The game confirms the early Script decision. Or if my script tells me that the strokes are not going to flow forever, then the game will play out a situation where the strokes do stop flowing, thereby confirming my Script. Thus, the predictable outcome of the game follows on from the early life decision, and justifies our beliefs in ourselves, in others and in the future as we envisage it. The outcome is, therefore, predictable and well defined, creating a self-fulfilling prophecy.

How do we know when a game is underway?

Often people are well into the game before they realise that a game is going on, and then it is almost too late to do anything. When both people involved in an interaction end up feeling hurt, misunderstood, resentful, angry or frustrated, they then realise too late that they have just participated in a game.

Sister Mary said she was feeling bored. Sister Liz suggested she go to the pictures to get out of the house. Mary said she had come to the end of her allowance and hadn't the money for the cinema. Liz offered to loan her the money. Mary thanked her but said that there was no good film on. Liz told her of a recent release that was supposed to be wonderful. Mary said she heard of the film but felt that she would prefer to go to it with someone as it was supposed to be a very emotional film. Liz offered to go with her. Mary thanked Liz, but said that she thought she would prefer to be alone for the time being. At this stage Liz got frustrated and told Mary that she better make up her mind and not go on complaining if she was not prepared to do anything about it. Liz asked if Mary wanted to stop being bored or what did she want. Mary was taken aback by Liz's outburst and said that all she wanted was some peace and quiet and that there was no need to be so unkind. Liz felt furious and just walked away. Both Sisters ended up feeling bad. This is a good example of a game which Berne called, 'Why Don't You...Yes, but'.

Why do people play games?

The short answer is that people play games to keep the strokes flowing and reinforce their Script. In many ways a game is a form of defence, providing the person with relief from debilitating feelings of anxiety and guilt (Woods, 2002: 190).

We saw in the Chapter 12 that without strokes, a person ceases to grow or develop in a healthy way. Chapter 13 examined how people structure their time to achieve the maximum number of strokes. Intimacy, we said, offers the greatest amount of positive strokes but, as Berne observed, there is often little opportunity for intimacy in daily life and he concluded that 'the bulk of the time in serious social life is taken up with playing games' (Berne, 1976: 79). This is true of community life, where often the structure of the community seems to favour withdrawal, rituals, pass-timing, activities and avoids psychological games and frequently prevents moments of intimacy.

When the desire grows for the maximum amount of strokes, games provide the opportunity to gain a significant amount. Of course, the strokes gained are negative strokes, but as we have seen, negative strokes are better than no strokes. Hence, other than in the context of intimacy, the next best source of strokes is the playing of games.

And as we noted above, games confirm a person's Script, leading to what Berne called the *payoff*. By payoff, Berne meant that the game brings out those early feelings that the person felt around the time of the formation of their Script. You will remember that we talked about a Script having a beginning, middle and an end – just like in a drama. Well, the payoff is the moment towards the end of the Script – Berne calls it the *final display* - when the outcome is realised and people feel those feelings that they learned to feel early on in life as the Script was being formed (Berne, 1972: 339).

A point worth noting is that games come from the Little Professor in the Child ego state (A_1). That Adult in the Child as we saw in Chapter 3, is the intuitive side of the young person who cleverly works out how to play the game. As grown adults, we often work out of the Little Professor when we find ourselves in the middle of a game. So, it is not simply a matter of us deciding to play or not to play a game; we simply find ourselves locked into a game before we can do anything about it. Avoiding games requires great awareness and the use of our Adult ego state (A_2) as well as our Little Professor! (A_1).

The Game Formula

Berne outlined the various stages that a game takes (Berne, 1972:43). He said that every game begins with a *con* (C), which we will explain below. Then following the con comes the *gimmick* (G), which is where the *con* hooks the other person into playing the game. Interchanges follow and can go on for some time, and are termed the *response* (R). Then there is a *switch* and *crossup* (X) where one of the players upsets the process and reverses the game plan. Finally, there is the *payoff* (P). So, Berne made the game to be summarised in a formula:

$$C + G = R \blacklozenge S \blacklozenge X \blacklozenge P \quad \text{(Formula G)}$$

So, if we take the game played by Sister Mary and Sister Liz, we can see the game being played according to the above *Formula G*.

Sister Mary begins with the *con*, saying that she is bored. This is the unconscious symbiotic invitation to Sister Liz to enter into a game (see Chapter 19). Sister Liz is hooked by the *con* because at an unconscious level she sees a hidden advantage in playing the game. This is what Berne calls the *gimmick* (Berne, 1963:319). Originally a gimmick was the device in a wheel of fortune that the operator was able to use to prevent people from winning a fortune! (*Ibid:*213). So, with the gimmick, Liz unconsciously feels that she will benefit in offering advice to Mary; it will put her in a superior position to Sr Mary But, in reality, the gimmick will prevent her winning. Once the con and the gimmick have happened, we then have a set of duplex ulterior transactions that continue for a longer or shorter period; this series of ulterior transactions is referred to as the *response* or (R) in the formula. They are called *ulterior* because the motivation for the transactions is not consciously evident to either member of the game.

The conversation between Sr Liz and Sr Mary could have continued indefinitely (R), but we saw that after some time Sr Liz expressed her frustration with Sr Mary, telling her that she had better make up her mind. This is the moment of the *switch* (S) when Liz sees that no matter what she suggests, Sr Mary is not going to accept any form of advice. The switch involves the switching of roles, where initially Sr Mary feels in the one-down position with Sr Liz in the one-up position; then, the switch happens and Sr Liz feels almost the victim, whereas Sr Mary begins to be the critical oppressor of Sr Liz, and takes on the one-up position.

Following directly from the switch we have the *crossup* (X), which Berne defines as 'the moment of confusion', where both Sr Mary and Sr Liz wonder what happened to both of them (Berne, 1972:43). Sr Mary thought she was sharing her difficult feelings of boredom, and Liz thought she was trying to help. With the *crossup*, both feel that the situation has changed and they cannot fully understand what has happened. In the end, both feel hurt and misunderstood.

Following the *crossup*, there is the *payoff* (P). By *payoff*, Berne meant what he defined as 'the ultimate destiny or final display that marks the end of a life plan' (*Ibid:* p.495). In other words, when we imagine the Script of Sr Mary, she could have a losing Script that says, "I cannot manage my life and people won't help me." In the game we described, we see how this Script belief is confirmed. With Sr Liz, her Script could be, "I'll never succeed", and again she experiences the game as confirming her Script.

So, Berne maintains that every game or series of ulterior transactions has to have all the elements of the formula for it to be classified as a game.

Berne in his book *Games People Play,* gave quirky names to the various games he identified (Berne, 1964). The game described above could be called 'Yes But' where Sr Mary poses the problem, and Sr Liz tries to suggest solutions only to be met with the 'Yes, but that would not work.' Related to this type of game is another game called *'Do Me something'* where the protagonist tries to enlist the help of someone else to do what the person can do for them. Some of the other games we will summarise below to give a flavour of how religious can play psychological games in community.

A Selection of Games

Blemish

Communities can have someone who is always finding fault with something or someone in the community. It might be the quality of food, the horarium, the way Br Michael eats his meals or many other things. There is a very strong Parent voice projecting faults onto others. The objective of this game is to ward off feelings of depression. The *Blemish game* gives a sense that the blemisher wants to hide from his or her own faults. Through the act of blemishing, the person does not have to connect with whoever is being blemished. Instead, they project their own faults outside themselves, and onto someone else or onto some situation. This is projection. (See Chapter 16).

Now I've got you, you son of a bitch (NIGYSOB)

This unpleasantly named game is played by a person who, having suffered constantly at the hands of a persecutor, finally reacts in a vindictive manner much to the surprise of the other person. Here is a case where the Victim becomes the Persecutor in retaliation for the many injustices he or she has suffered. In this game we have the classic switch very clearly evidenced. However, like the blemish game, NIGYSOB prevents the person looking at their own failings by projecting them onto others in a vindictive way.

Rapo

Some religious are inclined to flirt with religious of the opposite sex, or indeed with lay people. When the other person responds to the 'come on' by the religious, the religious gets indignant, pointing out that they never intended to imply the sexual approach. Such behaviour is not uncommon, and can leave the victims of the game hurt and embarrassed. In some cases a rapo game has also led to legal proceedings taken against the offending religious.

Wooden Leg

This game can be quite common in communities where a person uses a weakness they have to avoid doing difficult jobs. 'How could you expect me to cook the dinner, when I never was taught to cook?' would be one example of this game. Or they can use an illness or stress to argue against taking up some responsibility. The *Wooden Leg* is a good example of a victim game.

Kick Me

This religious finds himself or herself at the mercy of others in the community who persecute them. One religious keeps offering suggestions during the course of the community meeting, and finds that each time he comes forward, he is attacked or ignored. He cannot understand why people don't ever agree with him or why they usually attack him. Somehow, he seems to trigger the attacks. Unconsciously, he sets himself up to be eventually rejected. Here we have another victim game.

I'm Only Trying to Help You

We will see later in Chapter 18 how this game involves a type of symbiotic relationship where one person in the community, having tried many things to help out, finds that all her suggestions have been ignored. When the person she tried to help eventually reacts negatively to the offers of help, the reaction on the part of the helper is one of hurt and resentment. At an unconscious level, the helper may not want the other person to improve in case their assistance would no longer be needed. And so, the help offered seems always to be unhelpful and is therefore refused.

These are only a few of the games that Berne describes in detail in his *Games People Play,* but they give a flavour of how games can be played in community.

The Drama Triangle

Another way of looking at the games that people in communities or groups play is to use what Steve Karpman described as the *Drama Triangle* (Karpman, 1968:39ff). Karpman said that a game is like a drama, played out on the stage of life. Like any drama, there are usually at least three protagonists: The Persecutor (P), The Rescuer (R), and The Victim (V) (Fig. 23).

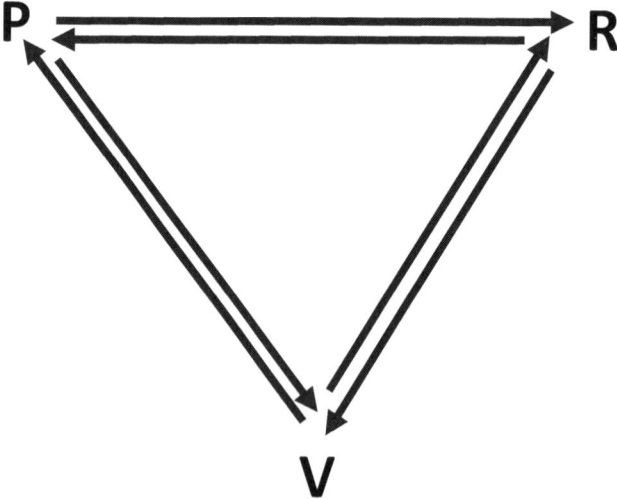

Fig. 23 The Drama Triangle

The *Persecutor* is the character that puts people down, criticizing them, blaming them, and making them feel inferior, shamed or simply hurt. The Persecutor ignores or discounts the value or dignity of the person, from an I'm OK –You're Not OK position, and seeks to *get rid* of the person with the problem.

The *Rescuer* is the character that discounts or underestimates the ability of other people to solve their own problems. So, the Rescuer jumps in to help even when help is not requested. The Rescuer is in the I'm OK –You're Not OK position, but unlike the Persecutor, does not wish to *get rid* of the person with the problem, but rather wants to *get rid* of the problem of the person, believing people cannot solve their own problems, and so need to be rescued.

Victims comes from an I'm Not OK- You're OK, or else from the I'm Not OK-You're Not OK position. Victims discount their ability to solve their own problems, looking for the Rescuer to jump in, and resenting the Persecutor who threatens to overwhelm them or criticise them.

The three actors on the Drama Triangle can move from one position to another during the course of a game. We saw that Sr Mary begins by being the Victim, where she is bored and does not know what to do. Sr Liz jumps in to rescue her, even though she was not asked specifically to do anything. She later then begins to persecute Sr Mary for being so passive. As the game progresses further, Sr Mary begins to persecute Sr Liz, giving her the impression that she is useless, and Sr Liz begins to feel like a Victim that is not appreciated.

The Drama Triangle is very useful in identifying what is happening in situations of conflict, and issues an early warning to the game players that trouble is brewing. Once this is recognised, the players have the opportunity to step off the Drama Triangle and put a new show on the road (Berne, 1961).

The Advantages of Games

We said earlier that people play games to keep up the supply of strokes coming to them and to confirm their Script. Berne offered six advantages that games offer to the game player (Berne, 1964: 50ff).

The first advantage we have already mentioned; games

confirm the Script of the person. So, when I have a belief that I am not important, each game I play will be undertaken to confirm that belief. So, by playing the game I maintain a certain psychic equilibrium or homeostasis where I do not have to change anything, especially my Script, and so experience a sense of relief that things are staying the same (Woods, 2002:190).

The second advantage is that when I play a game I avoid certain circumstances that I may have experienced in the past, and want to avoid a repeat of that event. If, for instance, I found that when I asked for something as a child, I was made to feel guilty or selfish, I now will not ask for what I want, and thereby avoid similar feelings.

A third advantage is that playing games supplies me with material for 'bitching' with friends. We have all heard conversations between friends where the line goes, 'He said ...and then I said' as the person describes in detail the way a game unfolded. This sort of sharing between friends is a type of pass-timing where such sharing appears to be a form of intimacy, but in reality is just a superficial way to converse.

A fourth advantage, like the third advantage, is where the 'bitching' is done in a bigger social circle. The person gathers an audience around them, and then goes into narrating how the game unfolded and how the narrator ended up being the victim. Such social complaining is done to gain some strokes of sympathy from an audience. Usually, such behaviour is itself a game that Berne called, 'Ain't it awful' (Berne, 1964:96).

The fifth advantage is that games are played to get strokes, and depending on the type of game played the strokes will change. If, for example, I am playing a game where I am the Persecutor, my strokes will be very different from those I get when I play the Victim.

And finally, the sixth advantage of games is that they keep me in my preferred life-position. If I am used to being in the I'm OK- You're not OK position, all my games will aim to maintain this persecutory position.

Degrees of Games

Berne identified three stages in games, moving from innocuous ones (First-Degree) to more problematic ones (Second–Degree) until finally arriving at disastrous ones (Third

–Degree) (Berne, 1964:57).

The first-degree game is the one that we are willing and even keen to talk about socially. So, when we return to the community after having had a 'fight' with a friend, we want to share the game in order to get some support and positive strokes from the community.

The second-degree game is the one where we experienced a game where we did not come out well from it, and maybe even were instrumental in making a fairly serious error of judgement. So, we want to hide the facts, and keep the game to ourselves. An example of this could be when we argued with the police over a speeding fine and got a bigger one for our protest!

The third–degree game, according to Berne, ends in the surgery, the courtroom or the morgue. It is difficult to imagine that religious would be involved in such games, but when we think of situations where religious are involved in the breaking of professional boundaries, there have been many instances of third-degree games being played by religious, who finally ended up in jail.

How to Stop Games

It seems that there are four approaches in dealing with games: ignore the game, expose the game, play the game, or play an alternative game (Dusay, 1966:136-7; Woollams & Brown, 1978:147ff; Stewart & Joines, 2012:270 ff).

Ignoring the game can be, at times, the wisest decision when there is more to be gained by avoiding conflict. Of course, the danger of doing this is that we allow the game to continue on other occasions, and give the impression that playing a particular game is acceptable. Many use the excuse of being tolerant to allow games to continue unchecked.

Exposing the game can be very effective if the person is open to hear the confrontation. By exposing, I mean noticing the *con*, the very first move in the game formula, and thereby stopping the game. Every con involves some type of discount and so, by catching the con, we expose the discount. If, for instance, a person begins complaining, and is about to invite you into a *'Why Don't You...Yes But'* game, the challenge is *not* to offer any solutions from your Nurturing or Rescuing Parent, but to stay in Adult, and ask the person what options they can think of, thus refusing to 'help' in any way. Explaining to the person that they may be discounting their own ability to solve their problem moves them away from the Victim mode.

Another way of exposing the game is simply to bring the psychological message of the game to the person's attention, and explain that they can get what they want by being more direct. So, if the person is playing the Game *'Kick Me'* where they want you to punish or criticise them, by drawing attention to their behaviour, it may stop the development of that game.

Playing the game with the person can be useful when the other person is not ready for a confrontation, or we cannot see an alternative at the time. When we play along with the game we are conscious of what is happening, and are therefore in our Adult. So, strictly, it does not become a game because both parties are not involved in ulterior transactions.

Playing alternative games is the fourth alternative approach, but it seems to me that such a strategy could be very manipulative. The idea, according to Woollams and Brown, is that by playing less harmful games, we ensure the other person gets some strokes without the negative fallout of the game they intended to play (Woollams & Brown, 1978:148).

Conclusion

In the final analysis, people play games to get their needs met. They then repeat the game strategies that worked when they were young, often because the alternative is not in their awareness. The challenge for members of a community is to discover ways to ensure a steady supply of healthy strokes that will no longer necessitate the need to continue playing psychological games. No community will be without game playing but the challenge is to keep them to a minimum in favour of clear communication. The important aspect of good communication is that we become aware of the games being played, and ever more alert to avoid being caught in the repetitive nature of the games that prevent the more authentic moments of intimacy.

Exercises

1. Identify a 'gamey' incident that you experienced with a member or members of your community or with members of another community, and describe what happened, and what you understand what was going on at a psychological level. The following questions are borrowed from Stewart and Joines, who in turn used the work of John James and Laurence Collinson (Stewart & Joines, 2012:259ff):

    i)   What keeps happening to me over and over again?
    ii)   How does it start?
    iii)   What happens next?
    iv)   What is my secret message to the other person?
    v)   And then what happens?
    vi)   What is the other person's secret message to me?
    vii)   How does it end?
    viii) How do I feel?
    ix)   How do I think the other person feels?

2. Using the same incident, describe the events using the game formula first, and then the Drama Triangle.

Chapter Fifteen

Rackets and Stamps

"Feelings are not supposed to be logical.
Dangerous is the man who has rationalized his emotions."
David Borenstein

Following on from games, we will examine in this chapter how racketeering, racket feelings and collecting trading-stamps are part and parcel of the game process that can take place in community, and how they fit our Script (Berne, 1964:127; 1972:167ff).

Br Philip, together with some members of his community, was at a meeting with their Province Leader, and in the course of the proceedings, Br Philip became very angry and resentful. Inside he could feel himself boiling with anger at the manner in which the Province Leader had made certain decisions without consultation. Br Philip kept his peace, because he feared the reaction of the Province Leader were he to express his opposition openly, and so he simply allowed the anger to simmer just below the surface.

On his way home after the meeting, he shared with two of the members of his community how angry he was about the way the Province Leader had conducted the session. To his amazement, he found one of the members had been delighted with the clear direction that the Province Leader had offered, while the other member was sad that the real point had been missed. Neither of them had been angry.

It is often the case that the same event can trigger a variety of feelings in different people when one would expect similar reactions. Examining the concepts of rackets, racketeering and collecting trading-stamps can best explain this phenomenon.

Racket Feelings

Racket feelings have been defined as 'repetitions of "permitted feeling" which were stroked in the past' (English, 1972:23ff). Fanita English explains how a young child growing up in a family gradually learns which feelings are permitted, and which are banned. For example, if a child begins to scream and shout with anger when his toy is taken away, he may discover that his parent either punishes him for being angry, or ignores the screams and shouts, and leaves him on his own with his anger. Gradually, the child learns that being angry and screaming only leads to punishment or isolation. By chance, the next time he loses his favourite tractor, he cries and shows real sadness. When his mother sees him being sad, she bends down, and picks him up, hugging him and kissing him. The Little Professor (A1) in the child comes to the logical conclusion that anger brings punishment, while sadness results in expressions of affection. So, gradually after many similar experiences, the child begins to express sadness to cover up his feeling of anger. Eventually, the child loses touch with what anger feels like, and now, as an adult, often when he is in situations that would normally warrant an angry reaction, he finds himself feeling sad. As a result, sadness becomes a racket feeling, covering the authentic feeling of anger.

Fanita English calls this process, the 'substitution factor', where racket feelings *substitute* for *other* feelings that would have been the more authentic reactions had those feelings in the person's past been allowed to be expressed (English, 1971:71ff).

English links the idea of racket feelings with the injunctions that we discussed in chapter 7 where the *Don't Feel* injunction is modified to *Don't Feel* certain emotions, while permission is given to feel 'substitute' feelings. So Script messages can create the situation where racket feelings are stroked and authentic feelings discouraged (English, 1971:67ff).

In the case of Br Philip, it turns out that he seems to feel anger quite easily when in the presence of superiors, and expresses it very frequently in explosions of uncontrollable fury, with his community members. And yet, he seems unable to show other feelings of fear or sadness or even joy when these emotions would be more appropriate. Anger for Br Philip is a racket feeling covering many other more authentic feelings.

Racketeering

English points out that we may fail to understand the difference between rackets and racketeering (English,

1976:78ff). Whereas the 'racket feeling' refers to the feeling that is being expressed in the moment as a substitute for a more authentic feeling, *racketeering* refers to the various transactions that are employed to bring about the artificial or inauthentic feelings. Racketeering refers to the sort of actions a person engages in so as to create racket feelings. A Racketeer seeks to 'hook' ulterior complementary transactions from the other person in order for him or her to feel the racket feelings. And when the Racketeer finds that he or she is not getting enough racket feelings, he or she will engage in a full-blown game.

If, for example, a community member is showing racket sadness, and others in the community seem to be ignoring him or her, then she or he will begin to play a game to escalate the feeling, so that the racket sadness is finally acknowledged by some of the members. The problem with stroking the person's racket feeling is that it simply compounds their inauthentic feelings.

The challenge, therefore, lies in seeking to uncover the authentic feelings behind the racket feelings so as to invite the person to be real. At the same time, we need to be conscious that a racket feeling cannot be easily dismissed simply because *we* judge it to be such. As we come to accept the feelings of others - both racket and authentic feelings - the hope is that the other person will favour the authentic over the racket feelings.

Trading Stamps

Berne wrote about the idea of emotional trading stamps following the practice he saw in supermarkets where people collected stamps as a bonus for spending money. They saved these stamps in a book, and eventually could 'cash them in' for various prizes. This practice gave him the idea of psychological trading stamps (Berne, 1964a: 127).

Imagine a community situation where Brother James is in the kitchen washing up the dishes when Brother Gregory comes in, and jokes that he is being the good housewife. Suddenly Brother James explodes, and tells Br Gregory in no uncertain terms that he is never to call him a housewife, and that he should keep his mouth shut if he has nothing positive to say. Br Gregory is stunned at the vehemence of the reaction, and can hardly get a word out to apologise. He beats a hasty retreat, and wonders what exactly did he say that upset Br James so much.

Br James in fact had reached the limit. Continually at table, he experienced the banter of the community to be toxic. Jokes that seemed to be light-hearted were, in fact, small hurtful barbs making many people feel embarrassed even when everyone seemed to be laughing. Br Gregory was the master of banter, and seemed ready on any occasion to make the funny comment at the expense of another Brother. Br James had had enough, and so he exploded. He had saved up his trading stamps of resentment, and now he was 'cashing' them in.

Berne called trading stamps the currency of rackets. He explained how the child is taught to feel certain emotions, which were stroked by the parents. These 'substitute' feelings are not expressed in the moment, but are collected and suppressed. Then some unsuspecting person does or says something that triggers the internal mechanism of the person that gives permission for the racket feelings to be 'cashed in'. The incident with Br James is a good example of this process.

In religious communities of men or women, there can be a lot of members who collect psychological trading stamps. Under the banner of tolerance, members of communities swallow hurts and resentments often for years and years. Feelings of hurt are buried, but buried alive only to emerge many years later. It is often sad to hear Brothers or Sisters, well into their seventies, talking about their novitiate days as teenagers, when the Director of Novices had shamed them or hurt them in some way. For fifty years, they had collected trading stamps, and find towards the end of their lives that the stamps are worth nothing. There can also exist what Berne calls *counterfeit* trading stamps where people imagine hurts that never existed in reality. Such stamps are also the currency of rackets and games (*Ibid*:127). When people feel good about themselves, they throw away their stamps!

Authentic Feelings

The discussion so far has dealt with racket feelings of anger covering hurt and sadness, or sadness covering anger and resentment. In a way, any one of the feelings could be a racket feeling covering another authentic feeling. This begs the question as to how we can identify an authentic feeling from a racket feeling?   When are anger or sadness or fear authentic feelings, and when are they racket feelings?

TA holds that there are four authentic feelings and neatly categorises them as *mad, glad, sad, and scared* or in more prosaic language: anger, joy, sadness and fear (Thomson, 1983:20ff). No doubt, there are other emotions not captured in this clever identification of emotions, but overall, these four emotional reactions are significant ones that can be examined here to distinguish authentic feelings from racket feelings.

George Thomson identified an authentic feeling as one that succeeds in resolving a problem and therefore is appropriate to the situation in which the emotion is experienced.   Another way of testing authentic emotions, he held, was to link the feeling with the time factor, and he maintained that if we look at the emotion, and see where in time it is occurring, we will have some indication as to whether the emotion is authentic or not. Hence, to test whether a feeling is authentic or a racket feeling, it is sufficient to ask, does it solve a problem, and is it linked to the appropriate time factor?

For Thomson, an authentic feeling of sadness is linked to *the past*, where I experienced some loss or tragedy.   For example, it would be authentic to feel sadness at the death of a dear member of the community. Sadness is authentic because it helps me deal with something that has just happened. When I feel sad, I am coping with the natural grieving for the passing of someone I love, and grieving takes time. In a way, I cannot come into the *present* until I have coped with the loss of the *past*. By being sad, I eventually solve the problem of dealing with the loss.

Authentic fear, on the other hand, is linked to the *future* where danger threatens to harm me or cause me trouble. When I am feeling afraid of a talk I have to give at a conference, this is an authentic feeling, as it warns me that I need to do some preparation and have the material ready on time. The feeling of fear is a *stimulus* to action, awakening my sympathetic nervous system to move towards either fight or flight. I move towards *fight*, when I get down to reading, researching and writing my talk. I move toward *flight*, when I decide I'm going to cancel my commitment to give the talk. Authentic fear is the key to either form of action. Authentic fear solves the problem of inaction and passivity.

An authentic angry feeling is linked to the *present.* When I get angry *in the moment* with a printer who promised to deliver an order within ten days, and who is now late with the order, this feeling is authentic *if* it expresses an emotion that has the chance to change the behaviour of the printer, and get him to honour his promise. By being angry, I want to see the promise honoured *now* and solve the problem instead of simply feeling resentment and agitation that does not change anything.

Thomson does not deal with the *glad* emotion or the emotion joy or happiness. Stewart and Joines suggest a reason for this (Stewart and Joines, 2012:233). They say that joy or happiness does not require any change, but simply lives the moment whether in the present, past or future.

Given Thomson's thesis that authentic emotions are linked to a time factor, then racket feelings of fear, anger and sadness will find themselves *out of step* on the time-line. So, if I am angry about the past when I can do nothing about changing it, according to Thomson, this is racket anger, possibly covering the more authentic feeling of sadness over the loss of something that occurred in the past. By being angry, I avoid getting in touch with sadness and resolving the sense of bereavement. Or if I am afraid in the *present* when nothing in the future would justify this feeling, then I am suffering from anxiety, a free-flowing fear that does not solve any problem, and covers an authentic anger at the situation. Were I in touch with *authentic* anger that emotion would actually galvanise me to solve the problem. And if I am sad about the present, here again I am experiencing racket sadness because I have not lost something.

Another way of testing authentic feelings is to see what I am escaping from, and what sort of assistance do I need at the particular time when I am feeling angry, sad or fear.

Carlo Moiso offers a neat way of connecting authentic feelings with the instincts of fight, flight and freeze as well as linking them with what a person is requesting from others when they feel a specific emotion (Moiso, 1984:69ff).

Fear attempts to escape or fly from something that threatens, and seeks reassurance from other people that things will work out. Therefore, I am being authentically fearful when I want to escape from a perceived danger, and request someone to calm my authentic fear.

Anger is linked to the fight response, where I want to change something that is happening. I am being authentically angry, therefore, when I am actively working to change the situation, and then requesting someone to behave differently as a result of expressing my authentic emotion.

And finally, sadness is linked to the freeze response where I want to receive some form of consolation or support in the moment of loss. My request is for someone to share my feelings of loss and provide me with the opportunity to be sad.

Conclusion

The challenge facing all of us is to be in touch with our authentic feelings, and express them in appropriate ways. Because our racket feelings are usually if not always out of awareness, it takes much work to uncover the authentic feelings in any given situation. By sharing our emotional responses in the community context, we have the opportunity to compare our emotional reactions with those of our fellow community members. This affords us the opportunity to see that what we feel may be very different from the way others feel, and in making the comparison, we can begin to get in touch with possible racket feelings. In doing so, we then have the challenge to discover the full range of feelings, and express them appropriately.

Exercises

1. In the presence of your community write down a list of resentments that you carry from the past. The other members of the community do likewise. Have some quiet music in the background. As you look at these resentments, ask yourself why are you still holding them *buried alive* in the present? What good are they doing you? What would you like to do with the resentments? Make a decision what you *will* do with them. Then as the music lowers, each one places the page in a container and the resentments are burned as a symbol of wanting to get rid of them.

2. You remember the egogram (Chapter 4) where you charted which ego state you had more of and which ego state you had less of. This time, draw what I call an emogram (emo for emotion!) where you list the four main feelings (mad, glad, sad and scared) – and you may want to add others – and make a chart that indicates which emotions you express more frequently and which you express less of (Gibson, 2007). So, just like the egogram, the emogram will show the pattern of your emotional expression.

3. A risky but valuable exercise is to share some current resentment you have with individuals in your community. Sharing these can contribute to healing and forgiveness.

4. Share incidents when you have racket feelings and how you struggle with specific authentic feelings.

Chapter Sixteen

Projection & Transference

"Don't Take Anything Personally.
Nothing others do is because of you.
What others say and do is a projection of their own reality,
their own dream."
Miguel Angel Ruiz

How is it that when someone enters into a room and meets people they have never met before, they immediately feel drawn to some people, while other people seem to put them off? Or how is it that in community, some religious seem to rub others up the wrong way without meaning to? It appears that we unconsciously feel more at home with some people, while others just don't seem to connect with us at all.

In any religious community setting, there is group of people who have been assigned to live together without any choice on the part of the members. Consequently, there will be some of the members who get on well from the outset, while others will take some time and effort to be able to make a connection. Understanding the process of how this attraction or lack of attraction works can go a long way to lessen the tensions that arise when we find ourselves disconnected from some of our fellow community members. The process of interpersonal dynamics involves a combination of transference and projection.

Transference

The Freudian understanding of transference involves the unconscious tendency to assign to others in one's present environment the feelings and attitudes associated with a parent or significant person from the past. When we find ourselves reacting negatively to someone whom we have just met, it may be that they remind us of someone in the past with whom we have had a negative experience.

The question is, why do we engage in this process of repeating in the present our experiences from the past? What is the function of transference? There are various motivations for employing transference, which we will briefly mention.

Sometimes we project our past onto someone in the present in order to identify with that person. In this case, we are usually talking about a positive identification with the person in the present because of the experience from the past that offered us support, protection and affection. Clarkson calls this *concordant transference*, where we seek to identify with the positive qualities of the other person by imitating them, entering into a mutually supportive relationship that we hope will replicate the good experiences from our past (Clarkson, 1991:101). In this case, we feel with and for the person and in TA terms, we are in touch with the other person's Child ego state.

When, on the other hand, we project onto another person the experiences of some historical person who treated us badly, or who failed to offer us the love and affection we needed for our emotional growth, we make this projection expecting that we will be treated equally badly by this other person, as we were by the historical person. Clarkson calls this *complementary transference* where we focus on the negative qualities of the other person, reacting to them as we did to the original parent or person who failed to provide us with the necessary emotional support in childhood (*Ibid*:101).

In either case, we can see that our positive or negative reactions to a person in community are not explainable simply by identifying the positive or negative qualities in that other person in the present moment, but are inextricably linked to our former experiences. In a sense, we are not reacting to the person who is before us, but are reliving some former experiences with a parent or significant other person in our past (Joines, 1991: 170ff).

Berne said that Scripts belong in the realm of transference where our present experiences are playing out our Script that was set down in our early childhood. He offered the simple diagram in Fig. 24 to explain how the transference worked in a therapeutic setting, and which we can extrapolate to explain what happens in community.

Person A   **Person B**

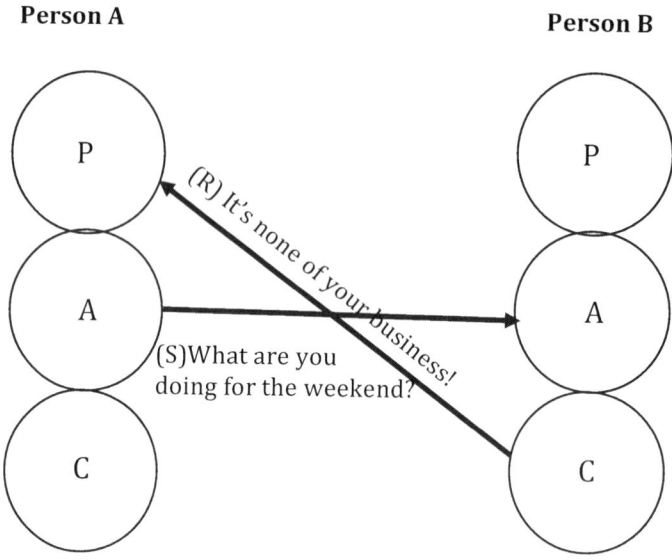

Fig. 24 Transference Transactions (Berne 1961)

Imagine a scenario where Person A in community asks Person B what they have planned to do at the weekend. This is an open question coming from the Adult of Person A and is motivated simply by interest in the welfare of Person B. However, Person B hears this question from a Child position, reminding him or her of a mother who was domineering and controlling. So, Person B transfers onto Person A the experience of the past, and reacts to Person A as they did historically to his or her mother. The reaction of Person B to Person A appears irrational and disproportionate to the original question coming from Adult. Naturally Person A feels shocked at the force of the reaction, and could express strong feelings in response to Person B's outburst. The interchange between these two community members has the potential to lead to ongoing conflict between the two members, unless one or other of the members understands what is behind the surface conflict. Ulterior transactions always have a psychological message behind the social message, and often the psychological message can be the result of transference.

The reason for transference lies in the need we all have to construct meaning, and organise our experience in a way that makes sense to us (Stolorow, Brandchaft and Atwood, 2000:37). We seek patterns in our lives, and transference is the method of assimilation where the new knowledge is made to fit into our already formulated Script. When we lack the familiar construct, we feel uneasy, and therefore employ transference to make a gestalt or pattern where we experience life as more predicable and familiar. Stern called this process *the representation of interventions that are generalised or* RIGS, where one event in the past prepares us to generalise our past reaction into a pattern of responses in the present (Stern, 2003:115). So, in the situations mentioned above, where we either find ourselves at ease with someone in community, or in conflict with a community member, it is valuable, indeed necessary, to begin to think about the possibility of transference as the cause of our reactions (Erskine & Trautmann, 1993:75ff).

Intimately connected with transference, is the mechanism of projection, which is used to transfer the experiences of the past and project them into the present. One of the reasons for this projection is the hope that the original conflict that occurred in the past can somehow be resolved in the present. By replaying the interactions in the present, the person tries to resolve the impasse from the past (Erskine, 1991:63ff).

This is one type of projection – the projection of a past figure onto someone in the present. But there is projection proper, where we project part of our ego states onto another person, and react to that person as if that part of ourselves belonged to the other person. It is particularly this form of projection that often creates difficulties in communication.

Projection

Br Fergus seems to be frustrated most of the time. He reacts impulsively to any hint of criticism, and takes everything personally. When people do not agree with him, he sees this disagreement as criticism of himself, and feels put down by the other members of the community. People are very wary of Br Fergus because the least innocent remark can be taken as a personal affront when nothing like that was intended. Everything becomes a drama with Br Fergus, and many in the community avoid him because it seems that every encounter leads to an argument. Br Fergus finds most of the community superficial, and not interested in him. He sees them as controlling and critical, and only accepting of him when he goes along with what the majority want. Most of the time, Br Fergus feels left out, ignored, and is very hurt by the way the community is treating him. And he cannot understand why his fellow Brothers are so thoughtless and indifferent.

At an unconscious level, Br Fergus is at the mercy of projection where his internal conflicts are being projected onto other people (Moiso, 1985:194ff). When Br Fergus was a young person growing up, his parents were highly critical of him. The messages from his parents were very conditional messages of him being OK only if he was perfect and pleased them. Some of the injunctions were: Don't Exist, Don't belong, Don't be close, Don't be a Child to name but a few of the unconscious messages young Fergus picked up from his parent.

Br Fergus' parents are now dead, but the messages that he received from his parents have been introjected into his Parent ego state (Fig. 25), and he still hears their voice telling him that he is not OK.

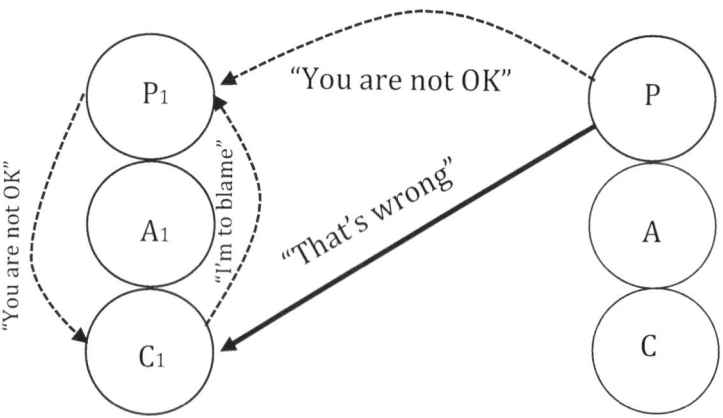

Fig. 25 Introjection

This internal dialogue of condemnation, and Fergus' feelings of being to blame for the Parents' rejection, creates within himself feelings of anger, hurt, resentment and lack of self-esteem. His

P_1 (Witch Parent) continues to criticize and control his C_1 (Somatic Child), creating tension and frustration within. This internal tension, begun in childhood, continues into adult life where now there is an on-going internal battle between his P_2 and C_2 (Fig. 26 overleaf). While the original introjection was employed to reduce the hostility between the child and the parent, and provided the child with a sense of control, now in the present, the introjection continues to create inner tension and frustration just as it did in the past (Little, 2006:10).

The internal war between Br Fergus' Parent ego state and his Child ego state (P_2 and C_2) leads to feelings of stress and frustration. This intrapsychic pressure becomes so strong that Br Fergus needs to seek relief by externally projecting the internal dialogue between his P_2 and his C_2 onto someone else (Moiso, 1985:197).

So, Br Fergus feels and acts towards other members of his community in a way that he felt towards his parents. Those same feelings of anger, hurt, resentment and frustration are now projected onto his community members, where he can now express these same feelings to them that he could not as a child express towards his parents (Erskine et al. 1988:12). This time, however, he can put the blame on the community members, when as a child he could not blame his parents because he needed to see his parents as the ideal parents he wished for. So, in Fig. 26 we see the *mechanism* of projection taking place between Br Fergus and a community member where the intrapsychic becomes interpersonal (Little, 2003:136).

In this diagram it is as if there is a screen in front of the ego states of the community member, and Br Fergus projects onto that screen the image of his own parents. So, Br Fergus does not see the community member in reality, but is seeing an image of his parents instead. He projects his internal dialogue of his introjected parents with the messages going on in his head – 'You are not OK' and 'I'm to blame' – externally onto the community member whom he now sees as his parent and not as a community member. He unconsciously projects his internal message of 'You are not OK' (a) onto the community member (b), and sends the ulterior transaction of "You are to blame" (d) as he interacts with the community member on a social level with the words, 'Did you lose it?'(c).

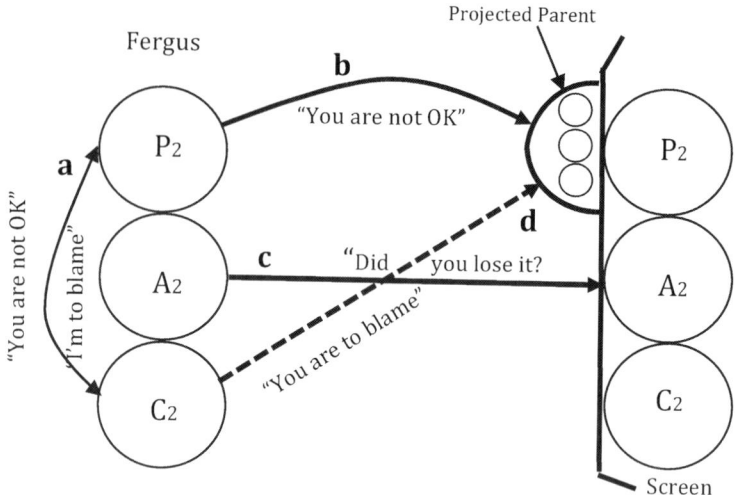

Fig. 26 Mechanism of Projection. (Moiso 1985)

Now he can blame the other person, and in so doing gain relief from the internal blame that is continually at war in his head.

The important thing to remember with regard to transference and projection is that they are both unconscious processes that are functioning out of our awareness. Because they are unconscious, we naturally put the blame on the other person for the feelings we have towards their behaviour or character. *They* are selfish. *They* are to blame. We simply cannot imagine that *we* are selfish or that *we* are to blame. We project onto others what is happening in ourselves.

Does this mean that every negative feeling and thought we have about another is just projection? Does the other person not bear some responsibility for the way we feel about them? These are interesting questions that merit some response. When are we not projecting, and when *is* the other person the cause of our reactions? In general, we could say with Jung (I think) that every relationship is a projection. But, for the sake of understanding community relationships, the following criteria may be of help in identifying projection and transference.

We can be fairly sure that there is either projection or transference when we have strong reactions to the other person. When our response seems to be disproportionate to the causal event, or even just very strong, then we can be fairly sure that we are projecting onto others what, in fact, is our own reality. If, for example, we view someone else as lazy and feel very critical and dismissive of that person, then we can be fairly certain that it is the laziness within ourselves that we are reacting to. We are externalising the internal Parent critic of our Child ego state onto the other person so as to relieve the internal war that is going on between our internal Parent and Child.

The fact that the other person may be lazy is not the point here. They may indeed be somewhat laid back, but it is our *reaction* to them that alerts us to the projection. Were there no projection, we could feel compassion, understanding and an Adult awareness that the person is failing to reach their full potential. But we would not be *reacting* to their behaviour as we do when we are projecting.

Another way of checking the level of our projections is to compare our reactions to certain people with the reactions of others to the same person. If we find that others have a very different reaction to that person, then we can be very sure that projection or transference is under way. And, of course, people can also project onto us, creating feelings of unease and tension within us, and impacting on our relationship.

When people project onto us and we begin to feel rejected, persecuted or ignored, it is worth remembering the advice of Don Miguel Ruiz in his book *The Four Agreements* when he warns the reader, 'Don't take things personally.' (Ruiz,1997: 51ff). He explains that whatever a person says about another person is more about critic than it is about the person they criticize. If the people being criticized take the comments personally, all it means is that they are agreeing with the observations of their critic. By taking things personally, we are acknowledging that the other's projection is true. He stresses that once we begin to take the other's criticism personally, it is at that moment that the poison from the other person enters into our blood stream, creating inner turmoil. In the face of criticism by another Ruiz suggests we engage in an imaginary conversation as follows:

> Whatever you think, whatever you feel, I know it is your problem. It is the way you see the world. It is nothing personal, because you are dealing with yourself, not with me. Others are going to have their own opinion according to their belief system, so nothing they think about me is really about me, it is about them (*Ibid:* 51).

The challenge facing each of us in community is to recognise that projection is going on all the time, and therefore we need to guard against any over-reaction we may experience in response to the way people treat us. It is when we begin to check fantasies and share resentments that the underlying dynamics of transference and projection have a chance to surface. It may be that someone may have a very negative reaction to another person, but as we have seen from our discussion of projection and transference, much of the reaction is due to fixated or archaic ego states. Therefore, the challenge facing each of us is to remember that when people react to us negatively it is very likely that they are engaged in transference or projection.

Projective Identification

Sister Margaret is normally a very jolly person, but she finds that when she is in the company of Sr Janet, she frequently feels sad. Sr Janet herself does not seem to feel sad in these moments when they are together, although very often Sr Margaret notices at other times that Sr Janet appears to have been crying. Even when Sr Margaret begins to feel sad in Sr Janet's company, and asks Sr Janet if she is sad, the response is often in the negative. This could be a case of projective identification.

Melanie Klein coined the term projective identification. She defined projective identification as 'an unconscious phantasy in which aspects of the self or an internal object are split off and attributed to an external object.' (Klein, 1997:1ff). This defence mechanism involves a situation where one person 'makes' the other person feel a certain emotion that they themselves are not able to experience (Hargaden & Sills, 2002). When the latter person feels an emotion that is very foreign to them, they wonder how they always seem to feel this emotion when in the company of the former person. What is happening is that the person who is not feeling the emotion has, in fact, projected it onto the other person who has to deal with this 'foreign' emotion.

The reason for projective identification is to allow one person (Sr Janet) to deal with the feeling of sadness by projecting it onto Sr Margaret, because she knows that Sr Margaret can handle the sadness, while sadness devastates Sr Janet. When Sr Margaret deals with the sadness with gentleness and patience, Sr Janet then seems to cope better with the sadness that lurks under the surface of her life.

Usually projective identification is discussed with regard to a client-therapist relationship. The client projects a feeling onto the therapist who is then able to metabolize the emotion and play it back in an acceptable form to the client. But it can happen in the community setting as described above. Awareness of this psychological dynamic can make us more compassionate to the person who projects their emotions onto us in the hope that we will be able to deal with this emotion.

The story goes that an important prelate went to visit the doctor for suspected depression. After many tests, the doctor told the prelate that he had not got depression, but that he was a carrier! Projective identification is a bit like this prelate who does not seem to have a particular emotion but brings out that emotion in his contact with other people.

Conclusion

Transference and projection happen all the time in community. Unless we understand these mechanisms we will find ourselves caught in interpersonal conflict that leads to disharmony and general frustration. When we understand transference and projection we have the capacity to slow down our immediate reactions, and begin to have a more compassionate view of others and of ourselves. The biggest challenge for each of us is to become reflective, pausing to allow ourselves to question what is going on when we feel strongly in response to the words, gestures and actions of others. When we manage to do this, we can avoid many mistaken judgements and unwise reactions.

Exercises

1. Think of someone who annoys, frustrates or angers you. Write down their qualities that cause this strong reaction in you. Then check with people in your community if they think you have any of these qualities. Be open to be surprised!

2. Think of someone who annoys, frustrates or angers you. Can you connect the reaction you have to this person with someone in your past who had the same effect on you? This could be an example of transference.

3. Can you think of someone who seems to react negatively to you? What is your reaction to them? What do you need to do to avoid taking their reaction personally?

PART THREE

Making the World Fit our Script

"Everyone takes the limits of his own field of vision
for the limits of the world."
Arthur Schopenhauer

I acknowledge Stewart and Joines for the title of Part 3, and for their general approach to discounting, passivity and symbiosis (Stewart & Joines, 2012:189). In this section of *Are We Together?* I will deal with how our perception of the world as expressed in our Script, determines, to a greater or lesser extent, the way we view the world. When we are in Script, we see the world in a particular way, and find it difficult to acknowledge that others may view things differently. As a result, when in Script, we ignore parts of reality that don't fit our way of thinking (Chapter 16), or we change our perception of reality to fit into our Script (Chapter 17). By ignoring parts of reality, we limit ourselves, and tend to depend on others in an unhealthy symbiotic relationship that either keeps us in our Child ego state, or ignores the Child ego state when we relate with others (Chapter 18).

The material in Part 3 is based on the work of the Schiffian school of TA (Schiff et al. 1975). The Schiffs focused mainly on the idea of passivity, where people fail to solve problems by the way they *discount* or ignore reality. Linking their approach with the more classical school of Berne provides a rich combination of insights that contribute to widen our fields of vision of how community works, and how our Script shapes our interpersonal dynamics.

Chapter Seventeen

Mind Blindness

"The eye sees only what the mind is prepared to comprehend."
Robertson Davies

The title for this chapter comes from a term coined by Baron-Cohen (1995) whose work focuses on the challenges of autism. He asks, 'Imagine what your world would be like if you were aware of physical things but were blind to the existence of mental things' (Baron-Cohen, 1990:81ff). When we are blind to certain aspects of reality we can be sure that the culprit for the blindness is our Script.

When we are in Script, we have a certain vision of life that is based on decisions that we made with the limited knowledge we gathered when we were very young. These early decisions are firmly rooted in our unconscious, and hence when we view the world as adults, we view it with the eyes of an earlier child who perceived reality from the narrow confines of childhood. As a result, we can be blind to the expanded world of the adult.

When a community comes together and begins to live its communal life, there can come a time when its way of living becomes stuck in the ruts of routine. When this happens, a community may fail to see that the only difference between a grove and a grave is its depth! So, a community may continue living a sort of life that has become impoverished by the humdrum of daily life. It is in such a situation that massive discounting can take place both on an individual basis and also as a community. Change is resisted because few see the need for it. This is a case of mind blindness at a group level. When mind blindness sets in, people begin to discount reality.

Discounting

The Schiffs saw discounting as an internal mechanism that minimized or ignored some aspects of reality (Schiff, 1975:16). This could involve ignoring some aspects of the self, of other people, or of the situation in general. When we are in Script, we have not a full view of reality, and so naturally we are going to have a limited frame of reference that fits in with the Script.

Discounting, according to the Schiffs, is defined as '*unawarely ignoring information relevant to the solution of a problem*' (Stewart & Joines, 2012:191; Mellor & Schiff, 1975:296 ff). The Schiffian school of TA emphasizes the idea of solving problems proactively, and focuses on the sorts of ways we avoid facing or solving problems. They designed what they called the *discount matrix* as a way of identifying and gauging the levels of discounts that a person in Script might be employing to avoid solving problems (Schiff, 1975:16ff).

For the purpose of this book, I have chosen to use another model for explaining discounting that may be more useful in describing the process of avoiding solutions to problems. The model is based on Julie Hay's 'Steps to Success', (the six 'S's) which outline the various stages a person needs to take in order to achieve a goal (Hay, 2007). Some people have used these same stages of Julie Hay to highlight the levels of discounting that a person in Script can go through (Mitchell, 2007:10). I think this model may provide a clearer guide to communities as they begin to reflect on levels of discounting (Fig. 27).

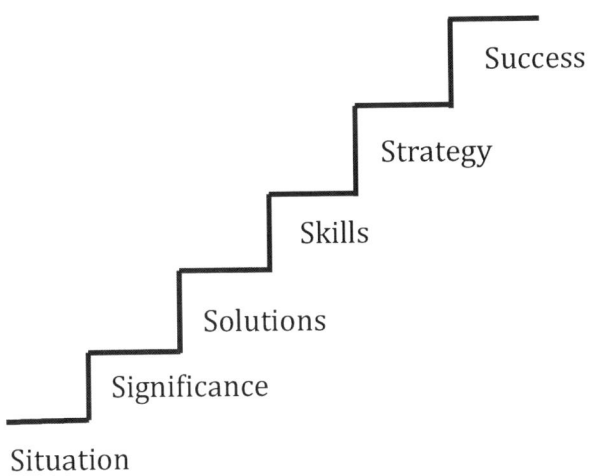

Fig. 27   A Model of Discounting (Hay, Mitchell 2007)

A Parable

To explore this model of discounting, imagine a group of religious that decided to examine how they interacted with the poor in their area. As they began the discussions, some of the levels of discounting kicked in. If we were to chart the levels, we can see how different members of the community were on different levels in this discount model.

The Situation

Some in the community could not see that there was a problem. They pointed out that when beggars came to the door, they were given food and money, and overall this was a valuable service to the wider community. This view discounted on the level of the situation in that these members did not recognise the level of poverty that existed in their area. Once a discount occurs at the level of the situation, no progress can be made until the situation is seen as problematic.

The Significance

Some members did acknowledge the situation, recognising that the community did not reach out to the poor like others religious did. They felt that the problem was not serious enough, and proposed to increase by 10% the amount they would allocate to the poor. Because the significance of the problem was being discounted, other than the increase in available funds, no significant change was going to take place. Fortunately, there were some in the community who felt that this was indeed an issue that was rather urgent, and felt that something should be done.

Solutions

Those who felt that something should be done, when challenged, were at a loss to know what exactly how things could change. They had a limited budget and could not see a way to augment this so as to have more for the poor. The words of Richard Bach seemed appropriate here: 'Argue for your limitations and sure enough they will be yours' (Bach, 1977,1988). In addition, some felt that they were not equipped to deal with the issues of the poor. And consequently, although these religious recognised the significance of the problem, they were at a loss to find a solution. In fact, they believed there *was* no solution. So, the discount was at the level of a solution.

Skills

This last group said that they had been teachers all their lives, and had no experience in interacting with the poor. They knew nothing about community development or community engagement, and they felt that they were too old to learn. They pointed out that many in the community were already involved in various aspects of parish life, and to begin to undertake a programme on community development was too demanding. In this case, these religious were discounting their own ability to learn new skills, despite having already undergone extensive training as teachers.

However, two of the community said that they already had read up on community development and felt that some plan could be put in place. They offered to draw up a proposal for the next meeting of the community.

Strategy

When the next community meeting took place, and the two volunteers were asked about the strategy that they had promised to draw up, they said that they had been busy and would have it for the following meeting. They also said that when they began to work out a strategy, they became somewhat afraid of all the things that needed to be done. As things turned out, no strategy ever saw the light of day. Even though one or two could see the need to reach the poor, and felt that it was vital to be associated with the poor, they did not pursue the matter. And even though a few could see possibilities, and had some skills to do something practical, they seemed to let things slide. Eventually, they said that a strategy was not necessary, and all they simply needed to do was to act purposely. As a result of discounting the need for a clear strategy, nothing practical was going to happen.

Luckily, however, there were two religious who began connecting with the local social services. They realised that the best strategy was to be collaborating with those already in the field of social work. Before long, they established a centre for homeless people that is still functioning and doing great work.

Success

Despite the success of the centre, established by these two religious, they seemed reluctant to take any credit for the work they had achieved. When people praise them, they change the subject quickly to focus on something else. It seems that they want to discount any idea that success should be acknowledged. When we discount our success, we deprive ourselves of the necessary strokes needed to keep us going through thick and thin.

Solving Discounts

From the example above, what emerges when we examine discounting is that a discount on any of the six levels can only be solved when that level of discount is being addressed. It is futile to address a level of discount if the previous levels have already been discounted. If, for instance, people are discounting on the level of the situation, there is no point in discussing the significance of the situation, or indeed the possible solutions to the problem. We need to identify the level of the discount, work with the discount and then and move from there.

Part of the challenge also in confronting discounts is to explore the internal dynamics that are causing discounts. Some of these will include: contaminations, life-positions, identification of the various ego states people may be tied to, and the games that are taking place. As people come to recognise their internal process, they may be more open to confront the discounts, and begin to account instead. By accounting we mean the acknowledgment of a problem, a situation or the existence of options in solving the problem.

How We Discount

Discounts can be mechanisms going on in our heads, or they may be observable behaviours that confirm the internal discounts. We will begin with examining the internal discounts first.

One of the ways we discount is when we view the situation with a certain level of *grandiosity*. Grandiosity involves maximising or minimising some aspects of others, the situation or ourselves. It could involve making mountains out of molehills, or making molehills out of mountains (Schiff, 1971: 71ff). We will see later that when we become grandiose, we use grandiosity to justify symbiosis, where we take over the control of things, or, alternatively, where we say we can't manage and rely totally on others. (See Chapter 19)

In the parable above, there was a fair degree of grandiosity, where the problem of dealing with the poor became so big, that people felt paralysed, instead of seeing the challenge as a possible project that could be done by the group.

Another way we discount is by *overdetailing*. Again, I suggest that many of the religious in their house were seeing too many details with regard to the outreach to the poor, instead of seeing the bigger picture. When we overdetail, we become overwhelmed, and then our thinking becomes ineffective, as we discount our ability to manage.

Or we can *overgeneralize* which led the religious to imagine that they had to feed *all* the poor, and *every* day. Such overgeneralizing leads them to view the task as a high mountain instead of seeing it as a large hill! Both overdetailing and overgeneralizing are types of thinking disorders that fail to see reality in any objective way.

From a behavioural point of view, the way that discounting can be detected is by observing what the Schiffs define as *passive behaviours* (Schiff, 1971:71ff; Schiff, 1975:12ff). For the Schiffs, passive behaviours are those behaviours that discount the person's ability to solve their problems.

The passive behaviours are: doing nothing, over-adaptation, agitation and incapacitation or violence. Passive behaviours are external manifestations of the internal processes of discounting, grandiosity and thinking disorders. We will comment briefly on each of the four passive behaviours.

Doing Nothing

Br Frank is part of a leadership group and is attending a meeting. The leader of the group is chairing the meeting, and as the session is coming to a close, he begins to itemise the tasks that have arisen from the meeting. Various members of the team volunteer to take on some of the jobs. Br Frank seems to be reluctant to volunteer for anything. The jobs are nearly all allocated, and the leader is beginning to wonder what is wrong with Br Frank. The leader comes to the last item and asks for someone to take on the task. There is a pause in the proceedings, and the rest of the team have realized that Br Frank has been noticeable by his lack of enthusiasm to roll up his sleeves. The silence continues for a while, until the leader asks Br Frank directly if he will do the job. Br Frank nods his head, and takes a note of what he was asked to do.

Br Frank is a good example of passive behaviour. He is *doing nothing.* Instead of taking an active part, he seems to be discounting his ability to solve any of the problems that the group is trying to manage. It seems that he has gone into a world of his own, has stopped thinking, or else has discounted his capacity to think and solve problems. It may also be, of course, that Br Frank is in his Rebellious Child ego state and expressing it by being overly passive.

Over Adaptation

Sr Mary is a member of a small rural community of five sisters. She seems very anxious to please the community leader. All the leader has to do is suggest an action or an idea, and Sr Mary agrees not only with the idea or action, but is first in to help out. After a day in school, she comes home and prepares the meal for the other Sisters. Normally, the Sisters take turns at the cooking, but very often Sr Mary volunteers to do the extra days, and especially the weekends. When many of the community want to relax, she is there to 'fill in'. How is this an example of discounting?

The principal factor involved here is the way Sr Mary *over adapts* to what she perceives are the wishes of the community. Instead of checking things out, she jumps in, and rescues the others even when nobody asks her to. She is always anticipating others' needs. But in the process, she is discounting her own needs. She is also discounting the fact that the group is using her. Her Child ego state adapts as a Compliant Child to the group, which she considers as Controlling Parents. Wishing to placate or please the Parent in the other members of the community, Sr Mary takes on an inordinate proportion of the community chores.

Agitation

At the conclusion of Mass, Br Dermot is ready to leave the church. The parish priest appears, and announces that he just wants to give the parishioners a breakdown of the financial balance sheet for the previous year in order to show accountability. Br Dermot is furious. He gives a big audible sigh causing people to look at him. Then he sits up in the pew, drumming his fingers on the front of the bench, and shifting his posture back and forth. The sighs continue unabated, and now he is beginning to tap his foot impatiently on the side of the kneeler. This is a good example of *agitation,* where Br Dermot employs nervous agitation in the face of frustration and annoyance. He could leave the church, and that would solve his problem. Other people slipped out silently, but Br Dermot keeps sighing, shifting and drumming his fingers and feet in response to his impatience. He is discounting his ability to solve the problem. He feels trapped, and seems blind to the possibility of simply getting out of the church. Agitation is a passive behaviour because it solves nothing, and builds up the frustration of the Rebellious Child.

Incapacitation and Violence

When Br Hilary gets frustrated, he drinks excessively. He could go to his room on a Friday evening after a particularly difficult time in school, or after a row with his superior and could consume a bottle of whisky on his own so that in the morning he is not fit for anything. This is an example of *incapacitation.* Instead of facing his difficulties in school, and working out strategies to overcome the problems with the students, he 'drowns his sorrow' to the extent that he becomes almost paralysed with drink. And instead of sitting down with his superior, he simply grumbles and frets without doing anything. He is discounting his ability to work things out, and also discounting the fact that he could get help from his brothers if he asked. The incapacitation is a sort of violence turned inwards that solves no problems, and makes Br Hilary even less able to function.

Sister Annemarie is like a time bomb ready to explode. When things don't go her way, she becomes furious, and often flings plates and dishes on the floor in a temper that is frightening at times. Many of the community are scared of her, waiting for the next outburst to happen. She has been advised to do an anger management course, but this suggestion did not go down well, and if anything increased the frequency of her outbursts. *Violence* in the Schiffian School is considered a passive behaviour because it involves discounting the various solutions to problems, and resorting to violent actions that solve nothing in the end.

Conclusion

By way of summary, we can say that mind blindness is caused by the internal mechanism that ignores some aspects of reality, and thereby maintains a rather dysfunctional frame of reference (see Chapter 17). The internal and external manifestations of mind blindness involve discounting either in thinking or behaviour, leading to a situation where problems are ignored or denied. The world is viewed, therefore, by an Adult with contamination coming often from both the Parent and Child ego states, leaving the Adult with diminished power to face the here-and-now reality.

Exercises

1. What are the current issues in your community that are being ignored, and at what level of discounting is this happening? Discuss.

2. Discuss in your community the sorts of changes that would make for a better community.

3. Which of the passive behaviours are you most inclined to use? Can you give examples when you used passive behaviours?

4. As you look at your religious organisation, how have you experienced passive behaviours or discounting?

Chapter Eighteen

Personal Perspectives

"Accustom yourself not to be disregarding
of what someone else has to say:
as far as possible enter into the mind of the speaker."
Marcus Aurelius

In fairly recent times, and before his resignation as the head of the Catholic Church, Pope Benedict XVI decreed that the language of the liturgy should be changed to better reflect the original Latin text. While attending Mass, I heard a young priest expressing great satisfaction that finally we would have language in the Mass that was a direct translation of the ancient Latin rite. From his perspective, this was an inspired move on the part of the Pope.

However, many religious were furious at this imposition of a clumsy and inelegant translation, and outraged at the insistence by the official Church on including several unintelligible theological concepts that would challenge the minds of the brightest theologians, but were a mystery to the ordinary parishioner.

The above situation where people have a very different reaction to the same event points to the subject of this chapter – our *frame of reference* (Mellor et. al., 1975:301ff). Simply put, our frame of reference can be defined as our point of view. It is about how we view the world wearing our own set of sunglasses. Some people wear green sunglasses, and therefore see the world with a tint of green. Others have red sunglasses and therefore the picture has a rosy tint! How does this happen?

The frame of reference is created from our Script where we have an unconscious life plan, and therefore will view reality through the eyes or lens of this Script.

The Schiffs defined the frame of reference as '*the structure of associated responses which integrates the various ego states in*

response to specific stimuli (Schiff, 1975:50ff).
Fig. 28 graphically captures this definition:

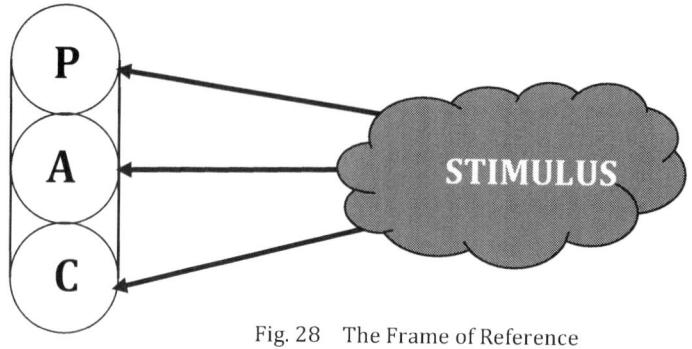

Fig. 28   The Frame of Reference

As we can see from Fig. 28, there is a stimulus that catches the attention of the three ego states, Parent, Adult, and Child. Each of the ego states responds to the stimulus in its own way. The Adult focuses on the here-and-now aspects of the stimulus, and sees and acts accordingly. But the external influences from the Parent ego state also have something to add to the picture, as does the archaic Child ego state. Both the Parent and Child ego states add some colour to the view, changing the overall perspective. So, when we have a frame of reference, all ego states combine to give the person their own unique view of the stimulus. And for each person the view will be different because each person has his or her own Script.

So, going back to the incident of the change in the liturgy, the priest hears of the proposed translation – the stimulus - in his Adult ego state, while his Parent ego state tells him how things *should* be according to the Controlling Parent of the Church. His Child ego state brings him back to his childhood, when he saw his own parents obeying the Parish Priest, and remembered how important it was to obey. Hence, the combined ego states are bound by a 'skin' to form a frame of reference from the unity of three ego states.

The religious hear the new language – the stimulus – in their Adult. Their Parent ego state tells them that they *should* obey, just like their parents did, while their Child ego state rebels like they did when their Controlling Parent confronted them in their childhood. Their Script became, 'Nobody is going to control my life.' The resultant response in the now is that the language perceived by their combined ego states, leads to their rebellion. The 'skin' that binds the three ego states together represents the combination of the ego states, and forms a very distinct frame of reference that views the translation as a crude way of controlling religious.

The Schiffs recognised that the Parent ego state plays a very important part in the formation of our frames of reference. Because our parents were the ones who shared their beliefs and prejudices, we are inclined to absorb these same beliefs and prejudices from them. For this reason, the Schiffs believed that sometimes there was a need for 'reparenting' in order for our frame of reference to change. In other words, when the Schiffs were working with severely emotionally disturbed children, they often replaced the 'crazy' introjected parent of the young person, and offered a new parent who would provide a new frame of reference (Schiff, 1975: 88ff).

Our frame of reference is therefore like tinted glasses already mentioned, which colour our whole perspective on life. The Schiffs said that the frame of reference provided 'an overall perceptual, conceptual, affective and action set, which is used to define the self, other people and the world.' (*Ibid*: 50).

Again from the incident above, we have the priest who reads the new text (perceptual), compares the changes with the previous text (conceptual), experiences the joy at the new version (affective), and begins to promulgate the adoption of the new missal (action set). The perceptual, conceptual and affective elements underpin his reaction to the new translation. All combine to create his frame of reference.

The Script and the Frame of Reference

When we think of Script, we remember that it is an unconscious life plan based on decisions made in childhood, reinforced by parents, justified by subsequent events, and leading to a chosen alternative (Chapter 1). By definition, the Script involves many discounts where young children pay attention to certain messages from their parents, and discount others. Although the children's perception of their parents was incomplete, they introjected *an* understanding of the parent behaviour, and this became their Parent ego state (P1). So, their frame of reference is going to reflect this incomplete perception they had of their parents.

In a sense, the Script *is* my frame of reference for the here-and-now, where I ignore some aspects of reality and favour others. The Script gives me my set of glasses with which I view the world, and as I view the world with a particular set of glasses, I will discount or ignore aspects of reality that do not fit in with my particular viewpoint.

When I said above that the Script *is* my frame of reference, I need to make a slight modification of that statement. Because the frame of reference also contains other definitions of reality that are not just Script based, there are aspects of the frame of reference that do not contain discounts. Complicated? Simply put, what we are saying is that most of my frame of reference is coloured by my Script, but the frame of reference is bigger than Script, and also includes aspects of my life that are not limited by Script (Stewart & Joines, 2012: 208).

With a frame of reference, therefore, we are going to view the world in a particular way. This means that the 'objective' reality (if such exists!) will have to be changed to fit my frame of reference. I will not see the objective reality but will *redefine* it in order to fit my pair of spectacles. This mechanism for changing 'reality' is called *redefining.*

The Function of Redefining

The Schiffs described redefining as 'the mechanism people use to maintain an established view of themselves, others and the world' (*Ibid*:55ff). Redefining, they said, was an internal mechanism to defend against anything that was inconsistent with their frame of reference. So, people redefine reality or distort reality so that it will fit into their Script.

For instance, take the priest we discussed at the start of the chapter. If his Script was 'I must do everything to please my parents', then everything that he does will be impacted by this original decision. So, when the new translation was introduced, his frame of reference only saw those aspects of the ruling of the Church that linked into his Script. He discounted the awkward phrases, the archaic theology, the unnecessary changing of words for the sake of change, because these aspects of the reality did not fit into his frame of reference. So, instead of pointing out these inconsistencies in the reform, he *redefined* the changes as a welcome innovation. Redefining occurs when a person distorts the perception of reality, and helps create new gestalts in order to fit into his or her Script.

One of the ways we can notice redefining taking place is by observing the verbal *tangential transactions* and the *blocking transactions* of people as they attempt to fit reality into their well-established Script. Tangential transactions and blocking transactions are neat ways of discounting the reality that seems obvious to most people, and then changing this 'reality' to fit a person's frame of reference.

Tangential Transactions

Tangential transactions take place when two people respond to each other from different perspectives (Schiff, 1975: 55: Mellor et al. 1975:303ff). So, if someone is asked a question that causes the person some discomfort, and especially when the question triggers their Script, then the other person will change the *frame of reference*, and answer another question that had not been asked. Imagine, for example, if the priest were asked, 'Do you not think the new liturgy is more like that of Trent?' Such a question puts him in an awkward corner, because his Script is 'I must do everything to please my parent.' To avoid this feeling of discomfort when his loyalty to his Church is under threat, the priest replies, 'The Council of Trent was a very important moment in the life of the Church.' That was a tangential transaction, where, instead of replying to the question that likened the liturgical changes to the imposition of the Council of Trent, the priest goes off on a tangent to answer a question that had not been asked, so as to maintain his equilibrium. Politicians are masters of the tangential transactions when they are in a tight spot!

Tangential transactions provide a good example of how discounting occurs on a behavioural level. When a person resorts to a tangential transaction, this provides the observer with a clear clue that the other person is struggling with maintaining the link between their frame of reference and the reality that is before them. And because the reality is at odds with their frame of reference, they want to change the reality. Consequently, they respond to a threatening question, by answering a more comfortable question even if this latter question had not been asked.

Blocking Transactions

A *blocking transaction* is another example of a mechanism that filters and structures external stimuli to help maintain our frame of reference. Like tangential transactions, blocking transactions provide us with a way of creating a gestalt that fits in with our Script, or helps maintain our Script. The essential element in blocking transactions is where the person, to avoid internal disorganisation or distress, will disagree with the definitions being used during the course of a conversation.

Going back to the incident mentioned at the beginning of the chapter where the religious were not happy with the imposition of the new translation of the Mass text. Were the religious asked why they did not simply obey the 'official Church', they would use a blocking transaction in reply by asking, 'What do you mean by 'official Church?' By challenging the definition of the word 'official', they are avoiding the discomfort of a situation that goes against their Script of 'Nobody is going to control my life.'

Blocking transactions are very effective ways of stopping a conversation, and putting the other person on the back foot. It distracts from the argument under way, and very efficiently brings the argument to a stop. Its aim is to avoid addressing the real issue because doing so would disturb a person's Script and threaten their frame of reference.

That said, both tangential and blocking transactions do not solve the situation, nor lead to a satisfactory resolution to a conflict. They simply discount the underlying core problem, and help maintain the frame of reference of both parties.

Conclusion

Often disagreements and misunderstandings in community are the result of differing frames of reference. The fact that each person has his or her own Script is a reality that we can find difficult to account for. So, when a discussion takes place, the very parameters for each person will be different, because the frames of reference are unique for each person. Hence, there is need for each person to stop, think, and then see the situation from the other's point of view. This ability to 'park' our viewpoint as we attempt to see things from another perspective is both challenging and at times frustrating. However, in order for a community spirit to grow and develop, this challenge is what we need to address.

Exercises

1. Try practising tangential and blocking transactions at your community sessions. Form groups of three, the one person being the observer, and the other two protagonists in the tangential transactions. One person is the interviewer, asking the interviewee questions on the importance of the vow of poverty. The other person uses tangential transactions to distract the interviewer from going where he/she wants to go. So, any question that the interviewer asks, the interviewee responds to a question they have not asked. At this stage, the interviewer goes along with the answers of the interviewee and continues ask other questions without trying to get the interviewee to stick to the questions asked. At the end of the process, the observer asks both parties what the process was like, and *then* tells them what it was like to observe.

2. After the first exercise, the same group form and this time the interviewer at his turn tries to keep the interviewee connected to the question. So, when the interviewee strays with either blocking or tangential questions, the interviewer brings them back to the topic in question. Again, at the end of the session, the observer asks both parties what the experience was like, and *then* shares what it was like watching the interaction.

Chapter Nineteen

Symbiosis

"We don't want to turn the safety net into a hammock
that lulls able-bodied people
into complacency and dependence."
Paul Ryan

Br Xavier is the superior of the community. He is an amazingly efficient man, taking care of the needs of the community members. He keeps an eye on everything so that the community members feel comfortable and relaxed. The timetable is made out for the year, and Br Xavier ensures that things are ticking along in line with the daily routine. There is always a good supply of provisions because each Saturday Br Xavier does a 'big' shopping, not forgetting to get some refreshments for the Friday night social. The finances of the house are in good shape because, although he is not the Bursar, Br Xavier keeps a steady eye on how the money is being spent, and realises that Br Brian is not very good at balancing the books. So, each month, Br Xavier sits down with Br Brian and together they do the accounts.

The community are very happy to have Br Xavier as their superior. He is kind and understanding, and anticipates all their needs. He seems to love doing all the jobs, and even when the community finds it difficult to manage their own laundry, Br Xavier gets a helper in to do the washing and ironing of the more elderly Brothers. They do notice, however, that Br Xavier never takes a break, and, at times, seems rather grumpy and distant especially when there is a lot to do. Luckily, there are some of the younger members of the community that seem to be able to jolly Br Xavier along, and Br Thomas especially seems to bring life to Br Xavier when he is in a bad mood.

The above description based on one or two of the more traditional community set ups, offers a good example of first order and second order symbiosis.

The concept of symbiosis refers to *where two people behave as though between them they form a whole person* (Schiff, 1977: 311ff). In the more classical school of TA, symbiosis means that neither person cathects the full complement of their ego states. You will remember from Chapter 6, that every person has *bound*, *unbound* and *free* energy distributed across his or her Parent, Adult and Child. So, when two people interact with each other, they are each working with three ego states – Parent, Adult and Child. This makes for six ego states potentially available to the interaction between the two parties.

In a symbiotic relationship, however, instead of having six ego states at the service of the interaction, there are only three functioning ego states at play. In Fig. 29 we see that the person on the left is using his Parent and Adult ego states and neglecting to pay attention to her Child ego state. The other person on the right is only engaging her Child ego states, while using the Parent and Adult ego state of the other person, and neglecting to engage her own Parent and Child ego state. The dotted circles indicate the ego states not in use.

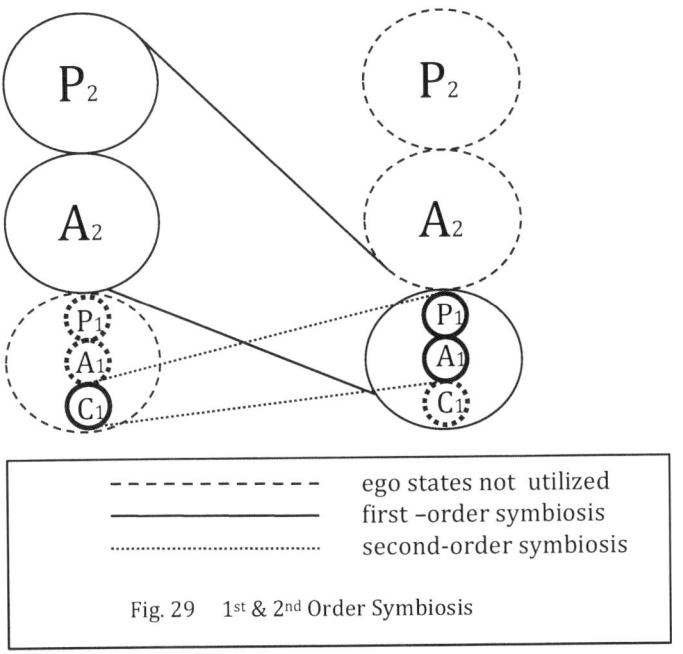

– – – – – – – – – –	ego states not utilized
———————	first –order symbiosis
····························	second-order symbiosis

Fig. 29   1st & 2nd Order Symbiosis

The first order symbiosis is where the P_2 and the A_2 represent the behaviour of Br Xavier. He is cathecting his Parent and Adult ego states to care for the Child ego state (C_2) of the community. The community have no need for their P_2 and the A_2 because everything they need is being supplied by the superior. So, instead of six ego states being in action, there are only three with Br Xavier unconsciously creating a dependency or a first order symbiotic relationship with the community. The community, as a result, retreats into a position of passive dependence where they over rely on the superior for all their needs.

In Fig. 29 above, you will also notice that in the C_2 on the right side, there are the earlier ego states of the Witch Parent, the Little Professor and the Somatic Child (see Chapter 3). These are the ego states of Br Thomas in the community. Even though Br Xavier is being Parent and Adult to the community, and neglecting his own Child needs, the presence of Br Thomas is forming an unconscious second order symbiotic relationship with the superior where, from Br Thomas Child ego state (C_2), he is using his P_1 and the A_1 (also called Fairy Godmother and Little Professor respectively) to support the C_1 of Br Xavier. In a sense, out of his awareness, Br Xavier *is* getting his basic Child ego state needs met by the support, banter and playfulness of Br Thomas.

Script and Symbiosis

Part 3 of *Why are we Together?* is focussed on fitting our vision of the world to the Script that we made early on in life. When we talk about symbiosis, we are showing how people discount part of themselves, ignoring or discounting one or more of their ego states in order to maximise gratification and minimize discomfort (Schiff, 1977:311). As children grow and relate with their parents, they learn to adapt to the parents in order for them to get their needs met. The Script is their life plan that they decided upon as the best solution to please their parents, receive love and acceptance, and feel OK about themselves however conditional that Okness might have been.

The Schiffs maintained that the goal of symbiosis is getting one's needs met. Usually people get their needs met by acting autonomously, and using all their ego states to work out the best way to live in the world (*Ibid*:311). However, when these needs were not met in childhood, the Little Professor (A1) cleverly strategized a way of satisfying the child's needs, and this involved creating a symbiotic relationship. By becoming either over-responsible and excluding the Child ego state, or alternatively, by being in Constant Child and remaining very dependent (see Chapter 5) on the parent, children hope to gain the support of their parents. Thus, symbiosis becomes a type of dysfunctional strategy of surviving by either over-care giving for others, or becoming very dependent on others by over-care receiving (Oller-Vallejo, 2002, 178ff).

When we enter into a symbiotic relationship with others, we are playing a type of game (Chapter 14). Games are attempts to re-enact symbiotic relationships that we did not resolve with parents, or they could be angry reactions to how our parents failed to provide us with everything we needed for healthy development (Lankford, 1972:15-17).

Also, when we engage in passive behaviours (Chapter 16) we are externally demonstrating our wish to establish a symbiotic relationship, discounting our own ability to employ the full-range of our bound, unbound and free psychic energy, and become dependent as a result.

A traditional community of religious Sisters or Brothers is potentially a glasshouse situation where unhealthy symbiotic relationships can grow and flourish. Because of the idea of *common life* where the physical needs of each religious are met, the danger is that religious become dependent on the institution to supply their every requirement. Religious often do not have to worry about where the money will come from, where they will get their clothes, or how they will pay for their annual holiday. They simply have to rely on the community to supply all their needs. Like all expressions of symbiosis, its main aim is to shift the responsibility for a problem or difficulty onto the other person, inviting them to solve the problem so that the individual does not have to take any personal responsibility.

Nowadays, it is true, religious communities are very different where members are held accountable for the way they live their lives. However, there is always the danger that symbiotic mechanisms can creep into a community in very subtle and unconscious ways. Because everyone has developed a Script, symbiotic dynamics are inevitable in any grouping of people, and even in friendship there will always be some element of the symbiotic relationship. Sometimes it is healthy, while at other times less so.

Unhealthy Symbiosis

When both people compete for the Parent or Child position then difficulties arise. In community, there may be a designated community leader, but sometimes there can be psychological and effective leaders in competition with the officially appointed leader. In Fig. 30, we see two people vying for the leadership position, and in competition to see who will be the Parent and Adult. The have excluded their Child ego state, and have serious Parent contamination of the Adult in their fight for Parent hegemony.

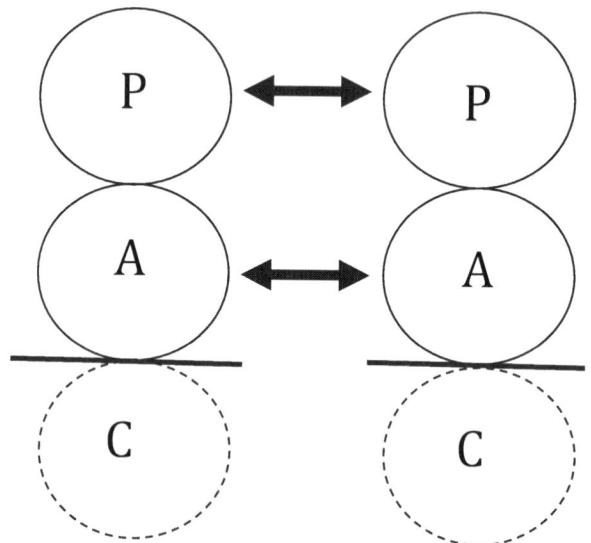

Fig. 30   Competitive Parent Symbiosis (Schiff, 1975)

When both compete for the Child position, then the situation becomes very unstable, and can result in anger, escalation, incapacitation and violence (Fig. 31.)   In communities where there are often outbursts of temper, or where one member of the community refuses to speak to another member, we then have two people in a competitive symbiotic relationship, with each one discounting their Parent and Adult ego states, and seeing the world from the Child frame of reference.

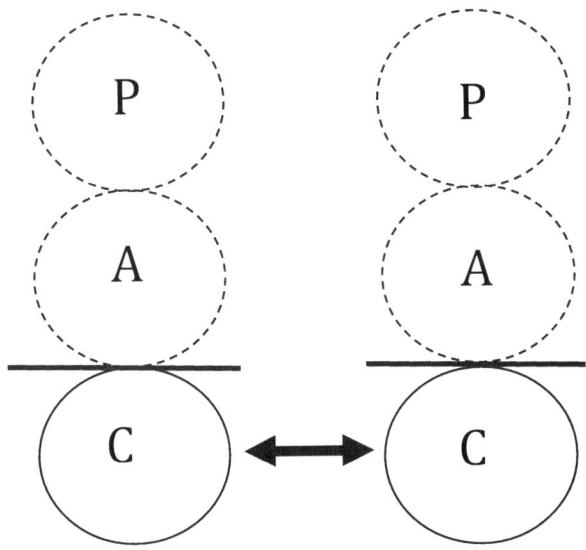

Fig. 31   Competitive Child Symbiosis (Schiff,1975)

Symbiotic Invitations

Another example of an unhealthy symbiotic relationship is what is known as *symbiotic invitations* (Hart, 1976:253-254). A symbiotic invitation begins with a passive ulterior stimulus, inviting the other person into a symbiosis. In plain language, the symbiotic invitation is where someone wants someone else to do something for him or her, and instead of asking directly, he or she will probably use one of the four passive behaviours, to get the other person to respond. This type of transaction is very common in community life.

For example, Sister Philomena would love a banana, but she doesn't feel like going into the kitchen as fetching it herself. So, she comments at table, 'I see we are out of bananas.' At that, Sister Pauline, jumps up, runs into the kitchen, and brings some bananas with her. Sister Philomena had just issued behind the simple social message 'I see we are out of bananas,' - an ulterior message to Sister Pauline on a non verbal psychological level –

"Please, Pauline will you get them?' -, and Sister Pauline obliged.

It is amazing how difficult people find it to ask for what they want. The dictum, 'Ask for 100% of what you want 100% of the time' which we mentioned earlier is easy to say, but difficult to put into practice. The symbiotic invitation is the Child ego state (Little Professor) seeking clever ways of asking for something without having to ask directly.

Healthy Symbiosis

A natural symbiosis occurs, for example, when a child is born. The infant has yet to develop its Parent and Child ego states, and relies or depends on the competence and the nurturing care of the Parent and Adult in the parent. As the child grows and develops, the parent begins to encourage the child to assume more and more responsibility in step with the child's physical, emotional and intellectual development. With time, the children assumes the tasks appropriate to their age, until they reach adulthood where they will, hopefully, have the capacity to have access to their three ego states. What began as a dependency becomes autonomy and interdependence.

In communities where someone becomes very ill, a healthy symbiosis kicks in. The invalided religious has lost the Parent and Adult capacity to fend for themselves, and needs the care and love of other members of the community to make up for this momentary dependence.

Conclusion

The Schiffs make the point that every significant relationship has an element of symbiosis to it (Schiff, 1975:6ff). Friendships involve symbiosis all the time. When the symbiosis is unhealthy, however, then relationships are affected because one party is not accessing all their ego states. In a symbiotic community, the quality of life is impoverished when some members wait for others to make the first move in showing affection, initiative or imagination. The challenge facing communities is for people to develop a healthy interdependence with each person contributing fully to the creation of a community spirit. When everyone in the community accesses all their ego states as they interact with each other, then the quality of communal living improves a hundredfold, and each member grows and develops into mature and vibrant religious people.

Exercises

1. Share with your community examples of people with whom you are in a symbiotic relationship i.e. people you depend on and without whom you would find life more difficult.

2. Practise giving symbiotic invitations to a partner in your group, and notice how they work!

3. Practise asking *directly* for what you want. Pay attention to the way you do this, and discover which way has the most beneficial result.

4. Share as to what aspects of your life do you feel challenged to confront with regard to levels of dependence.

PART FOUR

The Group Process

"A small group of thoughtful people could change the world.
Indeed, it's the only thing that ever has."
Margaret Mead

In the first three parts of *Are We Together?* we examined the individual human personality, and how the individual interacts within the social dynamics of a community. Transactional Analysis, by definition, was considered by Berne 'a unified system of individual and social psychiatry' that highlighted the intrapsychic (within the mind) and interpersonal aspects of the development of the person (Berne, 1961: 12). The term *Transactional Analysis* was designedly used by Berne to show how important the transactions that take place between people are, and how these transactions affect the development of the individuals and the community to which they belong.

We examine in Part 4 the nature of a group, using Berne's theory on the structure and dynamics of groups (Berne, 1963). Chapter 20 studies the nature of the group structure, and *certain* aspects of group dynamics. At the outset, I want to advise the reader that I am only taking a few of Berne's ideas with regard to the structure and dynamics of organisations and groups; a more extensive treatment is not within the scope of this book.

For Chapter 21, we borrow from the work of Scott Peck's theory of group development, and connect Scott's approach with that of TA. We will use Peck's four-stage development of groups that will provide a backdrop to integrate TA theory into the idea of the stages of group development. Chapter 22 outlines the role and value of leadership in a community when current models favour shared leadership. In chapter 23 we reflect the qualities of leadership necessary for the creation of a healthy and vibrant community spirit that is both caring and empowering for each member of the community to take individual responsibility for the quality of community life.

Chapter Twenty

The Nature of the Group

"We of alien looks or words must stick together."
C.J. Sansom

In recent years a number of religious communities have moved away from their established institutions and ministries, and begun to work in more rural and poor areas of the world where the needs are greatest. These communities were used to a fairly regular routine, with definite times for meals, prayers and work. But the needs were no longer that urgent in those developed parts of the world, and the life of the religious had become staid and comfortable without any real challenge. The members of these communities needed a new approach, and they felt that only by moving away from the established centres would they manage to do something new.

When they moved, they did not realize the challenge that they were facing. The supports and structures in the more traditional communities were no longer available, and certain strains and pressures began to surface both in the community and in the work.

Before long, messages were being sent to the leadership team, that things were not working out well. Sometimes, it was due to the pressures of small group living, and at other times, the problem was the task that the group had set out to accomplish. Either the work was too difficult, and the religious were not properly equipped to face the ministry, or external factors such as opposition from the local clergy were preventing the task from getting done.

Probably more crucial was the internal tensions that were arising as the groups began to struggle with the dynamics of the newly formed groups. It seemed that the stresses were not only coming from without, but also were happening from within.

The Group Work

Berne held that a group performs two different types of work (Berne, 1963:58). One aspect of the work is performed in the external environment; in this case the work of the community is to serve the poor in the rural areas. This he called 'the group activity'. The other work occurs within the group itself, which Berne called 'the group process'. The group process refers to the efforts that are required in order to maintain the healthy functioning of the group. Both aspects of the group dynamics need to be attended to for the task to get done, and for the group to grow and develop.

When the group process is healthy with good boundaries, and a certain level of equilibrium is achieved, then the focus can be on the task. When, on the other hand, there is internal conflict amongst the members, then the life of the group becomes the focus of the energy, and the task can suffer.

What often can happen when the internal life of the group becomes dysfunctional is that the members of the group simply focus on their individual work commitments, and become resigned to a community life that is merely going through the motions.

The Group Process

Berne held that the way a person saw his or her place within the group influenced the dynamic of the group process. He devised what he called the *group imago,* which identified where members situated themselves within a group (*Ibid*:28). Fig. 32 charts the configuration of an imaginary group.

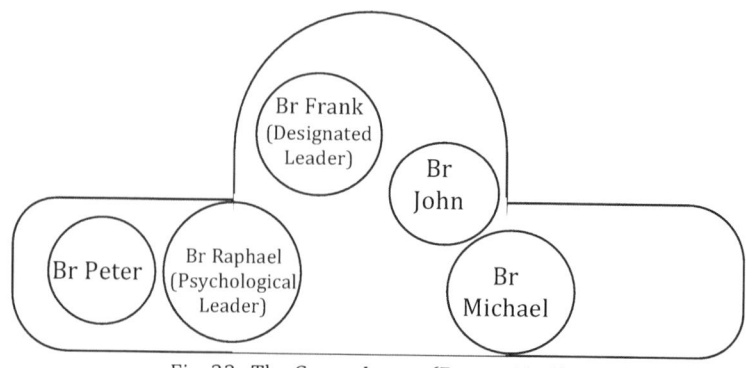

Fig. 32 The Group Imago (Berne, 1963)

In this imaginary community, there are two leaders: the designated leader (Br Frank) and the psychological leader (Br Raphael). We will discuss the various types of leaders later. Suffice it to say that having two leaders in a community will impact on the dynamics of the group. In the group imago, we see that Br John aligns himself with the designated leader, and they work very well together. Br Peter is more connected with Br Raphael, the psychological leader, and together they collaborate to create a good atmosphere in the community. Br Michael is more distant from the rest of the group, but he does feel a connection with Br John, and although they do not share at a very deep level, there is a respect and acceptance that makes Br Michael feel at home.

As part of studying the group process, it is also necessary to examine the sort of transactions that take place between the various members of the group. In Chapter 10 we examined the complementary, crossed and ulterior transactions that take place between people. Looking at the group imago involves reflecting on the types of transactions that occur between the various members of the community. What sorts of complementary transactions take place? When are there crossed transactions? How often do ulterior transactions occur? What sorts of games occur? Asking these questions gives an idea of the group process, and offers the group a fascinating if somewhat challenging view of how the group process is working.

The main consideration in this analysis of the group is whether the need to preserve the above structure becomes more important than the work at hand, or whether the task at hand is impacting on the quality of the interactions between the people (*Ibid:* 31).

The Major Internal Group Process

The major internal group process refers to the relationship between the leader(s) and the rest of the group. In Fig. 33, we see that same community mentioned above is now configured in a way that shows an internal boundary between the designated leader and the rest of the community. In many communities today, there is what is called 'shared' leadership, where each person takes their own responsibility for various tasks in the community. Whether this is the case or not, there will always be some members of the community who take on more of a leadership role, and when this happens, they take up the role of 'managing' the moments of conflict that will inevitably occur within a group. From the diagram we see that the role of leadership is somehow to control the pressure that comes from the group itself to 'upset' the equilibrium or the status quo. Whether we admit it or not, every group needs a level of stability, and it is the role of the leader to oversee the maintenance of this stability.

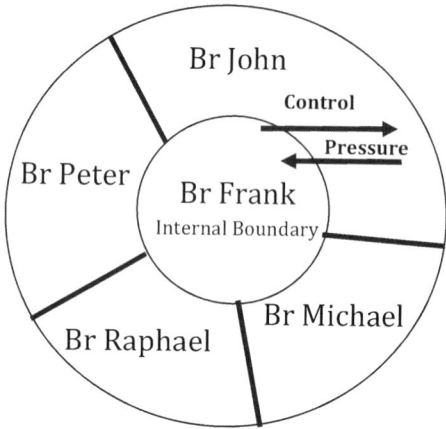

Fig. 33 The Major Internal Group Process (Berne, 1963)

The Minor Internal Group Process

The minor internal group process refers to the interactions that occur between the members of the community, as opposed to the interaction between the leaders and the group. In other words, how do Brothers Peter, Michael, Raphael and John transact with one another? From Fig. 34 we see that the transactions involve the stimulus and the response between the individual Brothers. When talking about the group process, we are simply indicating the reality that members of a group create their identity, and establish their boundaries as the group forms. Each member of the community will express him or herself in a particular way. People have their own egogram where they distribute their psychic forces in their own individual way (Chapter 4). This impulse for individuals to have their needs met is called their *individual proclivity* (*Ibid:* 57).

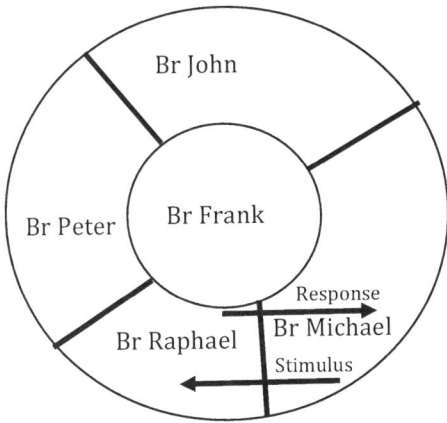

Fig. 34 The Minor Internal Group Process (Berne, 1963)

In Fig. 34, we can imagine that interactions between Br Raphael and Br Michael as shown in in the stimulus and response between the two members can impact positively or negatively on the major internal group process, and where the leader has the task of maintaining or facilitating the equilibrium of the group (Fig. 33).

An individual proclivity that is in harmony with the group will strengthen the groups; Berne calls this a *syntonic proclivity* (*Ibid:*102). Dystonic proclivities, on the other hand, pose problems for the overall balance of the group. When the amount of dystonic proclivities abound, the group is in trouble.

The External Group Process

Berne also comments on the external factors that can influence the structure of the group. In the case of communities, there are many factors impinging on the homeostasis or balance within the group (*Ibid:*35).

When members of the community are transferred to other communities, the life of the community changes radically; in fact, it is a new group. Other external factors can be more dramatic – Berne talks about hurricanes – but the task of the group is still the same, *viz.* to maintain a level of balance so that the group survives or thrives.

One of the problems in some religious communities is that they can live within a cocoon, ignoring the reality that surrounds them. In this climate of recession and of economic crises, of political and environmental upheavals, communities must not remain immune to the world in which they live.

The community is called to respond to the outside influences, and maintain the spirit of group in the face of the change that surrounds it. (Fig. 35)

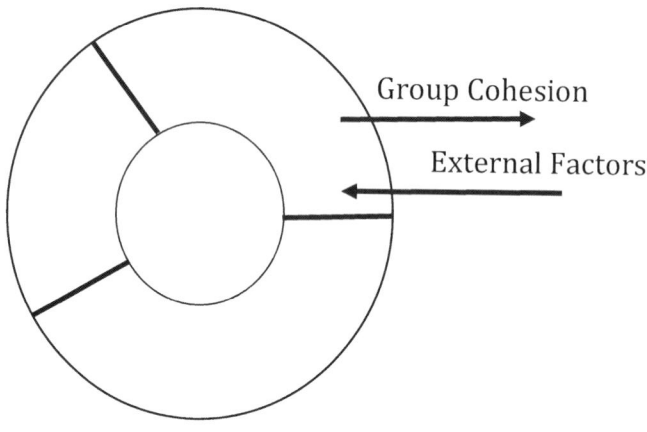

Fig. 35 The External Group Process (Berne, 1963)

The Group Dynamics

Berne said that the main concern of every healthy group is to survive as long as possible, or at least until its task is done (Berne, 1963:90). One Congregation put it nicely when they said, "We stay as long as we are needed and not as long as we are wanted." When the task in done, the reason for the group ceases to exist. While, therefore, there is work to be done, the quality of community living needs careful attention so that the members can fulfil their obligations and maintain a healthy quality of life. The group dynamics involve, therefore, both the task and the process in a healthy balance.

The two sets of influences that threaten the existence of a group are the internal forces and the external forces, as mentioned above. When there are external forces threatening the survival of the group, this threat becomes the real focus of the group – it is a matter of survival. The task becomes secondary, and the group gathers to support the individual and the group.

Many communities forget that constant vigilance is needed to regulate the quality of community life. Individual needs and concerns can threaten the overall health of the group – their proclivities – and communities need to be aware how important it is for the organisational structure – the community – to survive (*Ibid:*91). What often happens in communities is that the interpersonal transactions resulting from the individual proclivities impact negatively on the quality of the group. When the group fails to give attention to this internal pressure, the group process begins to deteriorate.

In the past, it was the role of the leader to 'control' this pressure, and bring the group to a healthy equilibrium. When the leadership is shared, the responsibility falls on each member of the group. One of the dangers when the responsibility for the cohesion of the group falls on the shoulders of all is that it becomes the responsibility of no one.

The Group Structure

An interesting way of viewing the group community structure is to link the elements of the group structure with the ego state model. Drego does this when she discusses the cultural parent and its impact on the individual and group (Drego, 1996: 58ff). I would like to take this idea of using the Parent, Adult and Child (PAC) model to show the elements of the community dynamic, and thereby indicate the interaction between three important elements of the community structure and dynamic: etiquette, technicalities and character (Fig.36 below).

The Etiquette

Berne maintains that 'the group etiquette is based on the general social etiquette and includes all items of etiquette which are different from the general etiquette, but are acceptable to the group' (Berne, 1963: 151).

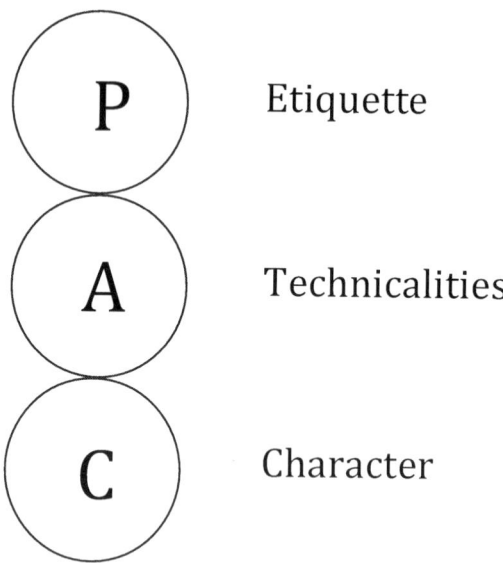

P	Etiquette
A	Technicalities
C	Character

Fig. 36 The Structure of Community (Drego, 1996)

So, for religious communities, in addition to the ordinary laws of the land, the main additional sources of etiquette are the Constitutions and Statutes of the Congregation. These define how the community and individual are going to live, and marks out the behaviours that are appropriate to religious life. In a sense, it is the contract between the members and the Congregation. In ego state terms, it is the Parent ego state outlining how the member is to behave.

Technicalities

Berne calls this 'the technical culture' and refers to the very concrete aspects of the life of the community. It also refers to the work that the community is engaged in (*Ibid:*150). It would include such things as the house, the furniture and the various pieces of equipment that the community uses in the day-to-day reality of life. Hence, the technicalities refer to the Adult in the group structure in the sense that the Adult deals with the here-

and-now concrete reality, and the technicalities deal with the physical and concrete aspects of the community.

Character

Group character, according to Berne, 'includes departures from the social contract'. This includes the various proclivities of the individual members that find expression in behaviour that disrupts the harmony and regularity of the group. This is the Child ego state energy, resisting the etiquette of the Parent, and demanding that the Child's needs and wants be taken into account. The character is a more primitive element of the community structure, and can subvert the rules and regulations of the Parent, just like the Rebellious Child does with the Controlling Parent.

Conclusion

The identification of the various forces at play in the life of a community provides us with an understanding of how communities are affected by internal and external influences. Both the internal and external forces will challenge both the community task and the community process. Since the community task and community process are equally vital in analysing the life of the community, the neglect of one aspect of community will immediately impact on the other side of the story.

The structure of the community involves certain ways of behaviour on the part of the members. The etiquette or the Parent ego state of the community, as contained in the Constitutions and Statutes of a Congregation, will determine to some extent how the community behaves. In counterbalance to the etiquette, are the individual proclivities of the members that can be in tension with the etiquette, and can sabotage the ideals as laid down in the Constitutions. The Adult of the community refers to the technicalities that we discussed, and this includes the actual structure and furnishings of the house, which also play a role in the creation of a community set-up.

Once the various structures of the community are established, the group then needs to study how the group is going to develop. This is the subject of the following chapter.

Exercises

1. You might like to draw your group imago. Do, this for yourself first, and then see how the others in the community draw theirs. This can be an interesting sharing, as it offers each one an insight into how they view their interactions with others, and then offers another view from the rest of the community.

2. Discuss the various external factors that impact on the life of the community. These factors can be divided into positive and negative ones.

3. In order for a community to grow and develop, the frequent use of a facilitator is very helpful. Discuss the idea of your community engaging a facilitator.

4. What individual proclivities do you think you have that might impact on the life of the community? Discuss this question with the community. Do the other members agree?

Chapter Twenty-One

Group Development

"Coming together is a beginning.
Keeping together is progress.
Working together is success."
Henry Ford

A Congregation of Sisters came together to form new communities, and develop relevant ministries in response to the changing needs of the world. For the first month they decided to live together and 'form community'. The experience was immensely positive for each of the group that gathered for this experience. At the end of the month, many of the Sisters were expressing sentiments like, 'This is the first time I have really experienced real community.' Every one seemed hugely enthusiastic about the process that they had undergone, and were keen to continue for another month.

However, as the months followed, and the group began to get used to each other, some cracks seemed to be appearing, and the euphoria of the early days was somewhat fading as interpersonal difficulties began to emerge. The group was changing, and not everyone was happy.

Group Development.

In this chapter, we will examine how groups develop, and how group theory can be useful in assessing where a group stands with regard to its development. Hill and Gunner report that more than 100 theories of group development exist (Hill & Gunner, 1973:355ff); from the early work of Kurt Lewin on the Individual Change Process, and Tuckman's Stages Model to Morgan, Salas & Glickman's Team model, we are not at a loss for finding a theory of group development. Berne's own theory of phases of the group is also worth studying but may be rather theoretical for the purpose of discussing community life (Berne, 1963:321ff). The theory, therefore that I have chosen to link to TA theory is that of Scott Peck whose four-phase model offers a valuable way to examine the stages of group development in a simple yet organic way (Scott Peck, 1988:86ff). In describing each of the phases, I will link Scott Peck's theory with the stages both in Berne and Tuckman for those who wish to explore group development further.

The Four Stages

According to M. Scott Peck, any group of people coming together to create a community goes through four very distinct phases. This development is not a linear process; some groups may skip a stage and have to revisit it later. The four stages he outlines are: pseudo-community, chaos, emptiness and true community.

Pseudo-Community

As the title suggests, a pseudo-community is characterised by conflict-avoidance where many strategies are employed to create a sense of cohesion. This is Berne's provisional group imago stage (Berne, 1963:321). A pseudo-community begins with an initial period of deep sharing, and superficial emotional enmeshment, while simultaneously discounting different frames of references, and avoiding any trace of resentments or disagreements (*Ibid*:86ff). This is the symbiotic stage where people depend on each other and can, at times, canonise dependence for fear of challenging individual responsibility.

The Life-position appears to be I'm OK – You're OK, where *getting on with* everyone in the group is a forced and dishonest strategy. Individual differences are discounted, and the core etiquette is, 'Don't offend anybody!' The complementary transactions seem at first to be Child-to-Child, and Nurturing Parent to Free Child.

The passive behaviour of 'do nothing' becomes a frequent characteristic of this phase when people do not want to change, or raise issues that could disturb or upset the peace. Discounting predominates where difficulties are ignored in the name of tolerance. This is Tuckman's *forming* stage (Tuckman, 1965, 387; 396).

However, what lies underneath the positive attitude of the pseudo-community are many ulterior transactions that never find expression or resolution. The Parent contamination forbids any disagreement, and the Child contamination fears any form of robust confrontation. There is little or no space allowed for the individual to express his or her views, for the group has to speak with a united 'we'. The games that people play are mainly done by the Rescuer.

Chaos

While the pseudo-community avoids conflict, the phase of chaos involves the emergence of individual differences, which, not infrequently causes the group to self-destruct (*Ibid*:90ff). Differences awaken the Rescuer who seeks to heal and convert the 'misguided' members in the vain hope that they will revert to the pseudo-community position. The game, "Why Don't You...Yes but.' features large in the discussions where advice is offered and then rejected. When this happens, the Persecutor takes over from the Rescuer, discounting the intrinsic worth of the dissenting voices, and persecuting the wayward for their refusal to accept the group etiquette. This is Tuckman's *storming* phase (*Ibid*.388; 396), or Berne's adapted group imago phase (Berne, 1963:321)

Complementary transactions from Controlling Parent to Rebellious Child escalate without any seeming end to the disagreements. There are many ulterior transactions that only highlight the psychological undercurrents that were lurking around in the pseudo-community phase.

The Life-position most evident is the paranoid one that seeks *to get rid of* the opposition. And immediately following this persecutory approach, the group falls into the Life-position of I'm Not OK- You're Not OK, where the group feels despair that it is *getting nowhere with* the situation.

The passive behaviours of agitation, incapacitation and violence can be frequently in evidence during the chaotic phase.

The fact that the group finds itself with frames of reference that are incompatible, move the group into Parent-Parent complementary transactions where prejudice feeds prejudice, and anger increases. This anger can often be directed to the designated leader of the group who is blamed for failing to give a direction to the group, and move it out of chaos. In the Drama Triangle, we have each of the actors – Persecutor, Rescuer and Victim – playing in a drama that often turns out to be a tragedy.

Emptiness

Scott Peck maintains that the way through chaos to true community is by going through emptiness (*Ibid*: 94ff). This phase involves members revealing the fragilities that lie beneath the surface. It means that people begin to uncover the contaminations that limit their Adult ego state from dealing with the here-and-now. At times, there can be feelings of I'm not OK and You're not OK, where the individual members feel somewhat isolated in the emptiness. It is when members accept the sense of being lost, that awareness begins to grow and develop. Tuckman's *norming* phase fits in here (Tuckman, 1963, 389; 396) as does Berne's operative group imago (Berne, 1963: 321)

The members relinquish the need to be in the Controlling Parent position, and move toward the Adult approach to life in their interactions with each other. There is more of the Inquirer and the Initiator roles being taken up (Chapter 11). The members begin to understand the dysfunctional dynamics that have created the chaos, and they leave behind the Pollyanna view of community life where problems were not allowed to exist. Crossed transactions are more frequent at this stage as people are willing to engage their Adult in robust conversations, and where people are prepared to agree to disagree.

Games are abandoned, and members begin to listen to the variety of frames of reference in the attempt to see reality from the other's point of view. The tangential and blocking behaviours give way to direct and honest interchanges.

The Free Child's fears and apprehensions are allowed to emerge in the group. Members are willing to admit that they can be in the 'I'm Not OK-You're OK position, and express their need of the support from the community in order to move to a healthier place. They humbly recognise that their individual proclivities are sometimes problematic for the group to handle, and they are willing to contract with the community to change their unhelpful behaviours for the sake of the community.

True Community

Following what Scott Peck calls the 'dying' of the Emptiness phase, the group moves into the true community phase (*Ibid*:103ff). Whereas the pseudo-community was conflict avoiding, true community is conflict resolving. The move to true community is a move to the I'm OK – You're OK position that recognises both the strength and fragility of each person in the community.

Peace pervades as members connect in a cohesive manner, and find that individual proclivities are let go for the sake of the group spirit in what Berne called the secondary adjusted group imago (Berne, 1963:321). Here, there is no attempt to heal or convert; instead dialogue becomes the common practice. Acceptance is at the core of the true community. It is at this stage that intimacy is achieved where the members reveal themselves as they are. There is increased awareness individually and collectively, and a level of spontaneity develops that never existed up to this phase. It is at this stage that the group enters the *performing* phase (Tuckman, 1965, 390; 396).

Facilitation

For a community to move through these four phases in an effective manner, the role of a facilitator is crucial. Many religious communities have attempted to 'go it alone' and have foundered on the rocks of resentment, hurt, and unexplored fantasies. It is highly recommended that communities engage a facilitator on a regular basis to 'walk' with the community on its journey to true community. In truth, it is doubtful if a community can grow in any real way without the influence of an external guide or facilitator.

Conclusion

Creating vibrant cohesive communities is probably the greatest challenge facing religious life today. In a world torn by strife, war, economic, social and religious crises, it seems that the breakdown of institutions is more the rule than the exception. Hence, the need for examples of people who can live together in love and harmony has never been more necessary. The early history of the church was marked by such groups who formed such strong loving communities to the extent that, according to Tertullian, onlookers would exclaim, 'Look, see how these Christians love one another!' How much more do religious need to demonstrate how communities, true communities are possible in a world of fragmentation and injustice!

We have seen how when a person enters a group, the reality is that the group enters that individual (de Graaf, 2013, 311). The group dynamic changes people, just as people change the group dynamic. Becoming aware of the stages in a group process goes some way to developing what Hargaden calls a *'third'* or triangular space which allows the person reflect on what is happening in a group, and attune to the individuals that make up the community (Hargaden, 2013: 284ff). By *third* Hargaden means any person or object that separates a symbiosis or enmeshment between individuals. *Third* allows a person to have a metaperspective of what is happening in the group process, where the person is able to stand outside of what is going on in the moment, and take a more objective view (*Ibid*: 287). This more objective awareness of the group dynamic facilitates the maintenance of clear boundaries and good game-free communication

Exercises

1. As you read through the TA elements of the four phases of community growth, check back in the various chapters of *Are We Together?* in order to revise the main concepts of TA.

2. Share your experience of the best community you have experienced and give the reasons for its success.

3. Discuss the value of having a facilitator and engage one!

4. Where do you situate your current community in the four-phase model, and give the reasons for your answer.

Chapter Twenty-Two

Leadership

"If your actions inspire others to dream more, learn more,
do more and become more, you are a leader."
John Quincy Adams

A religious Congregation was recently planning the establishment of a cluster of communities in the Far East, and had set up a team to oversee the rollout of the new project. In the initial planning stage, the question of whether or not to have community leaders appointed to the fledgling communities led to many differing views.

Some of the planning group felt that the new communities comprised groups of mature and well-prepared religious, and that there would be no need therefore for a designated leader for each community. The idea of 'shared leadership' was for them infinitely preferable, since it empowered each potential member of the new community to take responsibility for the growth and development of the community.

Other members of the planning group were of the opinion that when there is not appointed leader in a community, one of the members will effectively take on the role. While such a development could work in many cases, they felt the danger was that the 'lowest common denominator' would take over as leader. Lack of leadership, they felt, could lead either to a loose and directionless community, or to a rigid and fear-filled group that was dominated by the self-appointed leader.

In many religious Congregations, the question of leadership has undergone much scrutiny, and traditional models of authoritarian leadership have practically disappeared. Anecdotal tales of the ways superiors behaved in the past have coloured people's perceptions of leadership in general, and made religious suspicious of designated leadership in religious life, and particularly in community settings.

The title given to leaders in the past included such terms as Superior General, Superior and Provincial, two titles of which implied either someone at the head of an army, or someone who merited a higher place in an organisation than the ordinary member. However, these names have given way to: Congregation Leader, community coordinator or simply community representative. The question remains: what is the function, if any, of leadership in religious communities?

In this section we will offer a brief summary of Eric Berne's view on leadership and link it with TA theory in general. In *The Structure and Dynamics of Organisations and Groups*, Berne offers some ideas that may be of use in the general discussion on the role of leadership in religious communities (Berne, 1963).

Leadership Hunger

We already discussed stimulus hunger, recognition hunger and structure hunger (Chapters 1, 12 &13 respectively) as three fundamental needs of the human person to grow and develop. Berne maintains that there is also a *leadership hunger* that is very much linked to the structure hunger (Berne, 1966:230).

From structure hunger, Berne saw that leadership hunger often emerges. When time structuring is not functioning well, groups will begin to feel uneasy and dispirited. Sometimes there is almost a cry for 'someone' to take charge, and give some direction to the group. When people are 'lost' in a situation of mediocrity, a leader is often welcomed even when this may limit the freedom of the individuals (Berne, 1963:217). But even in ordinary circumstances, when the community is functioning well, the role and function of the leaders needs clarification.

The Role of Leadership

When Berne talks about a 'good' group leader, he identifies in rather strong and maybe anachronistic language the capacity of the leader to channel the various forces that impact on the community without obstructing the dynamics of the group (Berne, 1963:165). He said that the leader exercises the right degree of severity to control, without being intimidating! Strong language indeed!

If we can get behind the language of Berne, which was definitely of his time, and is not applicable *now* to religious life, we can see that Berne was pointing out an important aspect of any leadership – the maintenance of healthy boundaries, and the assurance of a natural equilibrium. In Fig. 37 we can see the various forces that impact on the life of the community. From the environment, the social, political, economic and religious influences have a significant effect on the community.

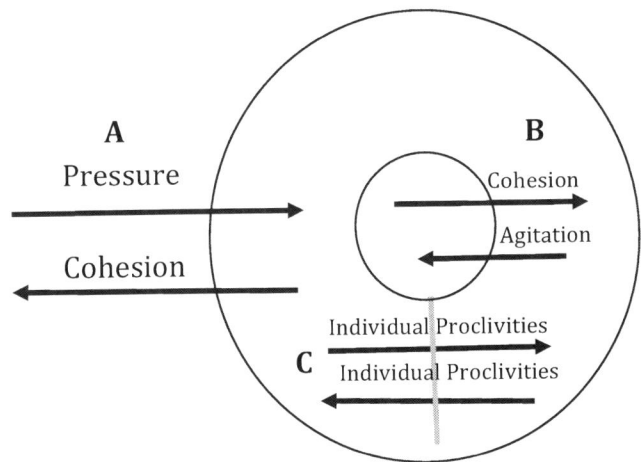

Fig. 37 The Group Forces (Berne, 1963)
(A) External Group Force; (B) Major Internal group Force;
(C) Minor Internal Group Force

In Berne's view, the leader is the one to manage the effects of external forces on the community (A). One of the external forces that can have a marked impact on the quality of community life is the multiplicity of ministries that can be present among the members. At times, each person can be so busy with differing timetables that it becomes almost impossible for the community to meet. Prayers are said privately, and sometimes even meals are taken at different times, simply because people are never together. In this situation, the challenge facing the leader is to negotiate times when the members will come together. If this is not done, the community degenerates into a lodging house for busy executives.

In addition, the leader has to ensure that a healthy level of cohesion can exist even in the moments when the group is at odds with the view of the leader (B). One of the roles of a leader is to hold the vision for the community. When members of the community 'forget' to honour the core values or religious life, or begin to allow external pressures to draw them away from the essentials of their vocation, the role of the leader is to alert them to the need to pay attention to the essence of their calling.

Another role for the designated leader is to manage the interpersonal moments of conflict within the community and restore group cohesion (C). The adage, 'two's company, and three's a row,' is never more true than when a group of people come together. Someone said that it remarkable that people with individual IQs of 150 have a group IQ of 30! We have seen that any group moves through various phases in its development, and the role of the leader is to manage the individual idiosyncrasies and maintain a healthy functioning group.

This role of the leader to maintain a group sense cannot be overestimated, and despite the frequent canonisation of shared leadership, there is little doubt that a good leader can be an invaluable asset to any group. Unfortunately, many leaders in the past have either used their power in abusive ways, or have been simply ineffective in their role as leader. This has resulted in many religious being very suspicious of having any type of leader, and insisting that shared leadership is the *only* way for communities to be managed.

Types of Leadership

Berne identifies a variety of leadership roles for each of which he gave a designation: primal, sub, responsible, effective and psychological leaders, each of which we will briefly describe and connect with their relevance to religious life (Berne, 1963: 145ff).

The Primal Leader

The Primal Leader in a Congregation is the founder of the organisation. The founder embodies the founding vision, and draws up the rules and regulations that guide the life of the group in the hope of nurturing the original inspiration.

Congregations will have their Constitutions that are based on the initial Constitution of the founder, but this Constitution will have been modified over the years to reflect the changing times, and the developing theologies that have evolved over the years. Before a Constitution can be changed, it needs the permission of The Vatican authorities to sanction the changes. This ensures that the spirit or vision of each founder is faithfully maintained.

The Subleader

Berne uses the term *subleader* to designate the leaders who follow the primal leader (*Ibid:*146). These leaders have a certain level of independent powers as laid down in the Constitutions, but are answerable to the Vatican for other decisions outside the scope of the Constitutions. The various Congregation leaders that are appointed for a specified time are *subleaders* in the language of Berne. Subleaders are vital for the maintenance of the vision or founding intention of the founders or primal leaders, but also for the reinterpretation of the original vision in the changing circumstances of society.

The Responsible Leader

For Berne, the responsible leader is the leader designated as such by the relevant authorities, and is responsible or answerable to them. He points out that often this position may simply be a named person, but does not imply that they actually perform key roles in the maintenance or facilitation of the group (*Ibid:*144ff). In many religious communities today there can be a named responsible leaders so that a 'contact' person is available to interact with outside agencies. Other than maintaining this role, many responsible leaders have no other function.

The Effective Leader

Berne characterises the effective leader as the 'one whose questions are most likely to be answered, or whose suggestions are most likely to be followed in situations of stress' (*Ibid:*17; 144). This is the person in the community who 'gets things done' and who sees to the smooth running of the community. In shared leadership communities, the effective leader is the one who provides an invaluable service to the group. He or she either does all the necessary tasks to make the community work, or ensures that one or other member of the community completes all the tasks. She or he is also the one who seems to have a solution to every practical problem. So, even when there is no one named as leader of a group, most functioning groups will allow the effective leader to emerge.

The Psychological Leader

The psychological leader, according to Berne, is the person considered by the group to have gifts that are almost superhuman! (*Ibid:*25). He can also be the responsible and effective leader, having the three roles and working effectively with them. More often than not, the psychological leader surrounds him or herself with at least one effective leader who can deal with the day-to-day management of the organisation or Congregation.

Berne goes overboard to likening the psychological leader to a God! What he describes is, in fact, that sort of leader who inspires the members of the organisation to live the spirit of the founder. By example, and by his or her capacity to express the vision in inspiring words, the psychological leader is able to draw people to the original vision, and invite them to internalise the values he or she proclaims.

Needless to say, there can be a type of psychological leader who can be a very negative influence in community. A leader who shows the qualities of the Critical and Controlling Parent impacts on a group in a way that leads either to rebellion or passive compliance. Hitler was such a leader! With such negative psychological leaders, a group is better off without any leader. When, however, the leader shows the positive aspects of the psychological leader described above, the group can only benefit.

Conclusion

John Quincy Adams' quotation at the head of the chapter is worth revisiting. He said, 'If your actions inspire others to dream more, learn more, do more and become more, you are a leader' (quoted in Lutteral, 2011). The leader of a Congregation or indeed of a community could well take the sentiments of

Adams as a yardstick for evaluating the effectiveness of his or her leadership.

People need leaders and, at the same time, it is important to recognize that within each of us are leadership qualities, and that we are all called to exercise leadership at various moments. The challenge is for us to unleash the potential within us to become effective, responsible and psychological leaders.

Exercises

1. Many communities are reluctant to name the effective leader and the psychological leader. It seems that there is a fear that by naming a person, we either put them on a pedestal or we disempower others to take on leadership roles. However, this exercise is inviting you to do just that: name who you think is the effective and/or psychological leader in your community. Write their name down and then discuss your choice with the rest of the community. When you reveal the name, give reasons for your choice. Affirm the person you have chosen.

2. If you have not been chosen as either the psychological or effective leader in the group, consider what you could do to move towards assuming these roles into the future. What would stop you becoming either of these leaders? Ask for suggestions from the rest of the community.

Chapter Twenty-Three

Identikit of a Leader

A leader is one who knows the way,
goes the way, and shows the way.
John C. Maxwell

Following on from the previous chapter where the advantage of having effective leaders in the community was discussed, we need to examine what sort of leader best serves communities, and what qualities and skills they need in order to fulfill their role as leader. Certainly, the combination of effective and psychological leader seems the ideal mix in creating communities that are vibrant and cohesive.

The challenge facing any leader of a community is to combine the ability to create connections with people, and, at the same time, to inspire them to action. Kohlrieser puts it well when he calls the leader to combine an approach of 'caring and daring' (Kohlrieser, 2012).

The caring aspect of leadership involves the capacity of the leader to bond with people in the community, and create a level of relationships that gives a sense of security among the members of the community.

The daring dimension of leadership focuses on the goals of the community, where the leader keeps his or her eye on the targets and objectives of the community. The daring leader will always focus on the horizons of achievement, never satisfied with simply maintaining the status quo. They will call the group to honour the ideals of the religious organization to which they belong, and challenge members to be faithful to their vocations.

The tension between safety and risk is paralleled with the balance between the caring and the daring; leaders need to create a certain level of security – caring - while ensuring that the community is working to its fullest potential – daring.

In order for leaders to have the capacity to both care and dare, they need to have established a secure base from which to operate. The idea of secure base comes from the work of John Bowlby and Mary Ainsworth who found that only when people felt securely attached to their caregivers could they form secure attachment later on in life (Kohlrieser, 2012:8). This secure base is primarily dependent on the connection with people, and only when this connection is achieved can a person focus freely on the goals or tasks at hand.

If leaders have people as secure bases but not goals, they may feel very secure but they will play it safe, and not take the risks (daring) necessary to maximize the community's potential. If, on the other hand, they have goals as secure bases but not people (Bowlby calls this 'avoidant attachment'), they often will experience considerable success in ministry, but be quite impoverished in terms of love (caring) and bonding to the members in the community (*Ibid*:14)

Secure base leadership builds trust and influences others by providing a sense of protection, safety and caring, and by providing a source of inspiration that together produce energy for daring, exploration, risk taking and seeking challenge (*Ibid:*18).

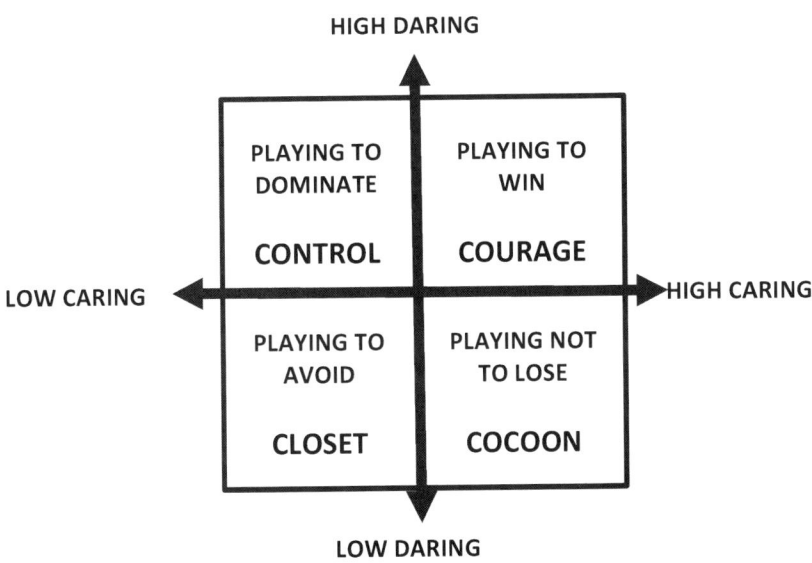

Fig. 38 Four Leadership Approaches (Kohlrieser, 2012)

From Fig. 38 above, we can identify four main approaches of leaders, each characterised by the level of daring and caring that they practise.

Kohlrieser, a trained transactional analyst, outlines the leadership approaches based somewhat on the life position grid of Franklin Ernst that we discussed in Chapter 2.

The I'm OK, You're OK leaders 'play to win' where they take the necessary steps to achieve specific goals (*Ibid:*145). They demonstrate a secure base in having a high focus on relationships (caring) as well as a determination (daring) to reach the highest levels of performance. They show a high level of trust in other people, and are open to be challenged by the members of the community. They courageously welcome differing views as to how the community is organised, and believe that the real victory happens when everyone has a part to play. As a result, the community is characterised by a creative and collaborative atmosphere where everyone is actively involved.

The controlling leader, on the other hand, comes from the paranoid position of the I'm OK- You're Not OK position. Instead of playing to win, these leaders play to dominate. Playing to dominate involves focusing on results at the expense of relationships. Controlling leaders believe that if you want to go fast – as an African saying goes – you need to go it alone. They forget the second part of the saying: 'If you want to go far, go together!'. These leaders are results-focused rather than people - focused (*Ibid:*149). The consequences of this type of leadership are that it fosters passivity and resentment on the part of the community members. Creativity suffers because the dominating leader demands conformity rather than individual initiative. This type of leader equates loyalty with submission, and forces people to 'toe the line' if they want to be part of the inner group.

The leader who works from an I'm Not OK – You're Ok position is fearful of failure, fear of making mistakes, and fear that they will lose the support of the community. They are playing not to lose. They focus on creating a warm and fuzzy community where no one will get hurt, and everyone will be nice to each other. Challenge is avoided in case someone in the community feels uncomfortable, and comfort is the highest priority. These types of leaders create a cocoon and over adapt to the expressed needs of the community members. Such passive behaviour avoids any level of goal setting or any degree of real engagement. This is a defensive form of leadership that harms no one, but has little effect on achieving real progress.

The leader who works from an I'm Not OK – You're Not Ok position is characterised by an avoidant attachment leadership style. In a sense, this approach is better defined as a lack of leadership. They play to avoid, hiding in the closet of their own fears and uncertainties. They neither connect with people, nor are they focused on achieving any real goals. In a sense, they are simply marking time until their term of office is over. They appear lonely and withdrawn, unable to connect, unable to express any real feelings.

Fig. 39 below further characterises the attachment styles of the four leadership approaches described above. Again, the influence of Bowlby, Berne and Ernst is clearly evident in Kohlrieser's classification of the four styles (Bowlby, 1988; Berne, 1963;Ernst, 1971):

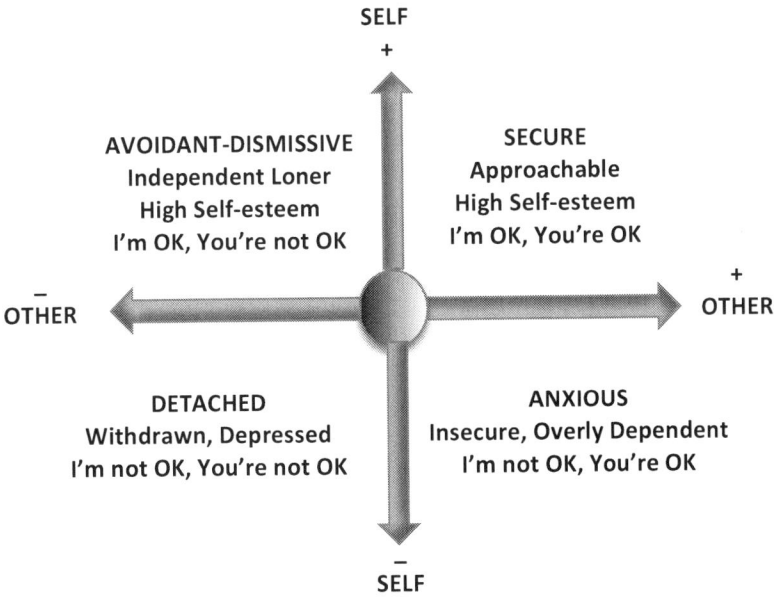

Fig. 39 Attachment Styles of Leaders (Kohlrieser, 2012)

In the above diagram, we see that leadership, in developing a secure base, necessitates the ability to become self aware, and aware of others. The way leaders in community connect with the members indicates the level of leadership that they can exercise. The more attached the leader is to the members of the community, the greater chance he or she has of working with the members of the community in a mutually enriching fashion. Whereas the avoidant, anxious and detached styles of leadership prevent the growth of the group, the secure leader provides the basis for the growth and development of the community as a whole as well as that of the individual members.

Characteristics of a Good Leader

Kohlrieser identifies nine characteristics of a good leader, and we can usefully apply these qualities to the good community leader (Kohlrieser, 2012: 35-41).

1. Stays Calm

The leader who can stay calm when under pressure is capable of dealing with situations that otherwise cause others to 'lose their cool'. Like the Inquirer (Chapter 12), the leader needs to be able to manage the external pressures that threaten the equilibrium of the community, and create a sense of cohesion. The ability to stay calm contributes to the members of the community perceiving the leader as dependable and predictable, one whom the community members can rely on. From the study of mirror neurons mentioned earlier, the calm of the leader can be transmitted to those who perceive the leader as centred and poised (Chapter 3).

2. Accepts the Individual

The I'm OK- You're Ok attitude of the effective leader promotes the health of the community, where each member is valued not only for what they do, but also for who they are. This type of leader is able to distinguish between the behaviour and the person, so that they, as leader, can when necessary point out the failures of the person, without shaming them or devaluing them in any way. The ability to view the person with positive regard prevents people taking any form of criticism personally. When there is respect between the leader and the members of the community, then the leader can offer clear direction to the group, and bring them on board in developing future plans. This kind of leader honours and appreciates the members of the community, and offers positive strokes that build up the spirit of the group.

3. Sees the Potential

Kohlrieser sees a key role of leadership is to go beyond acceptance of the person's inherent value, and possibly even beyond what the person expects from her or himself (*Ibid:*37). The secure leader has the capacity to motivate the members of the community to achieve more than they are currently delivering, and is able to draw out undiscovered or hidden talents. By offering from Adult some robust feedback to the members of the community, the secure-based leader challenges the members to be more, to be greater than they even imagine is possible, and to overcome any lack of confidence. These challenges are given in a spirit of support and encouragement, avoiding any sense of the Controlling Parent. The fact that the leader sees the potential in the community members boosts the members' belief in themselves, and unleashes their untapped potential.

4. Uses Listening and Inquiry

Most 'good' leaders are quicker to listen than to pontificate. They are aware that they have not got the monopoly on the wisdom of the group, and acknowledge that the individual members have valuable contributions to make for the benefit of the whole community. One facilitator described the best quality of community leader as a person who is 'relatively incompetent'. By this he meant that the leader who is prepared to allow others state their beliefs, hopes and expectations succeeds in creating a spirit of group involvement in the formation of the community. The leader has not got all the answers, and realizes that by listening and attuning to the members, many of the solutions can emerge easily and effortlessly, uncovering unthought-of ideas and suggestions.

5. Delivers a Powerful Message

Kohlrieser uses Karpman's idea of a 'bull's eye transaction' to describe the capacity of the leader to touch all the ego states of a person or group at the one time in a way that inspires and motivates the group to change (Karpman, 1971:83). By expressing authentic beliefs, the leader not only verbalises his or her convictions, but also models the message that is being transmitted. The bull's eye transaction succeeds in reaching the Parent, Adult and Child of the members of the community – connecting with the very core of the audience, and moving the minds and hearts of the group. Usually, good leaders have some core beliefs by which they regulate their lives, and which they find easy to express in ways that move the listeners to internalise these same values.

6. Focuses on the Positive

Leaders succeed in moving toward solutions, and away from problems. They have the capacity to see that there are many options to what may appear to be either/or choices. They continually think outside the box, refusing to be limited by the seemingly daunting situations that do not immediately suggest easy resolution. The phrase 'problems are opportunities for growth' is never more true than with the leader who feels secure to stay in the realm of the uncertain and the unknown. Such leaders instil a high level of confidence in the community members, and assuage feelings of panic and despair that can reign supreme in the less assured members when there is no secure leader present.

7. Encourages Risk Taking

The freedom of spontaneity is highly prized by the leader who demonstrates a high level of autonomy (Berne, 1964). Because there is little or no fear of failure, the dynamic leader is willing to risk making mistakes. Mistakes are simply considered as moments of insight and opportunities for learning for the future. The effective leader also is keen to give permission and protection to the members of the community to exercise their full potency without fear of failure (Crossman, 1966:152-4). Because the leader is prepared to take risks him or herself, much can be achieved that otherwise would be prevented through fear or anxiety of 'messing up'.

8. Inspires through Intrinsic Motivation

By 'intrinsic motivation', Kohlrieser is referring to the capacity of the leader to inspire the members of the community to achieve goals and objectives for no other motive than that of reaching a better quality of life. There is no other reward offered other than a sense of achievement and the increase in the level of self-esteem. Intrinsic motivation causes the members to take responsibility for the quality of their community life, and to undertake tasks for the simple reason that doing so will contribute to the quality of the community at large. The leader does not seek to manipulate the members to comply with the leader's wishes, but rather empowers the members to seek ways to enhance the group spirit. In a sense, the leader succeeds in transmitting his or her values to the rest of the group who, in turn, embrace these same values as their own.

9. Signals Accessibility

The person who identified a key quality of a good leader as one who is relatively incompetent (no. 4 above) also identified two other qualities of the good leader: someone who can lounge around the community room, and who can 'nurse a whiskey'. By these two qualities he was stressing the importance for the leader to be available to the members of the community. When leaders are 'too busy' to mix with the community, or who are so withdrawn that they avoid any real contact, they fail in a very essential quality of a leader – accessibility. The community leader has a very specific role to develop an attuned connection with the members of the community so that they become the conduit for a deep quality of sharing and communication.

Conclusion

There is much more that could be said about the role of a community leader, but for the moment, it may be sufficient to highlight the value of communities considering the idea of appointing a community leader. If communities can overcome their fears of having to deal with the Controlling Parent – the traditional view of 'the boss' – they may begin to appreciate that good leadership can only benefit a group that wants to grow and develop to their fullest potential.

Exercises

1. As you reflect on the qualities of a leader as outlined in this chapter, which of the qualities do you see in yourself, and in others in the community. Take some time to share the outcomes of your reflection, and allow others in the community to hear your opinions. Listen also to the other members of the community as they identify the qualities you have as a potential leader!

2. Take some time to reflect and share on past leaders of communities that you have experienced, and identify the level of caring and daring they demonstrated.

3. How could the members of your community be more caring and daring? Identify the behaviours that community members could adopt to practise caring and daring more effectively.

PART FIVE

The Adult

"Youth ends when egotism does;
maturity begins when one lives for others."
Hermann Hesse,

Keith Tudor commented that of the many writings on ego states in the *Transaction Analysis Journal* between 1962-1999, only 18 articles appeared on the Adult ego state compared with 70 on the Parent, and 27 on the Child ego states (Tudor, 2003:201). It seems that the Adult is inclined to take third place in order of importance! Despite the relative paucity of articles on the Adult, there is much to be said in this regard, which will bring together many of the TA theories into an integrated whole.

Part five focuses on the Adult as the culmination of development from the earliest years of infancy, through childhood and adolescence, until the person arrives at adulthood.

Chapter 24 will present the integrating Adult as a person who manages to decommission the archaic and introjected influences of Child and Parent ego states in order to live in Adult, and face the day-to-day challenges of life in a way that is aware, contactful and responsible. In Chapter 25 we see how the early influences of parents can have a very positive impact on the formation of a winning Script, and, by extension, on the beginning of a process of integrating the Adult ego state.

In Chapter 26, we explore the behaviour of the integrating Adult who is graced with permissions and allowers to live an adult life that is free from any sort of games or manipulative behaviours. Chapter 27 offers a glimpse of the spirituality of TA, and the role of spirituality in the development of the integrating Adult. Although Berne himself did not profess an explicit spirituality, we will see that he very much promoted the idea of self-transcendence which in contemporary terms points to an authentic striving to overcome the limitations of the material as we embrace a new consciousness.

The final Chapter tells of an experiment undertaken by a religious Congregation to transform their communities into cohesive and vibrant groups. The leadership of this Congregation also planned to initiate a ministry that would respond to the contemporary thirst for a relevant spirituality.

Chapter Twenty-Four

The Integrating Adult

"Clouds come floating into my life,
no longer to carry rain or usher storm,
but to add colour to my sunset sky."
Rabindranath Tagore

Sister Stan was the most integrated person you could find. She came across as warm, well grounded, with a sense of humour combined with an empathic approach to people. As a professional, she showed integrity and commitment in her work, and seemed always interested in seeking new ways to accomplish her duties. In community she was very pleasant, someone with whom you could relax and simply be yourself. She was an inspiring religious, and an impressive human being. She was a good example of the integrated Adult.

As we begin to spend some time reflecting on the growth of the mature adult, we will initially take Berne's view of the Adult ego state, and then further develop his ideas in the light or more recent thinking.

When Berne identified the Adult ego state he identified it by its role of 'marshalling and processing data and perceptions concerning the immediate situation' (Berne, 1961:30). By the immediate situation, he meant the current here-and-now reality that could be tested objectively (*Ibid:*77). The marshalling and processing he saw mainly as a cognitive process without any sort of emotional involvement. This part of the person's personality, Berne envisaged as organized, adaptable, and intelligent in the way that it responded to the data before it.

Having stressed the cognitive side of the Adult, Berne acknowledged the Adult with a set of feelings, attitudes and behaviour patterns that facilitated reality testing (*Ibid:*77). So, in addition to the cognitive side of the Adult, he included the affective and the behavioural aspects.

In his diagram of the three circles, representing the Parent,

Adult and Child, Berne places the Adult ego state between the Parent and the Child, for he sees the role of the Adult is to act 'as a buffer between the Child and the Parent' (*Ibid:*143). He does not consider the Adult as dominant, but rather as an aspect of the person that offers the option to move from one ego state to the other (*Ibid:*146). The Adult for Berne, in fact, is the ego state that ensures the survival of the person (Berne, 1964: 26).

Berne's description of the Adult gives the impression of an aspect of the personality that is clearly more rational than emotional, and it is this perception that can offer a very limited view of the Adult ego state. Berne does admit that 'in many cases certain child-like qualities become integrated into the Adult ego state' but overall, his presentation seems more to favour seeing the Adult as a data processor rather than a flesh and blood human being (Berne, 1961:196; 30). Consequently, it is difficult to deny that the Adult, for Berne, is more a thinking than feeling being. His view of Adult is more of the analytical Adult rather than the experiencing Adult (Kuijt, 1980: 232ff).

Keith Tudor offers a very refreshingly different view of the Adult that serves to flesh out a more holistic and dynamic view of the adult person (Tudor, 2003:201ff). He sees the Adult ego state as an integrating rather than an integrated personality. The growth process of the Adult ego state is for Tudor an on-going evolution that only concludes with the end of life. His view stresses the experiencing Adult. He describes the Adult as:

> '...A pulsating personality, processing and integrating, feelings, attitudes, thoughts and behaviours appropriate to the here-and-now at all ages from conception to death' (Ibid: 201).

The integrating aspect of the Adult ego state is the capacity of the Adult to be conscious of the past introjects from the Parent, and the archaic relics of the Child, while not being a slave to their dictates in the present. When we talk about contamination of the Adult, we mean an Adult who is unconscious of the Child and Parent contaminations, and believes he or she is living in Adult when all that is available is a contaminated and limited Adult (Chapter 5). In Fig. 40 we have a modified version of Tudor's diagram, showing how the Adult is transcending the limits of any form of contamination.

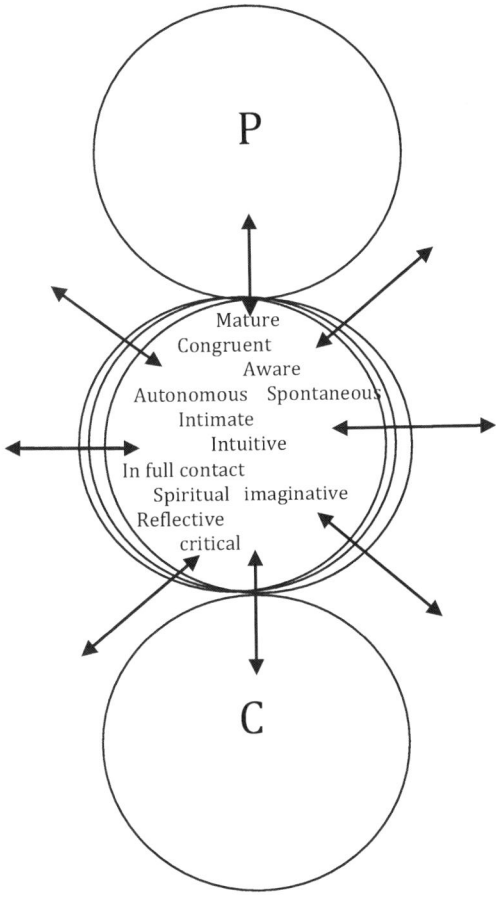

Fig. 40   The Integrating Adult (Tudor 2003)
(Adapted)

What Tudor is emphasising is that the Adult is far more than a data processor; the Adult is a vibrant and mature person, fully conscious and self-aware of what is happening at a intrapsychic, interpersonal and environmental level.   The diagram shows no contamination but instead we see the arrows flowing from the Parent and Child from the past into the Adult, and a similar flow from the Adult back to the Parent and Child.

The uncontaminated Adult is the person who is engaged in

experiencing, reflecting and integrating the various dimensions of his or her life, open to change, and characterised by a level of autonomy that is unfettered by distorted messages from the past. In addition, the uncontaminated Adult is open to the world, welcoming the richness of life to impact on his or her Adult, and offering the uncontaminated Adult many opportunities for growth and development.

Some of the words Tudor uses to describe the integrating Adult are: mature, congruent, autonomous, aware and reflective. Such a person has the ideal qualities for living in a religious community. It must be said here that the health of the community depends to a large measure on the maturity and integrity of the individual members. When the members are integrating Adults, the community becomes a place of growth and wholeness.

What does the mature adult do with the various contaminations that each person will have experienced due to the formation of their Script? If the Adult is uncontaminated by the Parent and the Child, does that mean that nothing from the person's past can penetrate the Adult? What about the Parent and Child of the integrating Adult?

Landy Gobes talks about the goal of therapy as the integration of Child ego states, and the decommissioning and assimilation of Parent ego states into the ongoing Adult ego state (Novey, Gobes et. al., 1993:163ff). Presumably she would also say that the aim of life is to achieve something similar, *viz.* to integrate the positive Parent and Child ego states into the Adult ego state. So, when we talk about the integrating Adult, we somehow have to deal with those parts of our past that need to be 'decommissioned' and those that need to be assimilated. The integrated Adult, therefore, draws from the Child and Parent ego state reservoirs in order to enhance and support healthy functioning (Clarkson & Gilbert, 1988:25).

The Functional Fluency Model of Susannah Temple (Temple, 1999:164ff) suggests to me a way of diagramming how the Adult incorporates the positive aspects of Child and Parent and decommissions the contaminated parts of these states (Fig. 41). While acknowledging Temple's Functional Fluency Model, I should point out that what I have suggested in the diagram below does not in any way reflect her thinking. I have simply taken her diagram, and modified it to graphically illustrate how the Adult can assimilate the positive memories from the past, and file away the negative experiences because they no longer are fit for purpose (Clarkson & Gilbert, 1988: 20ff). This filing away is not any form of repression, but simply a relinquishment of the negative impact that such memories held for the person in the past.

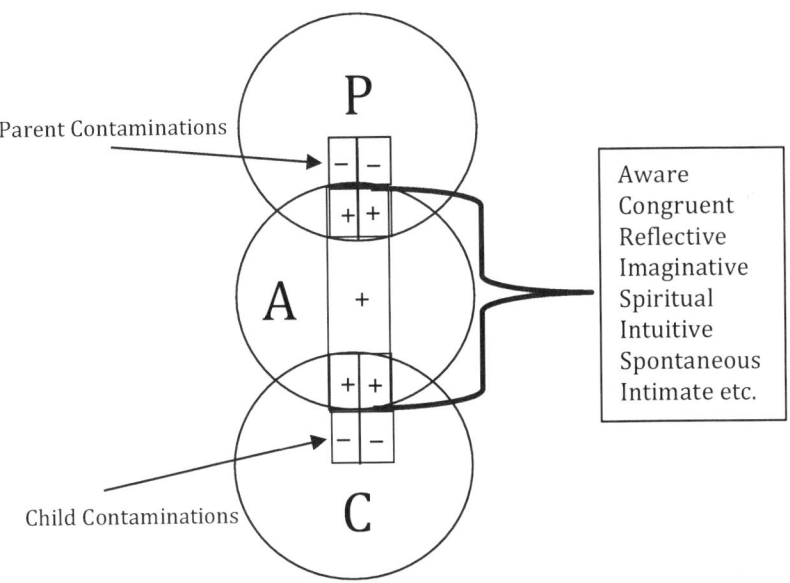

Fig. 41 The Integrating Adult Model (Gibson 2014)
(Adapted from Temple 1999)

In Fig. 41 we have the Parent and Child ego states intersecting with the Adult ego state to signify that these 'historical' Parent and Child ego states, as Clarkson & Gilbert call them, are part and parcel of our lives (*Ibid:*23). Our parents have impacted on us, and our memories from childhood are always with us.

With the integrating Adult ego state, however, the person functions without little or no intrapsychic (within the mind) control by an introjected Parent or contamination from archaic Child ego states (Erskine, 1991:63ff). Instead, the positive memories from Parent and Child go to contribute to our integrating Adult ego state, and those negative memories are 'let go' so that they no longer impact negatively on our Adult (Berne, 1961:69:175). They still remain in the Parent and Child, but they do not further contaminate the Adult. So, with the integrating Adult, the power of the negative contaminations is gradually abandoned and the positive historical 'contributions' from our past go to enrich our experience of the here-and-now.

As the Adult continues a process of integration, so the move towards autonomy goes on apace. Berne identified three aspects of autonomy that merit some comment: awareness, spontaneity and intimacy (Berne, 1964:158ff).

Awareness

Berne emphasises that awareness requires that we live in the here-and-now, without the distractions from the past or the future (*Ibid:*158). He identifies the person who is aware and conscious of how she or he is feeling and thinking in the moment. Erskine says that the Adult ego state integrates what is occurring moment-by-moment internally and externally (Erskine, 1991: 63ff). He comments that the Adult is working to its fullest capacity when it is free from 'the intrapsychic control of the introjected Parent of archaic Child ego states' (*Ibid:*63ff).

Such levels of awareness are very necessary for community members as they become conscious, not only of what is going on with the group, but also about what is happening for the members within the group. Self-awareness and awareness of the dynamic of the community is vital for healthy human relationships, and for the health of the community as a whole (Widdowson, 2008:58ff). When the community members are aware of what is going on intrapsychically and interpersonally, they are better able to handle potential moments of conflict or misunderstandings.

Spontaneity

The freedom to choose is what Berne means by spontaneity where he sees the person having a choice or option to connect with feelings from any of the ego states (Berne, 1964:160). People who are spontaneous do not play psychological games, and can express their feelings in the moment instead of having to adapt to others expectations. When Berne talks about a choice or option with regard to spontaneity, he is not referring to the choice that comes from the Adult alone. Rather he sees spontaneity as accessing the Parent and the Child in the integrating Adult where spontaneous, thoughts, feelings or actions are in play. The Free Child is spontaneous, and this is the energy that the Adult draws on when he or she is being spontaneous with the cooperation of a positive Parent.

A community without spontaneity is like a car without petrol; it can go nowhere! Spontaneity is the lifeblood of a community, investing it with energy, creativity and joy. When the members of the community can express themselves in the moment, and know they will be accepted, there is a sense of freedom in the group, and an atmosphere of lightness and affirmation pervades.

Intimacy

In *Games People Play,* Berne offers a definition of intimacy when he describes it as 'the spontaneous, game-free candidness of an aware person' (*Ibid:* 160). He talks about the uncorrupted Child in all its naiveté living in the moment as the basis for intimacy. For Berne intimacy is the function of the natural Child. In *Sex in Human Loving,* Berne gives the most comprehensive and succinct definition of intimacy. He says, 'Intimacy is a candid Child-to-Child relationship with no games and no mutual exploitation' (Berne, 1970:126). He says that intimacy often begins from the Adult ego state, and then overcomes the interference of the Parent, until the Child is in full control. This movement allows the person to move from the rational decision of the Adult to be open to others, and then to overcome the rules of privacy from the Parent, until the person can access the Free Child energy that promotes intimacy.

At a community level, the challenge of arriving at a stage of intimacy is not insignificant. We saw in Chapter 13, that many communities prefer to stay in the areas of withdrawal, rituals, pastimes and activities rather than risk moving towards intimacy. Intimacy in community is where people allow others into their most private of worlds. Someone said that intimacy could be renamed as 'into-me-you-see', where we invite our Sisters or Brothers to see into us without the normal masks and defences that we often wear or erect.

Conclusion

The integrating Adult as described above develops with the support of a positive family background, or else under the influence of deep friendships. When the Script messages from parents offer more permissions and allowers than counterinjunctions and injunctions, then the Script will be a winning Script (see Chapter 23). A winning Script is, therefore, the result of a person experiencing Parent messages that are life giving, rather than the death-dealing injunctions and counterinjunctions that we described in Chapters 7 and 8.

In the following chapter, we will explore the type of positive verbal and non-verbal messages that the parents of an integrating Adult send to their children from an early age. We will see how these positive reinforcements on the part of parents contribute to their children having a winning Script, and how communities can build up each community member by transmitting similar messages to their Sisters or Brothers.

Exercises

1. Describe to your community the person you know who is a good example of the integrating Adult. How does she or he behave that would identify him or herself as an integrating Adult?

2. You may also like to share the people you most admire either living or dead who have made a significant positive impact on society, and who were more inclined to work from Adult.

3. Share with your community the positive messages that you received from your parents and talk about how these have influenced you.

4. Share when you feel most in Adult – what are you thinking, feeling and how are you behaving?

Chapter Twenty-Five

The Good Script

"Parenthood...It's about guiding the next generation,
and forgiving the last."
Peter Krause

When we think of the integrating Adult, and the capacity of the Adult to decommission any trace of negative contaminations, while assimilating the positive memories of parents, it begs the question as to whether there is such a thing as a 'good' script. In fact, Berne *did* state in his early work that 'a practical and constructive script...may lead to great happiness' (Berne, 1961:116). But generally speaking, when we talk about Script in TA, it generally refers to mindless, or joyless Scripts, or losing or banal Scripts (Steiner, 1974:49ff). The winning Scripts are occasionally mentioned but not dwelt upon.

It is interesting to note, however, that not every writer sees Script as patterns that 'inhibit spontaneity and limit flexibility in problem-solving, health maintenance, and in relationship with people' (Erskine, 1980:102ff). Fanita English, for example, sees Script as (italics in original) '*a normal process* that occurs for all of us, at its own pace, not a pathological one' (English, 2010: 224). For her, Scripts are 'artistic productions with many hidden personal symbolic meanings for the persons who devise them' (*Ibid:*225). Loria sees Script as an evolving, and non-pathological process that is continually available for revision, and only finalized at the end of a person's life (Loria, 1995:165).

In this chapter we want to propose how a winning Script can come about. If one were to agree with the quotation at the head of this chapter, then the role of parents is significant in the formation of a winning Script. While still holding to the definition of Script which states that Script formation is based on the decisions made in early childhood. (See chapter 1), the positive reinforcement by parents of their children will, no doubt, contribute to the formation of a 'good' Script. In addition, the learning cycle of a child also contributes to the capacity of the child to overcome the negative influences of a child's background, so as to create a more positive life plan (Newton, 2006:186ff).

In Chapters 7 and 8, we showed how the verbal and non-verbal or conscious and unconscious messages from the parents impact on the decisions that the child will make. The unconscious messages or injunctions come from the Child in the parent, and are picked up by the pre-verbal child. Later on, the verbal counterinjunctions from the Parent in the parent give the message to the child that he or she is OK as long as he or she behaves according to the wishes of the parents. These behaviours we called the *drivers,* which drive the child to be perfect, strong, please others, hurry up or try hard in order to be accepted by parents.

In this chapter we will outline the verbal and non-verbal positive messages that are transmitted often out of awareness by parents, and received either consciously or unconsciously by their children. In this way both types of messages contribute to a winning Script that children adopt and live out in the course of their lives.

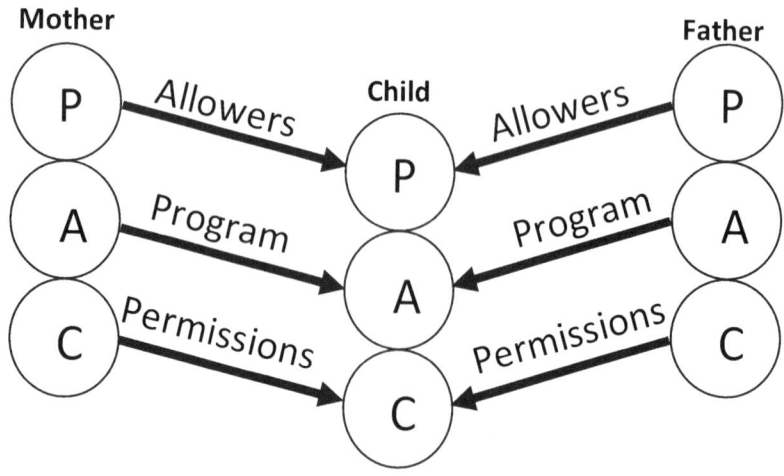

Fig. 42 The Winning Script Matrix

As we examine the positive parental messages that are

transmitted to children, we also reflect on how the transmission of positive messages can transform the quality of life in community. A winning Script can, therefore, be created in an atmosphere of positive affirmation and support.

In the winning Script (Fig. 42 above) there are *permissions* given instead of injunctions, and in place of driver messages, parents communicate *allower* messages to their children (Allen & Allen, 1975:72-74). We see in Fig. 42 that these verbal and non-verbal messages come from the Child or Parent in the parent to the Child or Parent in the child. Both types of messages contribute to the formation of people who dwell for a considerable portion of their life in an I'm OK-You're OK existential position. They have, in other words, a winning Script.

Some of the titles I have given to these permissions are not simply the reverse of the injunction, but indicate the real message of the permissions. So, for instance, with the *Don't Exist* injunction, I have suggested *'You are Welcome!'* instead of simply substituting 'Exist!' for its opposite. This alternative better describes what is involved in this permission, where the parents actively welcome their child at the moment of birth.

No doubt, the reader will be able to identify people who seem to live with some of the permissions described below. It would be difficult, of course, to find anyone who received *all* the permissions from his or her parents.

Permissions

The twelve permissions that counter the messages of the injunctions are: You are welcome; Be Yourself; Enjoy your childhood; Grow and Develop! Do it! Be a Winner!; You are important!; Belong! Be Close! Grow strong! Think Clearly! Trust your Feelings! We will briefly comment on each permission, connecting each one with the impact that the positive message can have on community.

You are Welcome!

Although the arrival of a child can, for some parents, be a moment of panic and dread, the arrival of an infant is for these parents a moment of unalloyed joy – the moment that the parents have been waiting for. They are excited that finally the child is born, and the Child in the parents rejoices in welcoming their infant into their home. They realise the challenges of child rearing, but they feel confident and relaxed that they will manage. They want the child to be happy, and their hope is that their child will grow to be a well-rounded and mature adult. But for the moment they are just ready to enjoy the adventure of bringing their child up. This sense of being welcomed into the world gives the child a sense of solidity and of security right at the outset, and prepares the child for life.

How welcoming are our communities? Often communities can tend to become inward looking, and protective of their privacy. Visitors to the community are seen as a nuisance, and even when new members arrive to join the community, they are expected to 'fit in' to the already established routine. A welcoming community, by contrast, is open and encourages both visitors and new members to become part of the community. When a new member joins, the community sees that it is a new community, and therefore everyone begins again to form itself in a way that is inclusive of the gifts and expectations of the new member. Anyone visiting this type of community is struck by the way the whole community comes together to welcome visitors, and is prepared to lay aside the timetable so as to make the visitor feel at home.

Be Yourself!

The parents greet the arrival of the infant with loving acceptance. They are not like the parents who have definite views as to what their child should be like. These parents are delighted with the newly born. They expected a boy, and a girl arrived, but the parents simply love the girl with no reservations. They immediately decide that the infant will be given a girl's name and not one that could be mistaken for a boy (e.g. Frances or Terri or Pat). They buy the most feminine of baby clothes, and stereotypically buy all the toys that a girl usually has. As the child begins to grow, the parents continually respect her feminine qualities, and come to understand how she, as a girl, sees the world. The child feels that her parents love her as she is. There are no unreal expectations that she should be other than the person she is becoming. As a result, she feels loved and accepted.

Communities are made up of many different types of

people: introverts, extroverts, thinkers, feelers, doers, poets, prophets and pragmatists! The great challenge in community is to accept, or rather to rejoice in the diversity of gifts and qualities of each and everyone. The existential position of I'm OK and You're OK breeds a quality of life where everyone in the community feels accepted and appreciated. Even though people have differing frames of reference, the community encourages this variety as an enriching dimension of the community. As a result of the message, 'Be Yourself', each member grows in confidence and in a sense of OKness.

Enjoy Your Childhood!

Unlike the parent who wants their child to be an adult before they have the chance to enjoy childhood, these parents enjoy the various stages that their child is going through. As she begins to crawl and then walk, the parents are there taking videos of the development of their child. They delight in the first words uttered by their daughter, and at each stage of development, the parents simply rejoice that she is growing and developing at her own pace. There are no expectations that she should walk earlier, speak sooner, or achieve any specific skill by a definite time; each stage is taken at the pace that suits their child. And the parents are excited at the process of witnessing her growth. They are enjoying the childhood of their daughter.

Communities often comprise religious who have varying degrees of experience. Some may have celebrated their Golden, or Diamond jubilees, while others may be hardly out of the novitiate. Sometimes, the wide age-gap can pose difficulties in community when the more mature members do not allow the younger members to be themselves, expecting that they will have the same level of maturity and commitment that the senior Sisters or Brothers have gained after many years in religious life. The challenge on the part of the more experienced Sisters and Brothers is to be patient and compassionate with the younger members of their community, and to allow them to make mistakes, move gradually along the road to commitment, and let them enjoy freedoms that maybe the older members never were allowed. In addition, the affirmation of the young members by the more experienced religious contributes to the overall atmosphere of spontaneity in the community. Thus, the young religious can begin to enjoy the vocation journey without any sense of being prematurely forced to grow up.

Grow and Develop!

These parents do not keep their child as a child, afraid that they will not manage when the child grows up. Instead, the parents support their child at every stage of her development. They encourage their daughter to overcome all the normal challenges that she will face, and the daughter knows that each challenge she faces and succeeds in meeting becomes a source of joy and celebration in the family. This leads her to face each new horizon with courage and confidence. Now as an adult, this daughter exudes a quiet confidence before the challenges of life.

Every member of the community should be given the gift of freedom to develop to their fullest potential. In the past, there was a tendency in communities to keep everyone 'humble' in the sense that any idea that people should be more intelligent, more creative, more artistic was contrary to the gospel message of being meek and mild. The permission to excel needs to be inculcated in communities, so that Brothers and Sisters rejoice in the successes and gifts that each one has, thereby enriching the quality and effectiveness of the communities.

Do it!

The parents of this young girl feel confident that the world into which she was born is safe enough to support her. Unlike the terrified parents who seek to protect their child by preventing her from doing anything, crying 'Don't' at every hand's turn, these parents encourage their daughter to 'go for it'. They offer their support without being overly protective, and allow their child to venture into the world, while ensuring the normal safeguards are in place. Moreover, these parents have a relaxed attitude to life, and this sense of calm is transmitted to their child who grows to be an adult who faces life with a determination and calm that allows her to deal with many challenges and difficulties.

One of the great dangers in community living is that we remain with inspiring ideas and challenging thoughts without putting these ideas and thoughts into action. The 'Do it' permission offers the members of the community the challenge to concretise the ideals that they process in very practical ways. Regular community meetings need to deliver real decisions as to how to improve the quality of life together. Each member of the community needs to hold one another accountable for the change that each wants to achieve. In addition, regular evaluation sessions serve to check if the aspirations of the community are being translated into action.

Be a Winner!

The parents of this child are successful parents themselves. They have achieved a lot in life, and see that their daughter also has great potential. While they avoid pushing her, or expecting that she match up to their expectations, these parents encourage her to succeed and celebrate the various moments when she does succeed. When she slips up, her parents are equally supportive, and offer reassurance that she can achieve great things and can overcome many obstacles. Gradually, their daughter grows in the expectation that she will be a winner, and eventually arrive at where she wants to go. She expects a lot of herself, not because she wants to please her parents, but simply because she knows she can achieve a lot.

Communities need to celebrate the successes of each other. A community must expect that the members become the best sort of religious that each is capable of being. Often, tolerance is viewed as a virtue, where we are encouraged to be patient with each other, and accept each other's faults. The problem with this approach is that we discount the capacity of the individual to overcome the limiting forces that are preventing the person from growth and development. By giving the message of 'Be a Success!' we encourage people to overcome obstacles to full human and spiritual growth. This encouragement is given by way of positive conditional and unconditional strokes to each community member.

You are Important!

Not like the parents who seem to grudge the success of their children, these parents demonstrate frequently to their daughter that she is important. She is important to her parents who love her, not only when she achieves success but simply because she is their daughter. They treat her in a way that encourages her to see her gifts and positive qualities. By their encouragement and support, they give her the impression that she can make her mark in the world. They inculcate in her a sense of her own worth, and, as a result, their daughter grows into a person who knows her own intrinsic value beyond anything she might achieve.

Many members of religious communities experience a very low level of stroking. Both Sisters and Brothers often spend much effort and energy in their work or ministry, and when they return to their communities, they often have to keep their concerns and worries to themselves instead of being able to share them with the members of the community. Somehow, they do not feel important enough to take the time of the community to process their successes and failures. Many, therefore, are inclined to maintain a level of privacy or even secrecy, which deprives them of the opportunity to receive support and encouragement. Communities need to transmit to each of the members that they are important and worthy of the affirmation of their Sisters or Brothers.

Belong!

This young girl grows up surrounded by friends and relations that love and cherish her. Her parents encourage her to mingle with the neighbours' children, and invite her friends to her home. She sees her parents maintaining close friendships with people they have grown up with, and learns from them that having friends is something of great value. More importantly, she feels a real sense of belonging to her parents, often being told how important she is to them. As she grows up, she is very aware of how much she feels part of her family, and how important key moments are in the life of the family that solidify this sense. Especially now, as her parents are getting older, this young woman still feels very connected to her parents who, right from an early age, made her feel she belonged.

Belonging is an essential element of community life. It is the extent to which Brothers and Sisters in religious communities feel a sense of belonging that the community will grow and develop. Belonging involves knowing each other, knowing each other's families and friends, and being welcoming to invite them into the community from time to time. In a real sense, the community needs to become a home where everyone feels free to be themselves. Belonging does not happen automatically. It needs the conscious efforts of each person in the community to engender a sense of closeness, and a feeling of being an integral part of the community.

Be Close!

Unlike some parents who hardly ever show affection either to each other, or to their children, this girl was fortunate to witness her parents being extremely affectionate and close. Right from an early age, she remembers being hugged and kissed when she came home from school, and when her father came home from work, he would invariably hug and kiss her. All the family members – her brothers and sisters – were very close as they grew up. Each would know what the other was doing. Each would be supportive of one another, so that when the children grew to adulthood, they continued to be in regular contact. As a result, this young woman finds it easy to be close to her friends and to her husband and children.

How do religious express their affection for each other? In the past, any form of what was known as 'particular friendships' was frowned upon. The idea was that religious had to love each member of the community equally. This approach led to a bland and superficial level of connection, where any real affection was stifled. Now, we are called to express both verbally and non-verbally our affection for each other. Religious are learning to pay attention to the 'matters of the heart', and to allow themselves to be touched by the affection of their Sisters or Brothers. A new spirit of gentleness is beginning to pervade the communities, where religious feel a new sense of attachment to their community members.

Grow Strong!

Just as some parents seem to favour sick children, only giving attention when the child is ill, these parents encourage their child to be healthy and strong. Unfortunately, parents who have psychological problems often visit the same problems on their children. Fortunately, this child has grown up in an environment of mature and balanced parents who provide their child with a level of normality that nurtures an inner psychological security, and makes her feel grounded and mature. As the child grows, she is able to face the normal challenges of life with a certain equanimity.

The emphasis on holistic living is often stressed in documents drafted at congregation chapters. Increasingly, religious are being encouraged to attend to their health, spiritual, emotional, physical and psychological. This emphasis on a healthy lifestyle is based on the belief that the effectiveness of ministry is in direct proportion to the health and wellbeing of the religious who are actively involved in outreach to the poor. Communities have put greater emphasis on a healthy life-work balance, and have called each member to accountability as to the way they live their life. Such an emphasis goes far to avoid such additions as workaholism, alcoholism, over-eating, unhealthy eating and so on.

Think Clearly!

Her parents enjoyed arguments, and so she grew up challenged to use her head, and work things out for herself. She could see how much her parents were open to challenge each other, relishing the intellectual tussles with regard to politics, religion or current affairs. This freedom to express their conflicting views, gave her the sense that intellectual challenges were stimulating and exciting. And so she took the permission to think for herself, to offer her own opinions, and found that these were always respected even if not agreed with.

Often religious communities can inhibit the divergent thinkers. An over emphasis on obedience and the common life often silences the person who is prepared to challenge the status quo. The old adage, 'keep the rule and the rule will keep you', while ostensibly passé, is often preached when people begin to question the manner in which the community is organised. Prejudice and established opinions frequently prevent some people from thinking for themselves. The healthy community, on the other hand, welcomes the 'out-of-the-box' thinking and encourages people to be innovative in their thinking. There are no 'sacred cows' that cannot be debunked; instead, everything is open to be challenged, and consequently, people feel free in community to re-assess the status quo in favour of fresh and alternative ideas. Such freedom fosters creativity and spontaneity. The result of clear thinking is that the ministry of the community becomes coherent and relevant because it is constantly under the scrutiny of clear thinking.

Trust Your Feelings!

'Trust your feelings!' was a phrase that her mother often told her. And so, this young girl grew up being very aware that feelings were a very good indication of what she was experiencing. Gradually, she learned a whole vocabulary of 'feeling' words so as to enable her to identify how emotionally she was feeling in different moments and with different people. This emotional literacy became invaluable for her as she began to enter into more serious relationships later in life. How different this experience was from those people whose parents seem to ignore feelings or even actively prevent their children from expressing them!

Increasingly, communities encourage the members to share feelings during their community meetings. There was a time when the more intellectually gifted ruled the roost, being quicker to lay out their reasons for adopting specific strategies, and ever ready to dismiss so-called 'stupid' ideas. Now, religious are coming to recognise that our feelings are probably better indicators of what directions we should take. As people get in touch with their feelings, they come to an intuitive knowledge, allowing the Little Professor to communicate what is happening at a psychological level. Sharing of feelings is now encouraged because people understand that our real identity is more easily revealed through the unique feelings that each of us experiences.

Allowers

Allowers are to drivers as permissions are to injunctions. The allowers are the verbal and conscious messages from the Parent in the parent to the Parent in the child (Fig. 42). Allowers come from an unconditional OK life position, whereas we saw that the drivers were messages from the parent to the child that the child was conditionally OK as long as they were perfect, strong, trying hard, pleasing others and hurrying up (Chapter 5). The allowers send very different messages to the young person from the parents: It's good enough; Share your feelings; Just do it! Please yourself! Take your Time! These allowers, when practised in community, engender a sense of self-esteem in the individual members, and foster a community spirit that is liberating.

It's Good Enough

It is not that these parents do not want their children to succeed. These parents transmit rather to their children that they do not have to have everything perfectly done. This message *allows* the child to make mistakes and to learn from them. The parents are not obsessed with detail, nor are they over demanding that their children be perfect. They guide their children calmly and in a relaxed manner, recognising that their children can do a good enough job. And they do not withdraw affection when the child fails; instead, they encourage them to get up and try again.

Religious life in the past was considered the 'way of perfection' and religious were encouraged to reach to the pinnacle of sanctity. This often led to scrupulosity, guilt feelings, depression and low self-esteem. Very few could reach to the heights of perfection, and those who could became intolerable to live with! Increasingly, religious are encouraged to take a gentler approach to life, aware of their own fragility, and more deeply conscious of a compassionate God who looks upon the saint and the sinner with equal love and acceptance. In this more compassionate atmosphere, religious have become gentler with each other, more accepting of the faults and failings of each one, and conscious that all are on a journey that requires patience and support along the way.

Share your Feelings!

When these parents see their children sad or angry or afraid, they are prepared to listen without unnecessarily reassuring them. These parents are good listeners, and allow their children express their feelings in a free and easy manner. The parents recognise that the child's feelings are unique to that child, and in accepting the children's feelings, the parents are communicating to their children that they are OK especially when they are mad, glad, sad, or scared. In other words, instead of the message 'Be Strong', they encourage their children to realise that their feelings are their friends!

How often religious live lives of quiet desperation, hiding their real feelings for fear of creating trouble or disturbing the peace! Very often in the past, the formation of religious involved controlling feelings or denying them for religious motivations. Feelings like anger, frustration, resentment and many of the uncomfortable feelings were considered 'wrong', and had to be subjugated by motivations of love and tolerance. The result was that feelings were buried, but buried alive, and the proverbial trading stamps were collected. In addition, when we think of racket feelings (Chapter 15), the challenge in community is to encourage people to express their authentic feelings in response to their experiences in the community. Normalising feelings goes a long way to supporting people express exactly how they feel. When religious feel free to share their feelings in community, the quality of community life grows exponentially.

Just Do It!

Since the Try Hard driver is the result of over-controlling parents, the parents who *allow* their child to complete tasks are those parents who avoid any sense of excessive control. They celebrate when their child accomplishes a task, and do not simply accept the fact that the child *tried* without completing a job. So, the parent does not bribe the child to do the work, nor does the parent readily accept unfinished or sloppily completed tasks. The child soon learns that actions speak louder than words, and that often words are excuses for actions that have not been completed. Parents call their children to be accountable for their actions, but in a spirit of love and acceptance.

Often on the pretext of tolerance, religious often fail to hold each other accountable. Consequently, when things are not done properly, or even neglected, there can be a real reluctance to confront the situation. And so, important issues can be overlooked. They are also inclined to display a significant level of passivity, where they simply avoid taking responsibility for fulfilling their obligations. Often this lack of accountability leads to high levels of frustration, and a sense of everyone being responsible and therefore no one being responsible. The allower 'Just Do It!' challenges them to complete tasks, take responsibility, and be proactive in taking necessary decisions. A community characterised by this 'Just Do It' allower, achieves the goals it sets in a planned and organised manner.

Please Yourself!

The parents, who demand that their children please them in order for the child to be accepted, are very different from the parents who encourage their children to live their lives independently, and not simply to please the parents. The child grows up, not constantly wondering if everything they do pleases or displeases their parents. Instead, the child picks up the message that they need to do things *not* just to please others, but because they want to do them, and because in doing them, they can please themselves, and achieve what they want in life.

Religious life often trains people to think of others instead of themselves. While this approach is laudable in many ways, the danger is that people over-adapt to the needs of others, and neglect their own normal needs. The passive behaviour of overadaptation (Chapter 17) eventually leads people to high levels of resentment, where their service is taken for granted, and they begin to feel used and abused. When people begin to take care of themselves, acknowledging their own needs and wants, then a more balanced approach to life can emerge. However, old habits die hard, and many religious find it very difficult to overcome the guilt of pleasing themselves.

Take your Time!

Relaxed parents make for relaxed children. Relaxed children are not synonymous with lazy children, or procrastinators. The message 'take your time' offers children the space to go at their own pace, and to complete a job properly without the pressure to 'hurry up'. Unlike the 'hurry up' person, the actual doing of the job for the relaxed person is more significant than the end point. In a sense, the journey becomes more important than the destination.

In more recent years, the pace of life even in religious houses seems to have accelerated to the extent that the more traditional peace and solitude have been replaced by constant activity and unrelenting rhythm. Whether this is due to the nature of society or simply the changing face of religious life, the allower 'Take your Time' is increasingly necessary for religious to remember, if they are to maintain any level of balance. It is especially when the community leader has a 'Hurry Up' driver that the rest of the community needs to counterbalance this with the opposite allower. In order for religious communities to be oases of tranquillity, the allower 'Take your Time!' is particularly useful to inculcate. It creates a spirit of calm and peace that facilitates the need that religious have of a self-reflective attitude to life.

The Program

As explained in Chapters 7 and 8, the program is basically the 'how to' that the parent employs to show the child the way to follow the injunctions or counterinjunctions. In the Winning Script, the program likewise offers the child a model to live the permissions and the allowers. It is in the way the parent models a way of life that the child learns to live accordingly.

Communities likewise are called to model the 'how to' of the permissions and allowers, so that new members gradually imbibe the spirit of a Congregation, picking up by osmosis that ethos of the group. It is only in a healthy community that the founding intention of the Congregation is realised.

Conclusion

What we have described in this Chapter points to the powerful impact of positive messages that parents can communicate to their children. By implication, we also show how communities can grow and develop in an atmosphere where positive messages rather than negative ones transform a community into a place of freedom and creativity. When religious in their communities communicate permissions and allowers to each other, the community atmosphere becomes transformed. Spontaneity and intimacy grow in a community that encourages these permissions and allowers, and invites each member to develop into fully autonomous and integrating adults.

Exercises

Share with the members of your community your answers to the following:

1. Which of the permissions do you find easy to give to others in your community? And which do you find difficult to give?

2. Which of the permissions would you like to receive from others in your community? And which do you find difficult to accept?

3. Which of the allowers do you find easy to give to others in your community? And which do you find difficult to give?

4. Which of the allowers would you like to receive from others in your community? And which do you find difficult to accept?

5. It may also be affirming for you to share who in your community embodies some of the permissions and/or allowers. And they can do the same for you.

Chapter Twenty-Six

A Game-Free Life

"I am not bound to win, but I am bound to be true.
I am not bound to succeed,
but I am bound to live up to what light I have."
Abraham Lincoln

Part Five of *Are We Together?* has dealt so far with the integrating Adult, viewing him or her mainly from the point of view of how they think and feel about themselves as individuals, and in relation to other people in community. We examined how the Adult ego state incorporated the positive aspects of the Parent and the Child in an integration that leads the person to be aware, spontaneous and intimate with self and others.

We also examined how early childhood experiences impact on the formation of the integrating Adult, providing the person with invaluable resources for them to make healthy decisions about their life, their view of themselves, of others, and of the future.

This chapter will focus on the *behaviours* of the integrating Adult, and identify the ways in which such a mature person can live in a religious community. Community life, we have seen, goes through various stages before it arrives at an expression of authentic living. It can, however, only become authentic if there are members who live and behave maturely in the context of community. The behaviour of the integrating Adult, therefore, can contribute much in facilitating the creation of communities that are wholesome places for religious to grow and develop.

When we discussed psychological games in Chapter 14, we took Steve Karpman's *Drama Triangle* as a very useful tool in identifying games that can have a deleterious effect on community. The Persecutor, Rescuer and Victim roles create various levels of difficulty in community and hinder the creation of any real possibility of authentic community.

In this chapter, we examine the *Winner's Triangle* as

opposed to the Drama Triangle in order to see an alternative and more mature way of maintaining healthy interpersonal communication that is not persecutory, rescuing, nor entering into the Victim mode. I wish to acknowledge the ideas of Vann Joines in this section, where he is always keen to emphasize the importance of saying 'yes' when we want to say 'yes', and 'no' when we want to say 'no', and being ready to change our minds (Joines, 2003).

The Winner's Triangle

Choy's model of the Winner's Triangle points to an alternative way of interacting in situations that normally could invite people into the Drama Triangle (Choy, 1990: 40ff). In drawing the Winner's Triangle, I will use a diagram that Adrienne Lee used when teaching the Winner's Triangle. In her diagram (Fig. 43) she superimposes the Winner's Triangle onto the Drama Triangle, thereby forming a star of David, and showing alternative responses that are on offer to the person

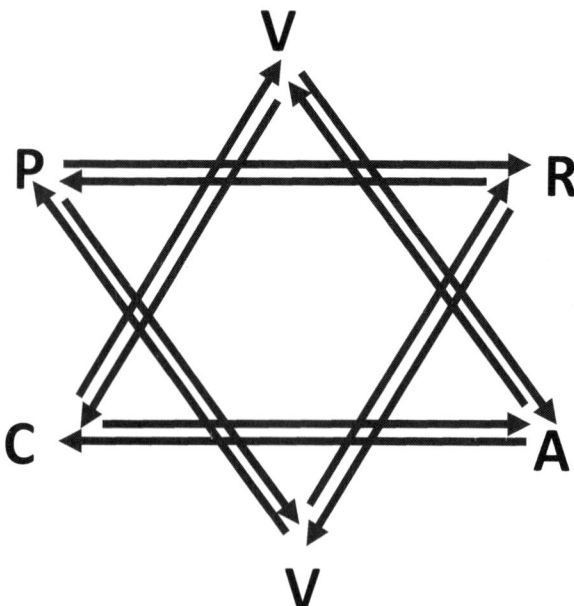

Fig. 43 The Winner's Triangle (Lee, 2003)

P=Persecutor; V (below)= Victim;
R=Rescuer; V (above)=Vulnerable;
A=Assertive; C= Caring

facing a situation of potential game playing (Lee, 2003).

Assertive People

Assertive people are those who express their ideas and opinions in a clear but non-aggressive manner. They do not persecute or put down the other person for having a different opinion, but simply state their own opinions in a clear and honest manner. They don't force their ideas on others, but neither do they water down their ideas to please others. Unlike the persecutors who attack people who disagree with them, assertive people can acknowledge the opinions of others even when other's ideas are diametrically opposed to their own.

When assertive people express what they want or need, they will do so directly. There will be no symbiotic invitations (see Chapter 19), where they send ulterior transactions from a passive and victim-like place in order to get the assistance of others. They simply state their wishes, and expect that these will be taken seriously and responded to with respect. They are also willing to pursue the necessary courses of action to get what they want. They do not give up when their initial request is denied, but persist in making their needs known to the community.

The assertive person will say 'no' when they want to say 'no' in a firm but respectful way. Often non-assertive people feel that they cannot say 'no' when they want to, and end up doing things that they would prefer not to do. In this way, non-assertive people find themselves more a victim than a person in charge of their destiny. Assertive people decide what they want and don't want without concern for how the other person may view their assertiveness. It is not that assertive people are insensitive to others, but they are clear when they wish to decline a request. And they are open to change their mind, and then instead of saying 'no', they can say 'yes' when they deem it appropriate. In this way they are flexible, ready to adapt to changing situations, and, at the same time, attentive to the needs of others.

When asked for feedback, assertive people are open to give clear feedback without equivocation. They believe that honest feedback is the best service they can give to others, and so they are direct, unapologetic and yet gentle in the manner of delivery.

Assertive people are also willing to share their fantasies and resentments. When they suspect that there are ulterior transactions going on in community (see Chapter 10), they will seek to find out what exactly is happening, and make explicit the hidden agenda. They are willing to share what they imagine is below the surface, being open to acknowledge that they may have misjudged the situation.

People know where the assertive person stands because they do not play games, or use ulterior transactions. Their social message matches their psychological message, leaving no doubt as to their intentions. As a result, people are inclined to trust assertive people, and go to them when in need of advice. They know they will get an honest response.

Caring People

Caring people are ready to respond to the needs of others rather than rescue them. They will be good listeners where they work to understand the other person who is in need, encouraging them to reveal their vulnerability, and express their needs directly. They invite the other person to be clear in what they want. They are caring and understanding when they hear the other being passive and manipulative, but they do not take over in order to solve the others person's problems. Instead, they continue to seek clarification as to what the other person wants.

They do not say 'yes' to a request when they want to say 'no', thereby running the danger of putting themselves in a victim mode. If they have to refuse a request, they do so in a manner that continues to show their care and respect for the person. And like the assertive person, they are ready to change their mind in the light of changing circumstances.

They do not do the thinking for others, but instead are patient in listening carefully to what the person has to say, without coming in too quickly with their own opinions and ideas. They are true 'inquirers' (Chapter 11). They do not make gratuitous suggestions when these are not requested, but seek to invite the other person discover the solutions to their own problems.

Caring people are also careful not to do more than their share of the work. Unlike the person who over adapts to other people and plays out this passive pleasing behaviour (see Chapter 17), the caring people will do their fair share of the necessary chores, but will not relieve the other person of *their* own responsibilities. They will not take over, nor invite the other person to become passive or a victim. Instead, they are keen to empower the other to take responsibility for their life. In this way, they avoid the unhealthy symbiosis we discussed in Chapter 19.

Vulnerable People

Unlike the Victim who easily moves into the Child ego state, vulnerable people stay in Adult, and use their Adult thinking to reflect on their difficulties, and seek solutions. Instead of depending on others, vulnerable people will be ready to reveal their needs, without abrogating his or her responsibly to seek ways to have their needs met.

They do not hide their weaknesses or faults, but are ready to be open and honest in how they present themselves. They are neither better nor worse than they appear. In this way, they feel free to be themselves.

Vulnerable people are very much in touch with their feelings, and use their feelings as information that will facilitate greater awareness of how they are in a given situation. Their consciousness of their emotional life is a real strength, which takes them from the victim stance to the vulnerable stance. As they share their feelings, they get in touch with the core of their identity, and come to own their reality. In this way they are free.

Conclusion

In describing the elements of the Winner's Triangle, we have painted a picture of the authentic person. Religious who become authentic help create communities of health and wholeness. Such communities can model a way of living that the world needs to witness. Repeating the words of Abraham Lincoln quoted at the head of the chapter seems an appropriate conclusion to this chapter on a game-free life: "I am not bound to win, but I am bound to be true. I am not bound to succeed, but I am bound to live up to what light I have" (Lincoln, www.brainyquote.com).

Exercises

1. Share a time when have you said 'no' when you wanted to say 'no'.

2. This could be a moment when you could share resentments. The important thing to remember when sharing resentments is that you are sharing how *you* feel. It is not a blaming exercise. The other person needs to be able to hear the resentment without explaining, or making excuses and, above all, they need to avoid taking the comments personally.

3. Sharing fantasies is also another exercise that demands we take a risk. Checking things out exposes us to being wrong. It also challenges the other person to be honest in their response to the fantasy. Often there will be some truth in the fantasy. Can we admit that small piece of truth?

4. Often the sharing of fantasies and resentments can conclude with some type of gesture of reconciliation.

Chapter Twenty-Seven

TA and Spirituality

"Knock, And He'll open the door.
Vanish, And He'll make you shine like the sun.
Fall, And He'll raise you to the heavens.
Become nothing, And He'll turn you into everything."
Rumi

Although Berne was born a Jew, he did not focus much on the explicit spiritual dimension in his theory of TA. However, he did talk about 'Physis' which he described as 'a force of Nature, which eternally strives to make things grow, and to make growing things more perfect' (Berne, 1947:94). He called this force, 'a creative force' creating a form of growth that is 'orderly and progressive' (*Ibid:*94). Berne, who was writing from a psychoanalytic viewpoint at the time, considered Physis, together with the Superego as opposing forces to childish *Id* wishes (*Ibid:*137).

In *What do You Say after You Say Hello,* he draws the winning Script (Fig. 44 over) with an arrow coming up from within the Child ego state, and cutting through the Adult and Parent ego states (Berne, 1972:155).

Berne seems to be emphasising the self-transcendence of the person in the process of growth and development. As the Physis arrow begins in the Child ego state, and rises through Adult and Parent ego states, we understand Berne is stressing the inner energy of the ego states to liberate the free energy to achieve maximum growth.

In this sense, he seems to have been open to a form of spirituality that transcends the limits of the here-and-now (James, 1981:54ff).

Some say that his emphasis on autonomy points to a certain 'open door' to the spiritual development of the person (Kandathil & Kandathil, 1997:24ff).

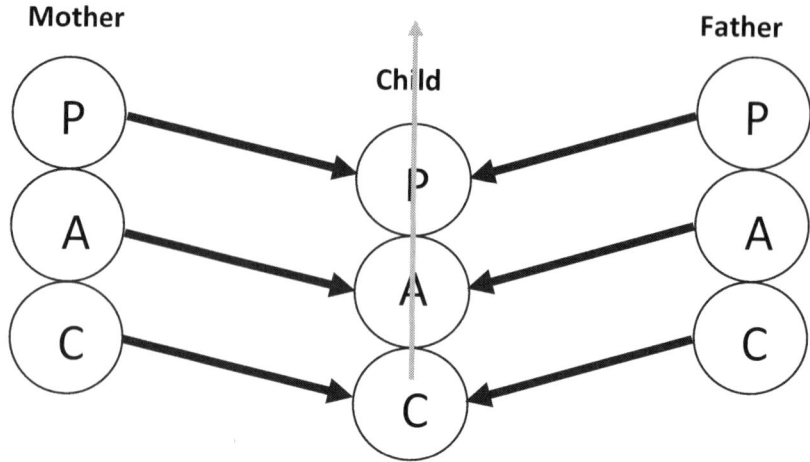

Fig. 44 Physis (Berne, 1972)

The idea of autonomy is taken up by the Kandathils where they link it to the document *Gaudium et Spes* from the Second Vatican Council (Flannery, 1992) which says, 'Only in freedom can man (or woman) direct himself (or herself) to goodness' (Par. 17). I am reminded of the words of St. Paul to the Ephesians; 'May he give you power through your spirit for your hidden self to grow strong' (Eph. 3:16). This hidden self could well be described as that inner force to grow and develop.

It was Albert Einstein who said,

> "A knowledge of the existence of something we cannot penetrate, our perceptions of the profoundest reason and the most radiant beauty, which only in their most primitive forms are accessible to our minds — it is this knowledge and this emotion that constitute true religiosity; in this sense and in this sense alone, I am a deeply religious man"(Seelig, 1954:8-11).

Berne did not express himself as a spiritual man like Einstein, but his theory of Physis at least indicates his awareness that there is a force within the human species that draws the person beyond.

Ilia Delio in her study of cosmic spirituality states: 'this new world is within our reach if we awaken to the power of love within us as the power to create anew' (Delio, 2013, 198). Berne in his healthy life position of I'm OK-You're OK points to interpersonal relationships of love and mutual acceptance, and in this sense, he appears open to the self-transcendence of the person.

Interestingly enough, there are about half dozen or more articles in several editions of the *Transactional Analysis Journal* on the question of spirituality. So, although Berne underplayed it, some of the writers from the TA world have intuited the value of the spiritual especially in the area of psychotherapy (Trautmann, 2003:33ff). Isaacson discusses religious Scripts as an element of a person's overall Script (Isaacson, 1974: 38ff), while Gilpin shares a personal journey of faith as a transactional analyst (Gilpin, 1995:29ff).

Fanita English identifies three motivational forces that impact on the growth of the person: the survival, the expressive and the quiescence motivators (English, 2003:55ff). The quiescence motivator relates to spirituality, and to the connection between the person and the Cosmos, inviting us to connect with the universe, and move between the survival motivational force, and the expressive motivational forces. She stresses the importance of the spiritual for a healthy flow in life.

The element of spirituality can be intimately connected with the concept of I'm OK-You're OK, where we experience the unconditional love of God who accepts us even when our behaviour is often not OK (James & Savary, 1974:49ff). This experience of being loved by a gracious God opens us to look on the world as OK, with the potential to provide for everyone in a way that is just and loving. TA, in a sense, gives us permission to be holy and holistic, integrating the spiritual and the psychological (Drego, 2005:7ff).

John Philip Newal further highlights the integrating nature of the spiritual dimension of life when he says,

> '...to be unconscious either of the oneness of life or the radical individuality of everything that has being is to fall out of relationship with the wholeness of which we are a part.' (Newell, 2011: 29)

The Physis of Berne and the quiescence of Fanita English all point to the transcendent nature of humanity. Whereas not every person follows a specific religion, and many reject any form of organized religion, English stresses that it would be remiss to ignore the basic spiritual nature of people, and of all of creation.

In these days, there is a growing consciousness of the unity of all life and especially with the earth. As John Philip Newell again observes: 'Our oldest unity is our relationship with the earth' (*Ibid:*143). As we grow in our appreciation of the groanings of the earth in the face of global pollution and neglect, we are being called to adopt an I'm OK-You're OK position towards the earth and the universe, where we *get on with* the universe by honouring its right to be treated with respect and reverence.

Neglecting the spiritual dimension of life, limits us in our view of humanity, and reduces the person to an entity that is without soul. When people come together, be it in a religious community or in any group, it is important to see the whole person, and to offer encouragement for the whole person to grow and develop in spirit, mind and body.

The development of transpersonal psychology includes as a constitutive element of personal growth, the spiritual dimension of life (Rowan, 2005). To quote Joseph Fabry:

> To maintain or restore health, we must consider all three dimensions. The spirit, like the body and the psyche, is part of every person, not just the religiously inclined. The spiritual dimension, which Frankl calls the *noös,* contains such uniquely human attributes as our will to meaning, our goal orientation, our creativity, our imagination, our intuition, our faith, our vision of what we can become, our capacity to love beyond the psychophysiological, our capacity to listen to our conscience beyond the dictates of the superego, our sense of humour. It also contains our self-detachment or ability to reach out to people we love and causes in which we believe. In the area of the

spirit we are not driven; we are drivers, the decision makers (quoted in Rowan, 2005:10).

Physis, while not making the spiritual explicit, seems to sit well with the idea of transpersonal psychology. Also, Berne discusses the role of intuition, which again is part and parcel of what transpersonal psychology deals with (Berne, 1977).

As we conclude our study of TA within the context of *Are We Together?* there is no doubt that the place of spirituality must take centre space in the lives of the religious community members. The challenge is for religious to integrate the spiritual and the human so that both find full expression in the life of the individual. Without a firm awareness of our humanity, our spirituality will, at best, become a process of placing spiritual bandages on psychological wounds, and degenerate into empty practices that fail to be integrated into our day-to-day living. Without a deep spirituality, on the other hand, religious men and women living together in community lack the very dynamism that motivates religious life (Morris, 1996:254ff). Discounting the spiritual means discounting an essential dimension of life.

When we stress the spiritual nature of life, we are emphasising a type of Adult spirituality that is growthful, liberating and mature. Religious are called to leave behind a Child ego state belief in a 'God of the gaps' that resorts to spirituality when faced with the normal challenges of life. Like the soldiers caught in the trenches or fox holes of World War I, who prayed when they were in danger of death, but later, when they escaped, abandoned any contact with God, some religious simply use God to solve their immediate difficulties instead of forming a mature relationship with the divine.

Other religious have a Parent view of the God who punishes and demands obedience (Morris, 1972:92-93). This is the Controlling God whose omniscience is used as a threat when we do wrong or fail to live up to the dictates of the Church. Such a God engenders fear and compliance for some, but eventually leads to a rebellious refusal to believe in any form of religious practice.

The invitation is instead to develop an Adult spirituality that is open to a loving God who invites people into the fullness of life (Edelman, 1973:50-51). This God seeks to become an integral part of our lives, requesting that we engage with Godself from a Free Child position, and in response to a Nurturing divinity that reaches out to us with transformative love. Such a grounded spirituality is liberating and integrating, transcending the limitations of the merely human, and pointing to the inner capacity of the person to become a new creation interconnected with all humanity, and with the entire universe.

Conclusion

The adage that says, 'Grace builds on nature' is never truer than when we are discussing the quality of community living. It is when religious Sisters and Brothers succeed in creating loving and human communities that their spirituality develops into a mature and integrating response to the Christian call to love and unity. The call of Jesus –'That they may be one' (Jn.17: 21) – finds realisation when people adopt an I'm OK, You're OK position, and creates gospel communities that witness to the power of love and compassion.

Exercises

1.   Share what you mean by your spirituality?

2.   What aspects of your spirituality do you connect with your humanness?

3.   How do you relate 'Physis' to your spirituality?

4.   How has your spirituality developed over the years?

5.   What is your image of God, and how has it changed?

6.   In terms of ego states, how do you see God?

Chapter Twenty-Eight

A Case Study

"Do not wait to strike till the iron is hot; but make it hot by striking."
William B. Sprague

The three leadership teams (comprising 15 Brothers) of a religious Congregation had decided to amalgamate their three Provinces into one Province because of declining membership. They struggled with how to make the move, or decide on what sort of structure the new combined Province would take. In addition, they discussed at length what overall direction the new entity would have, but found it difficult to come up with a clear plan. They were stuck. After many meetings they did not seem to be making progress, and felt a certain frustration at the impasse. They therefore decided to avail of the services of an organisational consultant, in the hope that such professional assistance could offer a way out. Eventually they found a consultant in Holland who agreed to take on the project. Jane Zuidema of Open Mind Management was the organisational consultant.

She immediately saw that a group of fifteen would not work, and had not worked in bringing a definite plan to be implemented. She encouraged, therefore, that a small group should be chosen to become the architects of the new Province, and to take some time out to plan for the future. The fifteen Brothers agreed to this strategy, and a process was put in place to select five members from the fifteen to form a team or focus group.

The focus group met, and decided that if they were going to achieve any real progress in the re-organisation of the three Provinces, they needed to live together, and spend a significant amount of time in imagining what the future would be like. They realised that part of the reason for the impasse had been that the three leadership groups, with all their current work, simply hadn't had enough time to dream for the future. So, in the end, the focus group decided to form a community, and devote two days a week to the restructuring project, while carrying out their leadership duties in their respective Provinces on the other three working days.

The five members of the focus group established a new community, and began the process of planning. Early on in their deliberations, they came to the conviction that creating a healthy community spirit was an essential ingredient in the plan for the future. And so, they engaged a TA psychotherapist to work with the group to ensure that the group was going to function well, and achieve the task for which they were mandated to complete. Lorna Johnston of the Change Institute from Calgary in Canada was the TA psychotherapist.

The work of the organisational consultant and the TA therapist became vital in the work of the group. Gradually, the group formed into a vibrant and cohesive unit, and began to work at imaging a new vision for the new amalgamated Province. They called themselves the New Life in Mission Group (NLMG).

The NLMG explored the needs of society, inviting people from all walks of life to share what they felt the society most needed in the current climate. It was quite interesting to discover that most of the invited people who came to these conversations, pointed out the urgent need in Irish society for some way to answer the spiritual hunger of people who were not being satisfied by the practices of the official church. It became clear to NLMG that the way forward would need to be very different from the current structures of the Congregation that focussed heavily on the schools ministry. The Congregation needed a new paradigm to respond to new needs.

After two years of planning, and with the assistance of the two consultants, the NLMG came up with a plan that they called New Life in Mission. The plan consisted of establishing new communities that would focus on the spiritual search, and would establish three spirituality centres in Ireland and England to respond to the spiritual hunger that had been identified.

The NLMG spent considerable time teasing out the details of what the new communities would look like, and how they would live as religious in a new way that would prioritise the spiritual search. They drew up a detailed plan for the new communities, and a strategy for establishing spirituality centres.

Each member of the three Provinces was invited to consider becoming part of these new communities. The NLMG held meetings in Ireland and England, explaining what was involved in living the new vision. When the NLMG concluded their tour of visits to all parts of the three Provinces, they invited Brothers to apply for membership of the new communities, on the understanding that they would have to undergo an interview, and some intense training before being accepted as a member of the new communities.

About forty Brothers came forward to enter into the selection process. They were interviewed, and when the detailed outline was presented to them, about thirty agreed to enter into the preparation stage. It became clear to some of the Brothers that the vision for the new communities was too challenging, and they therefore withdrew their names from the list.

The thirty Brothers who passed the selection process were invited to embark on a training course for membership of the new communities. The TA therapist (Lorna Johnston) was engaged to lead the training, and to be involved in designing the process of final selection for the communities.

The thirty Brothers met for three sessions of three days each where they began to share on their hopes and fears with regard to coming on board for the New Life in Mission Communities. Early on, some of the candidates withdrew, indicating that they felt that the process was too intense, or that simply they felt unable to give the level of commitment that was being required.

After the three sessions, it was agreed that the remaining twenty-five Brothers would assemble for a month, under the guidance of the Lorna Johnston and undergo training for membership of the New Life in Mission communities.

The training consisted of introducing the candidates to Transactional Analysis, outlining the essential elements of the theory in a very practical way, and showing how the theory of TA could be used to develop communities that were vibrant and cohesive. Each day for the month, the group engaged in exploring how to communicate at a deeper level, how to manage conflict, and how to live a style of community that was very different from what they had been accustomed to.

The content of the months training in TA is reflected in the various chapters of *Are We Together?* Giving the group the various theories, techniques and tasks as described in *Are We Together?* proved to be invaluable in the formation of the communities.

The candidates grew in awareness of the need for intimacy, spontaneity and fun in order for the community to be life giving and supportive. As the month progressed, one the members withdrew while the rest continued to enter into the training with enthusiasm and commitment.

At the end of the month, the group formed themselves into three communities and agreed to commit to the New Life in Mission project for the following number of years. The new communities were encouraged to focus primarily on the formation of the group, before they embarked on establishing the spirituality centres. It was felt, that unless the communities first became models themselves of what they wanted to promote for others, their message would not be authentic.

As the three communities began their life together, they continued to avail of Lorna Johnston who visited the communities three times during the first two years of their existence. Her role was to encourage the members to practise what they had learnt during their month's training in TA, and to deepen the quality of their lives together.

The NLMG who had accompanied the communities along the way, continued to walk with the communities, encouraging them in the work of community building.

The result of this careful preparation was that the three groups formed very healthy and welcoming communities where they experienced a level of intimacy that they had never experienced before in all their years as members of the Congregation.

After about a year, it became clear to the NLMG planners, that while the communities were developing well, and creating a welcoming and enlivening group, the task of establishing the spirituality centres seemed to be low down in the priority of the communities. The NLMG themselves were divided as to the importance of this aspect of the project.

Some of the NLMG planners were convinced that when the communities were ready, they would then embark on the project. Others believed that the actual formation of the communities had become the ministry, and that there was no need to develop another project other than forming the community of New Life in Mission. The mission had become the community itself. Others again felt that the project of establishing spirituality centres – the group task - was being neglected in favour of the group process. This divergence of opinion on the part of the planners meant that the original idea for the establishment of the spirituality centres was put on hold.

Some of the members of the New Life in Mission communities became impatient with the lack of progress in the creation of the ministry, and decided to leave the communities in order to engage more actively in ministry. Most of the new communities, however, were satisfied with the experience of community and, mainly because of their advanced ages, were not concerned that the establishment of the spirituality centres was not being progressed. It seemed that the group process took centre stage, and the group task was considered less important.

There was further training and more invitations to Brothers to enter into the New Life in Mission process, and two additional communities came into being. Today, there are now five New Life in Mission communities in existence. These communities continue to be a real sign of hope for the Congregation.

There is still the problem that ministry is being underplayed. The Brothers are aging, and it appears likely that they will not be able to establish any ministry that will respond to the spiritual needs of the people. However, it must be said that the quality of community life in the new communities can be seen as small shoots of hope for the future. It may be that the simple presence of vibrant cohesive communities may bring about a change in the environment in which the communities are situated. Maybe this is their ministry.

As the NLMG reflected on the process of setting up the New Life in Mission communities, they agreed that the one essential element in the whole planning process was the decision to engage both the organisational consultant and the TA therapist.

These two women, Jane and Lorna provided the necessary challenges to the group as these Brothers embarked on training to be communities with a difference.

TA as a theory was very useful in helping the Brothers understand their own intrapsychic dynamics, and also the interpersonal transactions that they experienced in the process of forming community. These communities continue to grow in their appreciation of TA as a tool for community development.

Almost as a by-product of the intense planning for the establishment of the New Life in Mission communities, was the decision to amalgamate the three Provinces without delay. The amalgamation took place soon after the formation of the New Life in Mission Communities.

References

Allen, T.R, & Allen, B.A. (1975) 'Script, the Role of Permission.' *Transactional Analysis Journal.* 2(2): 72-74.

Allen, J.G. & Fonagy, P.(Eds) (2006) *Handbook of Mentalization-Based Treatment.* Chichester: John Wiley.

Badenoch, B. (2008) *Being a Brain-wise Therapist. A Practical Guide to Interpersonal Neurobiology.* New York, London: W.W. Norton & Co.

Bacon, F. (1909) *'Of Great Place.'* In: F. Bacon (2001) *Francis Bacon, Essays Civil and Moral. The Harvard Classics (1909-1914. Vol.3 Part One).* New York: Bartleby. XI

Bach,R. (1977,1999) *Illusions. The Adventures of a Reluctant Messiah. An inspirational classic of profound and enduring wisdom.* London: Random House.

Bader, E. & Pearson, P. http://www.couplesinstitute.com

Baron-Cohen, Simon (1990) 'Autism: a specific cognitive disorder of 'mind-blindness'. *International Review of Psychiatry* 2: 81–90.

Barr, J. (1987) 'The Therapeutic Relationship Model: Perspectives on the Core of the Healing Process.' *Transactional Analysis Journal.* 17 (4): 135-140.

Beck, A.T. (1975) *Cognitive Therapy & Emotional Disorders.* International Universities Press.

Berne, E. (1947) *The Mind in Action.* London: Lehmann.

Berne, E. (1957) *A Layman's Guide to Psychiatry and Psychoanalysis.* New York: Ballantine Books.

Berne, E. (1961) *Transactional Analysis The Classic Handbook to its Principles.* New York: Grove Press.

Berne, E. (1962) 'Classification of Positions.' *Transactional Analysis Bulletin.* 1(3): 23.

Berne, E. (1963) *The Structure and Dynamics of Organisations and Groups.* New York: Ballantine.

Berne, E. (1964a) 'Trading Stamps.' *Transactional Analysis Bulletin.* 3 (10): 127.

Berne, E. (1964) *Games People Play. The Psychology of Human Relationships.* London: Penguin.

Berne, E. (1966) *Principles of Group Treatment.* New York: Grove Press.

Berne, E. (1970,1973) *Sex in Human Loving.* London: Penguin.

Berne, E. (1972) *What do You Say, after You Say Hello.* London: André Deutsch.

Berne, E. (1976) *Beyond Games and Scripts.* New York: Grove Press.

Berne, E. (1977) *Intuition and Ego States The Origins of Transactional Analysis* (P. McCormick, Ed.) San Francisco: TA Press. Pp. 1-32.

Blackstone, P. (1993) 'The Dynamic Child: Integration of Second-Order Structure, Object Relations, and Self-Psychology.' *Transactional Analysis Journal.* 23(4): 216-234.

Bowlby, J. (1988) *A Secure Base.* New York: Routledge.

Bruce, T.T. & Erskine, R.G. (1994) 'Counterfeit Strokes.' *Transactional Analysis Journal.* 4(2): 18-19.

Camus, A. (First Published in 1942. This edition: 2005) *The Myth of Sisyphus.* London: Penguin Books.

Capers, H. & Holland, G. (1971) 'Strokes Survival Quotient – or Stroke Grading.' *Transactional Analysis Journal.* 1(3): 40.

Chapman, G. (2009) *The Five Love Languages. The Secret to Love that Lasts.* Chicago: Northfield Publishing.

Cheng, N. (1995) *Life and Death in Shanghai.* New York: Penguin.

Choy, A. (1990) 'The Winner's Triangle.' *Transactional Analysis Journal.* 20(1): 41-46.

Christian Brothers, (1984)*Constitutions of the Christian Brothers.* Private Publication.

Clark, B.C. (1991) 'Empathic Transactions In The Deconfusion Of The Child Ego States.' *Transactional Analysis Journal.* 21(4): 312-315.

Clarkson, P. (1991) 'Exploring Transference and Countertransference.' *Transactional Analysis Journal.* 21(2): 99-107.

Clarkson, P. & Gilbert, M. (1988) 'Berne's Original Model of Ego States: Some Theoretical Considerations.' *Transactional Analysis Journal.* 18(1): 20-29.

Cornell, W.F. (1988) 'Life Script Theory: A Critical Review from a Developmental Perspective.' *Transactional Analysis Journal.* 18(4): 270-282.

Cox, M. (1999) 'The Relationship between Ego State Structure and Function: A Diagrammatic Formulation.' *Transactional Analysis Journal.* 29(1): 49-58.

Covey, S. (1989) *The Seven Habits of Highly Effective People.* London: Simon & Shuster.

Crossman, P. (1966) 'Permission and Protection', *Transactional Analysis Bulletin,* 5(19): 152-154.

De Graaf, A. (2013) 'The Group in the Individual: Lessons Learned From Working With and in Organizations and Groups.' *Transactional Analysis Journal.* 43(4): 311-320.

Delio, I. (2013) *The Unbearable Wholeness of Being. God, Evolution, and the Power of Love.* New York: Orbis Books.

Drego, P. (1996) 'Cultural Parent Oppression and Regeneration.' *Transactional Analysis Journal.* 26(1): 58-77.

Drego, P. (2005) 'Acceptance Speech on Receiving the 2004 Eric Berne Memorial Award.' *Transactional Analysis Journal.* 35(1): 7-30.

Drucker, P. (n.d.). BrainyQuote.com. Retrieved March 10, 2014, from BrainyQuote.com Web site: http://www.brainyquote. com/quotes /quotes/t/Peterdruck/121295.htm

Drye, R.C. (1974) 'Stroking the Rebellious Child. And Aspect of Managing Resistance.' *Transactional Analysis Journal.* 4(3): 23-26.

Dusay, J. (1966) 'Response.' *Transactional Analysis Bulletin.* 19 (5): 136-137.

Dusay, J.M. (1977) *Egograms. How I See You and You See Me.* New York: Harper & Row.

Edelman, K.M. (1973) 'Is theology Adult?' *Transactional Analysis Journal.* 3(1): 50-51.

Egan, G. (1994) *The Skilled Helper (5ᵗʰ Edition). A Systematic Approach to Effective Helping.* Belmont: Brooks Cole.

Ekman, P. (1980) 'Biological and Cultural Contributions to Body and Facial Movement in the Expression of Emotions.' In: A. Rorty (Ed.) *Explaining Emotions.* Berkeley: University of California Press.

English, F. (1969) 'Episcript and the 'hot potato' game.' *Transactional Analysis Bulletin.* 8(32): 77-82.

English, F. (1971) 'Strokes in the Credit Bank for David Kupper. (sic) *Transactional Analysis Journal.* 1(3): 27-28.

English, F. (1972) 'Rackets and Real Feelings. Part II.' *Transactional Analysis Journal.* 2(1): 23-25.

English, F. (1976) 'Racketeering.' *Transactional Analysis Journal.* 6(1): 78-811.

English, F. (2003) 'How are You? And how am I? Scripts, ego states and inner motivators.' In: Sills, C. & Hargaden, H. (Eds.) (2002) *Key Concepts in Transactional Analysis Contemporary Views.* London: Worth Publishing. pp. 55-72.

English, F. (2010) 'It Takes a Lifetime to Play Out a Script In: R.G. Erskine (Ed) (2005) *Life Scripts. A Transactional Analysis of Unconscious Relational Patterns.* London: Karnac. pp. 217-238.

Ernst, F.H. (1971) 'The OK Corral: The Grid for Get-On-With.' *Transactional Analysis Journal.* 1(4): 33-42.

Ernst, F. (1982) 'The Annual Eric Berne Memorial Scientific Award Acceptance Speech.' *Transactional Analysis Journal.* 12(1): 5-8.

Erskine, R.G. (1988) 'Ego Structure, Intrapsychic Function, and Defense Mechanisms: A Commentary on Eric Berne's Original Theoretical Concepts.' *Transactional Analysis Journal.* 18(1): 15-19.

Erskine, R.G. (1991) ' Transference and Transactions.' *Transactional Analysis Journal.* 21(2). 63-76.

Erskine, R.G. & Trautmann, R.L. (1993) 'The Process of Integrative Psychotherapy.' In: R.G. Erskine, (1997) *Theories and Methods of an Integrative Transactional Analysis: A Volume of Selected Articles.* San Francisco: TA Press. pp. 79-95.

Erskine, R. G. (1996) 'Methods of Integrative Psychotherapy.' *Transactional Analysis Journal.* 26(4): 316-328.

Erskine, R.G.; Clarkson, P.; Goulding, R.L.; Groder, M.G.; Moiso, C. (1989) 'Ego State Theory: Definitions, Descriptions, and Points of View.' *Transactional Analysis Journal.* 18(1): 6-14.

Flannery, A. (1992, New Revised Edition) *Vatican Council II: Basic 16 Documents.* Dublin: Dominican Publications.

Fonagy,P.;Gergely,G.;Jurist, E.L. & Target, M. (2004) *Affect Regulation, Mentalization, and the Development of the Self.* London; New York: Karnac.

Fowlie, H. (2005) 'Confusion and Introjection: A Model for Understanding Defensive Structures of the Parent and Child Ego States.' *Transactional Analysis Journal.* 35 (2): 192-205.

Freud, S. (1922) 'Beyond the Pleasure Principle.' in: S. Freud, M. Edmundson, & J. Reddick (2003) *Beyond the Pleasure Principle and Other Writings.* London: Penguin. pp. 43-102.

Fuller, T. (n.d.). BrainyQuote.com. Retrieved April 20, 2014, from BrainyQuote.com Web site: http://www.brainyquote. com/quotes /quotes/t/thomasfull121295.html

Gibson, D. (2007) 'The Emogram.' Pending publication.

Gilpin, V. (1995) 'My Professional and Spiritual Development as a Transactional Analyst.' *Transactional Analysis Journal.* 25 (1): 29-34.

Gobes, L. (1990) 'Ego States – Metaphor or Reality?' *Transactional Analysis Journal.* 20(3): 163-165.

Goulding, B. & Goulding, M. (1979) *Changing Lives through Redecision Therapy.* New York: Grove Press.

Hargaden, H. (2013) 'Building Resilience: The role of Firm

Boundaries and the Third in Relational Group Therapy.'
Transactional Analysis Journal. 43(4): 284-290.

Hargaden, H. & Sills, C. (2002) 'Deconfusion of the Child Ego State
– a Relational Approach'. In: C. Sills & H. Hargaden (Eds.)
(2003) *Ego States. Key Concepts in Transactional Analysis
Contemporary Views.* London: Worth Publishing.

Harman, K. (2010) 'How Important is Physical Contact with Your
Infant?' *Scientific American.* May.

Harris, T. (1967) *I'm OK, You're OK.* New York: Grove Press.

Hart. E.W. (1976) 'Symbiotic Invitations.' *Transactional Analysis
Journal.* 6(3): 253-254.

Hay, J. (2007) *Reflective Practice and Supervision for Coaches.*
Berkshire: Open University Press.

Head, M. (2013) *Workshop Presentation.*

Hill, W.F. & Gunner, L. (1973) 'A Study of Development in Open
and Closed Groups.' *Small Group Behaviour.* 4(3): 355-381.

Holloway, W.H. (1972) 'The Crazy Child in the Parent.'
Transactional Analysis Journal. 2 (3): 32-34.

Iacoboni, M. & Siegel, D.J. (2004) 'The Implications for Mirror
Neurons in Psychotherapy. In: Siegel, D.J. (2007) *The Mindful
Brain. Reflection and Attunement in the Cultivation of Well-
Being.* New York; Norton.

Isaacson, C.E. (1974) 'Religious Scripts.' *Transactional Analysis
Journal.* 4 (2): 38-40.

Irwin, T. (Ed.) (1999) *Nicomachean Ethics of Aristotle (2nd Edition)*
Indianapolis: Hackett.

James, M. (1981) 'TA in the 80s: The Inner Core and the Human
Spirit.'*Transactional Analysis Journal.* 11(1): 54-65.

James,M. & Savary, L.M. (1974) *The Power at the Bottom of the
Well. Transactional Analysis and Religious Experience.* New
York, San Francisco, London: Harper & Row.

Jerrold, W.J. quoted in: J.Wood (1899/2012) *Dictionary of
Quotations.* London New York: Warne&Co; Bartleby.com

Johnston, L. (2003) *Workshop sessions.*

Joines, V. (1991) 'Transference and Transactions: Some Additional Comments.' *Transactional Analysis Journal.* 21(3): 170-173.

Joines, V. (2002) *Workshop presentation.*

Joines, V. (2003) *Hand-out for workshop presentation.*

Joines, V. & Stewart, I. (2002) *Personality Adaptations.* Melton Mowbray & Chapel Hill: Lifespace Publishing.

Kafka, F. (2008 edition) *Letter to my Father.* Toronto: Garamond Press.

Kahler, T. (1975) 'Drivers: The Key to the Process of Scripts.' *Transactional Analysis Journal.* 5(3): 280-284.

Kahler, T. (1978) *Transactional Analysis Revisited.* Little Rock: Human Development Publications.

Kahler, T. (2008) *The Process Therapy Model.* Little Rock: Taibi Kahler Associates.

Kandathil, G. & C. (1997) 'Autonomy: Open Door to Spirituality.' *Transactional Analysis Journal.* 27 (1): 24-29.

Karpman, S. (1968) 'Fairy Tales and Script Drama Analysis.' *Transactional Analysis Bulletin.* 7(26): 39-43.

Karpman, S. (1971) 'Options' *Transactional Analysis Journal.* 1(1): 79-87.

Kay, S. (2005) *The Phantom.* Coral Springs: Llumina Stars.7

Klein, M. (1997) *Envy and Gratitude and Other Works (1946-1963)* London: Vintage.

Kohlrieser, G., Goldsworthy, S. & Coombe, D. (2012) *Care to Dare. Unleashing Astonishing Potential through Secure Base Leadership.* New York: San Francisco: Jossey-Bass.

Kuijt, J. (1980) 'Differentiation of the Adult Ego State: Analytical Adult and Experiencing Adult.' *Transactional Analysis Journal.* 10(3): 232-237.

Kupfer, D. & Haimowitz, M. (1971) ' Therapeutic Interventions, Part 1. Rubberbands Now.' *Transactional Analysis Journal.* 1(2): 10-16.

Lair, J. (n.d.) livinglife fully.com Retrieved February 24, 2014, from livinglifefully.com Web site: /praise.htm

Lankford, V. (1972) 'Rapid Identification of Symbiosis.' *Transactional Analysis Journal.* 2(4): 15-17.

Larkin, P. (1991) *Collected Poems.* London: Marvel and Faber & Faber.

Lee, A. (1998) 'The Drowning Person.' In: Tilney, T. (1998) *Dictionary of Transactional Analysis* London: Whurr Publications.

Lee, A. (2003) 'The Winner's Triangle.' *Workshop Presentation*

Lewis, C.S. (1961) *A Grief Observed.* London: Faber and Faber. pp. 52-53.

Lincoln. A. (n.d.). BrainyQuote.com. Retrieved March 26, 2014, BrainyQuote.com Web site: http:// www.brainypuote.com/ quote/a/abrahamlin163082.html

Little, R. (2005) 'Integrating Psychoanalytic Understandings in the Deconfusion of Primitive Child Ego States.' *Transactional Analysis Journal.* 35(2): 132-146.

Little, R. (2006) Ego State Relational Units and Resistance to Change. *Transactional Analysis Journal.* 36 (1): 7-19.

Loria, B.R. (1990) 'Epistemology and Reification of Metaphor in Transactional Analysis' *Transactional Analysis Journal.* 20 (3): 152-162.

Loria, B.R. (1995) 'Structure, Determinism and Script Analysis: A Bringing Forth of Alternative Realities.' *Transactional Analysis Journal.* 25(2): 156-168.

Lutteral, M. (2011) 'John Quincy Adams perfectly defined leadership.' In: *North Bay Business Journal.* October 24.

McKenna, J. (1974) 'The Stroking Profile.' *Transactional Analysis Journal.* 4(4): 20-24.

Mellor, K. & Schiff, E. (1975) 'Redefining' *Transactional Analysis Journal.* 5(3): 303-311.

Mellor, K. & Schiff, E. (1975) 'Discounting' *Transactional Analysis Journal.* 5(3): 296-302.

Mindell, A. (1995) *Sitting in the Fire. Large Group Transformation Using Conflict and Diversity.* Portland: Lao Tse Press.

Mitchell, L. (2007) 'An Example of a Section of the Written Exam.' *ITA News*. 29(Feb.) 10-11.

Mitchell, L. (2014) The Link Centre website: http://www.thelinkcentre.co.uk

Moiso, C. (1984) 'The Feeling Loop.' In: E. Stern Ed. (1984) *TA: The State of the Art. A European Contribution.* Dordrecht: Foris Publications. pp. 69-75.

Morris, D. (2002) *Peoplewatching.* London: Random House.

Morris, D.G. & Morris, F.R. (1996) 'The Anatomy of Belief.' *Transactional Analysis Journal.* 26(3): 254-261.

Morris, F.R. (1972) 'Is Theology Adult?' *Transactional Analysis Journal.* 2(2): 92-93.

Newell, J.P. (2011) *A New Harmony. The Spirit, the Earth, and the Human Soul.* San Francisco: Jossey-Bass.

Newton, T. (2006) 'Script Psychological Life Plans and the Learning Cycle.' *Transactional Analysis Journal.* 36(3): 186-195.

Noriega, G. (2005) 'Transgenerational Scripts: the unknown knowledge.' In: R.G. Erskine (Ed) (2005) *Life Scripts. A Transactional Analysis of Unconscious Relational Patterns.* London: Karnac. pp. 269-290.

Novellino, M. (1984) 'Self-analysis of Countertransference in Integrative Transactional Analysis' *Transactional Analysis Journal.* 14(1): 63-67.

Novey,T.B.; Porter-Steele, N.; Gobes, L.; Massey,R.J. (1993) 'Ego States and Self Concept: A Panel Presentation and Discussion.' *Transactional Analysis Journal.* 23 (3): 123-138.

O'Donohue, J. (1998) *Eternal Echoes. Exploring the Hunger to Belong.* London: Random House.

Oller-Vallejo, J. (2002) 'In Support of the Second-Order Functional Model.' *Transactional Analysis Journal.* 32(3): 178-183.

Presentation Sisters (2012) *Our Way of Life.* Private publication.

Proust, M. (n.p.) www.goodreads.com Retrieved January 12, 2014 from: https://www.goodreads.com/quotes/7810-let-us-be-grateful-to-the-people-who-make-us.

Putman, R.D. (2001) *Bowling Alone: America's Declining Social Capital.* New York: Simon & Schuster.

Rowan, J. (2005, 2nd Edition) *The Transpersonal: Spirituality in Psychotherapy and Counselling.* London & New York: Routledge.

Ruiz, D.M. (1997) *The Four Agreements: A Practical Guide to Personal Freedom.* California: Amber-Allen Publications.

Samuels, S.D. (1971) 'Stroke Strategy 1. The Basis of Therapy.' *Transactional Analysis Journal.* 1(3): 23-24.

Schiff, A.W. & Schiff, J.L. (1971) 'Passivity' *Transactional Analysis Journal.* 1(1): 71-78.

Schiff, J.L. in collaboration with Schiff, A.W.; Mellor, K.; Schiff, E.; Schiff ,S.; Richman, D.; Fishman, J.; Wolz, L.; Fishman,C. & Momb,D. (1975) *Cathexis Reader. Transactional Analysis Treatment of Psychoses.* New York, Evanston, San Francisco, and London: Harper & Row.

Schiff, S. (1977) 'Personality Development and Symbiosis.' *Transactional Analysis Journal.* 7(4): 311-316.

Schore, A.N. (2003) *Affect Regulation and the Repair of the Self.* London: Norton.

Schore, A.N. (2012) *The Science of the Art of Psychotherapy.* London: Norton.

Scott Peck, M. (1990) *The Different Drum. Community Making and Peace.* London: Arrow Books.

Shriver, L. (2003) *We Need to Talk about Kevin.* New York: Perseus Group.

Seelig, C. (Ed.) (1954) A. Einstein, Ideas and Opinions, based on Mein Weltbild. New York: Bonanza Books, pp. 8-11.

Shmukler, D. (1991) 'Transference and Transactions: Perspectives from Developmental Theory, Object Relations, and Transformational Processes. *Transactional Analysis Journal.* 21(3): 128-135.

Siegel, D. J. (2013) *Brainstorm. The Power and Purpose of the Teenage Brain.* New York: Penguin.

Steiner, C. (1974) *Scripts People Live. Transactional Analysis of Life Scripts.* New York: Grove Press.

Stern, D.B. (2010) *Partners in Thought. Working with Unformulated Experience, Dissociation, and Enactment.* New York: Routledge.

Stern, D.N. (1985; 2003) *The Interpersonal World of the Infant. A View from Psychoanalysis and Developmental Psychology.* New York, London: Karnac.

Stern, D.N. (2004) *The Present Moment in Psychotherapy and Everyday Life.* New York, London: W.W. Norton.

Stewart, I. & Joines, V (2012) *TA Today. A New Introduction to Transactional Analysis* 2nd Edition. Melton Mowbray & Chapel Hill: Lifespace Publishing.

Stolorow, R.D.; Brandchaft, B. & Atwood, G.E. (2000) *Psychoanalytic Treatment: An Intersubjective Approach.* London: Routledge.

Strachan, D. (2007) *Making Questions Work: A Guide to What and How to Ask for Facilitators, Consultants, Managers, Coaches, and Educators.* San Francisco: Jossey-Bass.

Summers, G. & Tudor, K. (2000) 'Cocreative Transactional Analysis' *Transactional Analysis Journal.* 30(1). 24-40.

Temple, S. (1999) 'Functional Fluency for Educational Transactional Analysis' *Transactional Analysis Journal.* 29(3): 164-174.

Thomson, G. (1983) 'Fear, Anger and Sadness.' *Transactional Analysis Journal.* 13(1): 20-24.

Trautmann, R. (2003) 'Psychotherapy and Spirituality.' *Transactional Analysis Journal.* 33 (1): 33-36.

Tuckman,B.W. (1965) 'Developmental Sequence in Small Groups.' Psychological Bulletin. 53(6): 384-399.

Tudor, K. (2002) 'The Neopsyche: the integrating Adult State.' In: C. Sills & H. Hargaden (Eds.) (2002) *Key Concepts in*

Transactional Analysis Contemporary Views. London: Worth Publishing. pp. 201-231.

Wallin, D.J. (2007) *Attachment in Psychotherapy.* New York, London: The Guilford Press.

Widdowson, M. (2008) ' Metacommunicative Transactions.' *Transactional Analysis Journal.* 38(1): 58-71.

Williamson, M. (1992) *Reflections of the Principles of A Course in Miracles.* New York: Harper Collins.

Wilson, A. (1990) *The Piano Lesson.* Middlesex: Penguin.

Winnicott, D. W. (1965) 'Ego distortion in terms of true and false self.' In: The Maturational Process and the Facilitating Environment: Studies in the Theory of Emotional Development. New York: International UP Inc. pp. 140-152.

SUGGESTED READING FOR A STUDY OF TRANSACTIONAL ANALYSIS

BASIC TEXTS

James, M. & Jongeward, D. (1996) *Born to Win: Transactional Analysis with Gestalt Experiments.* Cambridge: Perseus Books. Interesting and Enjoyable.

Sills, C. & Lapworth, P. (2011) *An Introduction to Transactional Analysis: Helping People Change.* London: Sage. A short introduction to TA.

Steiner, C. (1974) *Scripts People Live: Transactional Analysis of Life Scripts.* New York: Grove Press. Written by one of the early TA colleagues of Eric Berne. Worth reading.

Stewart, I., & Joines, V. (1987 2nd Edition, 2012) *TA Today: A New Introduction to Transactional Analysis.* Nottingham: Lifespace. The best textbook for introducing people to TA and suitable for students and lay people alike.

Stewart, I. (1996) *Developing Transactional Analysis Counselling.* London: Sage. A very valuable resource for therapists who have a good understanding of TA.

Tilney, T. (1998) *Dictionary of Transactional Analysis.* London: Wiley-Blackwell. A great book to revise TA theory once the basics have been covered.

Tudor, K. (Ed.) (2002) *Transactional Analysis Approaches to Brief Therapy or What do you say between saying hello and goodbye?* London: Sage. Useful essays of various aspects of TA for the student of TA.

Widdowson, M. (2010) *Transactional Analysis: 100 Key Points & Techniques.* London & New York: Routledge. An excellent book for people who are already familiar with TA theory.

Woollams, S. & Brown, M. (1978) *Transactional Analysis.* Ann Arbor: Huron Valley Institute Press. A Classic TA textbook that requires careful reading.

FURTHER SELECTED READING FOR THE ADVANCED STUDENT:

Cornell. W.F. & Hargaden, H. (Eds) (2005) *From Transactions to Relations: The Emergence of a Relational Tradition in Transactional Analysis.* Oxford: Haddon Press. An excellent series of essays for the more advanced students.

Fowlie, H. & Sills, C. (2011) *Relational Transactional Analysis. Principles and Practice.* London: Karnac Books A mixed bag of interesting articles.

Hargaden, H. & Sills, C. (2002) *Transactional Analysis: a relational perspective.* New York: Brunner-Routledge. A key text for advanced students of the relational model of TA.

Stewart, I. (2nd Edition, 2000) *Transactional Analysis Counselling in Action.* London: Sage. A very useful book for all therapists.

Great material on TA to be found in the *Transactional Analysis Journal, available from Sage Publications.*

Author Index
(numbers in bold refer to chapters)

Subject Index
(numbers in bold refer to chapters)

Made in the USA
Charleston, SC
28 September 2014